We hope you enjoy this book. Please return or renew it by the due date. You can renew it at **www.norfolk.gov.uk/libraries** or by using our free library app. Otherwise you can phone **0344 800 8020** - please have your library card and PIN ready. You can sign up for email reminders too.

NORFOLK COUNTY COUNCIL
LIBRARY AND INFORMATION SERVICE

NORFOLK ITEM

30129 079

D1352130

The complexity of Dickens's life and character never diminished his Christian charity and advocacy of the poor. Hooper's new biography reveals a different Dickens, one who wrote "expressly for his children" The Life of our Lord. *At the heart of this is a man who loved Jesus, acknowledging that there was none so good, so kind, so gentle, and so sorry for people who did wrong. Hooper gives us a Dickens who, in the midst of his complex and divided life struggled to translate his faith into practical social good.*

REVD CANON PROFESSOR DAVID JASPER,
Professor of Literature and Theology,
University of Glasgow

Charles Dickens

Faith, Angels and the Poor

***

KEITH HOOPER

LION

This book is dedicated to my father, a writer himself, who, in April, was called home by the author and finisher of his faith; my son, Nathanael, of whom I am so proud; my daughter, Abigail, who is truly her father's delight; and the one I love, who has taught me that birds do, indeed, fly at night.

Published by Lion Books
an imprint of
Lion Hudson IP Ltd
Wilkinson House, Jordan Hill Road,
Oxford OX2 8DR, England
www.lionhudson.com/lion

ISBN 978 0 7459 6851 3
e-ISBN 978 0 7459 6852 0

First edition 2017

Acknowledgments
Scripture quotation taken from the Holy Bible, New International Version Anglicised. Copyright © 1979, 1984, 2011 Biblica, formerly International Bible Society. Used by permission of Hodder & Stoughton Ltd, an Hachette UK company. All rights reserved. "NIV" is a registered trademark of Biblica. UK trademark number 1448790.

A catalogue record for this book is available from the British Library

Printed and bound in the UK, August 2017, LH26

Contents

ACKNOWLEDGMENTS

The author would like to thank all the staff at Wroughton library, especially Lucy, Jan, Jane, and Natasha, for their support during the writing of this book. Their assistance has been invaluable. I would also like to thank my wonderful proofreader for the first draft, Elsa.

A Timeline of Charles Dickens's Life

YEAR	MONTH	PERSONAL/FAMILY LIFE
1812	7 February (Friday)	Charles John Huffam, second child of John and Elizabeth Dickens, born in Portsmouth.
	4 March	Baptised at St Mary's parish church Kingston, Portsea, Portsmouth.
1814	Christmas Day	John Dickens posted to London. The family move to 10 Norfolk Street, St Pancras.
1816	Christmas Day	John Dickens transferred to Sheerness. The family go with him.
1817	April	The family move to 2 Ordnance Terrace, Chatham, Kent.
1821	Spring	Family move to 18 St Mary's Place, Chatham. Dickens attends William Giles's School in Clover Lane.
1822	September	John Dickens recalled to London. The family move to Camden Town. Charles remains with the Giles family.
	December	Charles rejoins his family.
1824	February	John Dickens imprisoned in the Marshalsea for debt.
1824	February–March 1825	Dickens sent to work at Warren's Blacking factory.
1825	Spring	Dickens resumes his education at Wellington House Academy. Family move to 29 Johnson Street, Somers Town.
1827	Spring	Dickens forced to leave Wellington House due to family finances. Starts work as a solicitor's clerk at Ellis and Blackmore.
1828	November	Moves to Charles Molloy's solicitors. Teaches himself shorthand.
1829		Begins work at Doctors' Commons.
1830	May	Meets and falls in love with Maria Beadnell.

1831		Appointed political journalist on the *Mirror of Parliament*.
1832	Spring	Takes on a second journalistic role on the *True Sun*. Leaves after a few months.
1833	May	End of Maria Beadnell romance.
	December	First story, "A Dinner at Poplar Walk", appears in *The Monthly Magazine*.
1834	August	Leaves the *Mirror of Parliament* and starts as a political journalist at the *Morning Chronicle*.
	September–December	A series of five sketches appears in the *Morning Chronicle*.
1835	January–August	Twenty *Sketches of London* appear in the *Evening Chronicle*.
	May	Dickens gets engaged to Catherine Hogarth.
1836	September–January	A series of twelve sketches, *Scenes and Characters*, publishes in *Bell's Life of London*.
1836	8 February	First book, *Sketches By Boz*, appears.
	31 March	Opening number of *Pickwick Papers* published.
1836	2 April	Charles and Catherine marry at St Luke's Church Chelsea. Following a week's honeymoon in the village of Chalk, near Gravesend, they return to 15 Furnival's Inn, Holborn, an apartment they share with Dickens's brother, Fred and Catherine's sister Mary.
	November	Dickens leaves the *Morning Chronicle*.
1837	6 January	Dickens' first child, Charles Culliford Boz born. (1)
	31 January	*Oliver Twist* begins publication in the *Bentley Miscellany* (Dickens is the editor).
	April	Dickens family move to 48 Doughty Street, Bloomsbury.
	7 May	Mary Hogarth, aged 17, dies suddenly. Dickens is heart-broken.
	17 November	*Pickwick Papers* published in one volume.
1838	6 March	Mary (Mamie) Dickens born. (2)
	31 March	First number of *Nicholas Nickleby* appears.
	9 November	*Oliver Twist* published in one volume.
1839	23 October	*Nicholas Nickleby* published in one volume.
	29 October	Kate Macready Dickens born. (3)
	December	Dickens family move to 1 Devonshire

		Terrace, Regent's Park.
1840	25 April	First number of *The Old Curiosity shop* appears.
1841	8 February	Walter Landor Dickens born. (4)
	15 December	*The Old Curiosity Shop* and *Barnaby Rudge* published as single volumes.
1842	4 January – 1 July	Catherine and Charles Dickens tour America.
	18 October	*American Notes* is published.
1843	January	First number of *Martin Chuzzlewit* appears.
	19 December	*A Christmas Carol* published.
1844	15 January	Francis Jeffrey (Frank) Dickens born. (5)
	July	*Martin Chuzzlewit* published.
	July–June 1845	The Dickens family move temporarily to Genoa, Italy.
	14 December	*The Chimes* published.
1845	28 October	Alfred D'Orsay Tennyson Dickens born (6)
	December	*The Cricket on the Hearth* published.
1846	March	*Pictures from Italy* published.
1847	May–February	The Dickens family move to Lausanne, Switzerland and then Paris.
	October	First number of *Dombey and Son* appears.
	December	*Battle of Life* published.
	18 April	Sydney Smith Haldimand Dickens born. (7)
1848	April	*Dombey and Son* published.
	2 September	Dickens's older sister, Fanny, dies of tuberculosis.
	December	*The Haunted Man* published.
1849	15 January	Henry Fielding Dickens born. (8)
	1 May	First number of *David Copperfield* appears.
1850	30 March	First number of Dickens's weekly journal, *Household Words*, appears.
	16 August	Dora Annie Dickens born. (9)
	November	*David Copperfield* published.
1851	31 March	John Dickens dies.
	14 April	Dora dies.
	November	Family move to Tavistock House, Tavistock Square, Bloomsbury.
1852	March	First number of *Bleak House* appears.
	13 March	Edward Bulwer Lytton Dickens born. (10)

1853	September	*Bleak House* published.
1854	April August	First number of *Hard Times* appears. *Hard Times* published.
1855	December	First number of *Little Dorrit* appears.
1857	June August	*Little Dorrit* published. Dickens first meets Ellen Ternan (Nell).
1858	May	Dickens and Catherine separate.
1859	30 April 30 December	First number of Dickens's new weekly journal, *All the Year Round*, containing the opening instalment of *A Tale of Two Cities*, appears. *A Tale of Two Cities* published.
1860	1 December	First number of *Great Expectations* appears in *All the Year Round*.
1861	August	*Great Expectations* published.
1864	May	First number of *Our Mutual Friend* appears.
1865	November	*Our Mutual Friend*, Dickens's last completed novel, is published.
1867	9 Nov – 1 May 1868	Dickens completes a reading tour of America.
1870	15 March April 9 June (Thursday) 14 June September	Dickens gives his final public reading at St James's Hall, London. First number of *The Mystery of Edwin Drood* appears. Dickens dies at Gad's Hill Place of a cerebral haemorrhage. Buried in Poets' Corner, Westminster Abbey. Sixth, and final, part of the unfinished *Mystery of Edwin Drood* appears.

INTRODUCTION

Charles Dickens was a genius. Arguably the greatest novelist in the English language, he was also an accomplished political journalist, public speaker, performer, editor, and social reformer. More than this, in his life and work, he encapsulated the spirit of the age in which he lived. When, in 1844, Richard Horne's *A New Spirit of the Age* appeared, the first seventy-six pages were dedicated to the then 32-year-old author. To read a Dickens novel today is to be transported into a different world. The readers of his day had a similar experience when he exposed them to the harsh, uncompromising wilderness endured by the poor.

Born in a newly built suburb of Portsmouth, the story of how Charles Dickens rose from obscurity to become an international literary celebrity is as compelling as any of the plots that appear in his fifteen novels. One of any number of aspiring young writers, he was to reach the pinnacle of his profession. Though driven by a desire to secure financial security (on his death, his estate was valued at around £93,000, around £4.5 million today), he was also motivated by his faith, which impelled him to care for those trapped in a cycle of poverty and to communicate aspects of his beliefs to his readers. The Russian writer, Fyodor Dostoevsky, described Dickens as being "a great Christian man", but this spiritual aspect of his life and career has been relatively ignored by those who have written about him.

The Victorian age was something of a paradox. Traditionally, it has been viewed as a golden age of religious observance and activity; a time when individual and corporate faith held sway over much that took place. In one sense this was true. In the first twenty years of Queen Victoria's reign, the physical landscape of towns and cities was transformed by an unprecedented building programme of new churches and chapels. Missionaries were being sent in ever increasing numbers throughout the British Empire, and the preoccupation with religion was apparent in all aspects of life, including Dickens's chosen profession: at least a third of the books published in 1845 were of a religious nature.

Yet, the Religious Census of 1851, which recorded church and chapel attendance on Mothering Sunday of that year, seriously challenged this belief in the religious devotion of the Victorian Age. Highly controversial and, no doubt, to an extent, statistically flawed, it revealed that only 50 per cent of the population attended a service on that day. As Horace Mann, the individual responsible for overseeing the census, rightly concluded, the majority of the poor and labouring classes living in towns and cities had little or no interest in religion.

Victorian Britain experienced a huge population explosion, which was made worse by mass urban migration. The population of London alone increased by two million between 1831 and 1871. Whereas, in 1801, 80 per cent of people lived in rural communities, by 1901, the year Queen Victoria died, the figure was reduced to just 25 per cent. Within the towns and cities, the resources and infrastructure were wholly inadequate, and heart-breaking deprivation and poverty ensued for hundreds of thousands of people. The situation was accentuated by two factors. Firstly, Victorian society was strictly segregated on social grounds. Two parallel worlds existed, and the inhabitants of the relatively wealthy one, by and large, knew as much about the lives of the poor as they did about the Eskimos living in the North Pole. This was the case in the cities; in the villages, the landowners had always felt more of a responsibility for the local poor. This division was exacerbated by the widely held belief that God ordained an individual's status; a view clearly stated in the third verse of Cecil Frances Alexander's popular children's hymn, "All Things Bright and Beautiful" (1848):

The rich man in his castle,
The poor man at his gate,
He made them high and lowly,
And ordered their estate.

The role of the Church, many believed, was to maintain the divine order. The poor should accept their lowly position and be content, and those of a higher social position need not intervene on their behalf. Far from discouraging segregation, the seating inside parish churches each Sunday embraced it. Those who could afford to pay pew rents occupied the best seats, while the poor were hidden away at the back, or in the gallery. At times, this preferential approach was even applied to the distribution of communion.

Secondly, many within the Church believed that the suffering experienced by those living in poverty was a direct result of their immorality. The solution to their ills rested not in improved housing, sanitation, better wages, or education, but in persuading individuals to adopt biblical values. Dickens's faith, however, was of a practical nature. He was convinced that individuals, and society as a whole, had a Christian responsibility to care for the underprivileged; there was little point preaching to the starving and ignorant, when what they needed was an improved standard of life and, above all, hope.

In his sermon at Westminster Abbey on the Sunday after the writer's funeral, Dean Stanley revealed how "the distress of the poor pierced through Dickens's happiness and haunted him day and night". He saw himself as the voice of the voiceless and the conscience of the nation. Acting as their guide, through the pages of his books and journals, he took his readers into that other world. Having done so, he exposed the chronic failings and abuses of the Poor Law system, and those involved in its operation. Finally, through a series of charitable individuals, he demonstrated how compassionate intervention transformed the lives of those in need. His commitment to Christian charity was no less fervent in his own private life. Family, relatives, friends, and complete strangers, all had good cause to be grateful.

Dickens was not interested in the minutiae of doctrine. His was a simple faith, based primarily on the life and teachings of Christ, as revealed in the four Gospels. He produced his own version for the use of his children.

In the postscript to his last completed novel, *Our Mutual Friend*, Dickens refers to himself as being "the story-weaver at his loom". This perfectly describes the way he wove religious content into the fabric of his writing. First, and foremost, he was a great storyteller, and like the seventeenth-century philosopher, John Locke, he understood that Christianity was best observed in people's lives. Among the 2,000 or so characters that populate his work are a select group of angels. In his first three novels, *The Pickwick Papers*, *Oliver Twist*, and *Nicholas Nickleby*, "charitable angels" demonstrate the ideal and effectiveness of individuals enacting their Christian responsibility towards the poor. Following on from this, he uses a collection of "female angels" who manifest various Christ-like attributes: self-sacrifice, love, kindness, compassion, grace, and mercy. His work also contains a group of negative angels used to expose the failings of those, who, in his view, practised a form of false religion.

Writing to his friend, the Reverend David Macrae, Dickens provides insight into the importance he placed upon the religious content of his work: "with a deep sense of my great responsibility always upon me when I exercise my art, one of my most constant and most earnest endeavours has been to exhibit in all my good people some faint recollections of the teachings of our great Master, and unostentatiously to lead the reader up to those teachings as the great source of all moral goodness."

In what is effectively a spiritual biography of Dickens's life, I have attempted to shed light upon his personal faith and how it was expressed in his work. There has, in the later stages of the book, been no attempt to conceal his most noteworthy fall from grace or to disguise his faults. Flawed, as we all are, his was far from a perfect life. Yet, he did earnestly and most effectively seek to fulfil what he saw as his divine vocation.

It is difficult to accurately assess the impact his writing had upon Victorian society. However, there can be no doubt as to his enduring popularity and the gratitude he received from those he sought to represent. On 30 December 1853, Dickens walked out onto the stage at Birmingham Town Hall, to read *A Christmas Carol* in aid of the city's industrial education initiative. At his special request, the tickets had been reduced in price to encourage the less well-off to attend. On addressing the audience as "My dear friends", he was greeted by an avalanche of applause and cheering. They realized that they, and tens of thousands like them, had a friend and advocate who would plead their cause and not rest until positive action was taken upon their behalf.

Dickens had a calling for which he was especially equipped. Unlike most writers of the time, his was not a comfortable childhood. He had felt the pain of bitter disappointment and experienced the shadow of debt and poverty within his own family. Yet he achieved greatness, not only in his literary success, but by virtue of the influence he had upon the hearts and minds of his readers, and, as a result, upon society as a whole.

Faith was as much a part of his life as creativity and imagination. He wrote to entertain, challenge, inform, educate, and to make a difference. The enduring popularity of his work testifies to his brilliance as a writer. The purpose of this book is not to claim that Dickens was a religious writer. He was not. Rather, he was an outstanding author, who sought to express his Christian ideals through his work.

LADY OF JOHN DICKENS ESQ.
A SON

On Monday, 10 February 1812, a prominent London newspaper, the *Morning Post*, carried a brief birth announcement of a son having been born to a nondescript family in the Portsmouth area. Fifty-eight years later (14 June 1870), it was to feature a leading obituary stating how the same unnoticed child had, through his "sheer force of genius, done more than any other that lived in his time to make English literature loved and admired".

The appearance of Dickens's birth in the *Morning Post* was unusual for a lower middle-class family living outside the capital. While lacking the flourish of the announcement placed in the provincial newspapers on the same day, it reveals something of his father's social aspirations. Following their London wedding on 13 June 1809, at St Mary's-le-Strand, John and Elizabeth Dickens had been delighted with their first matrimonial home. Situated in Landport, on the edge of Portsmouth, 1 Mile End Terrace, with fields and country lanes behind, was the first of four newly built Georgian terrace brick properties. Having been satisfied that John Dickens would make an excellent tenant, the owner of the house, Mr Pearce, agreed to lease him the property for £50 per year. Overlooking Cherry Garden Field, the two-bedroomed house proved to be a desirable home for a young couple looking to establish themselves within respectable Portsmouth society. The following year, at the end of October, their first child, Frances Elizabeth (Fanny) was born.

Around sixteen months later, Elizabeth Dickens gave birth, probably in the front bedroom, to her son, Charles, on Friday, 7 February 1812. Throughout his life, he considered the day of his birth to be of particular significance. He adopted a policy of specifically making important decisions on Fridays. He was married on that day, started his books on that day, and completed the purchase of his dream house on that day.

The timing of Dickens's birth has been the subject of speculation. It is likely that Dickens was born late at night, close to midnight. In the absence of direct autobiographical evidence, we find much of his story within his novel, *David Copperfield*. When he writes that David was born on a Friday, at the chimes of midnight, we can reasonably assume he was referring to his own birth. On Wednesday, 4 March, just under four weeks after he was born, his parents took their son to be baptized at their local parish church, St Mary's, Kingston, Portsea.

Dickens's three names, recorded in the St Mary's parish register of that day, were Charles, John, and Huffham (a misspelling of Huffam). He refused to use the second and third, and never forgave his parents for giving them to him. The first was the Christian name of his mother's father, Charles Barrow; the second, that of his own father; and the third, the surname of his godfather, Christopher Huffam.

Charles Barrow's life resembles that of a character from one of Dickens's novels. Born in 1759, the son of a successful Bristol wool merchant, he enlisted as a lieutenant in the Navy. Following this, he moved to London and, in 1788, aged twenty-nine, he married Mary Culliford, the daughter of a musical instrument maker. A few years later, he joined his father-in-law, Thomas Culliford, and a William Rolfe, as a partner in their musical instrument firm. In 1797, following the retirement of his wife's father, he left the business, taught music, and ran a circulating library for four years.

Then, at the age of forty-two, he embarked on a new career within the Navy Pay Office. Within a year, from the lowly position of an extra clerk, Barrow progressed to the senior post of "Chief

Conductor of Monies" – and his income increased from £130 to £350 per year. Occupying a whole suite of rooms, he was responsible for salaries and incidental expenses. In doing so, he was empowered to sign bills worth £900 each, to allow money to be transferred to the naval establishments at Plymouth, Portsmouth, Chatham, and Sheerness. His son, Thomas, followed in his footsteps, starting on 15 April 1805, the same day as another young man, John Dickens, also began working in the Navy Pay Office.

John soon became a regular visitor at the Barrow family home, where he met Charles Barrow's second eldest daughter, Elizabeth, who was sixteen at the time. John Dickens fell in love with the sweet-tempered, energetic, hazel-eyed girl. She had, however, more than just outward beauty to commend her. Well-educated, she possessed certain qualities that were to be inherited by her eldest son, Charles.

About six months after his daughter's marriage, in 1809, Charles Barrow's employers became suspicious, and their concerns were soon alarmingly confirmed. On 11 January 1810, oblivious of the investigation into his conduct, he submitted his usual account. Confronted by a board of treasury officials, he was accused of embezzling the huge sum of £5,689 (around £290,000 today). Barrow confessed, citing the burden of ten children and the expenses of a constant illness in his defence. A few days later he resigned, imploring his employers not to instigate criminal proceedings. His pleas were ignored. To escape an inevitable prison sentence, he fled, initially to Brighton, with the view to escaping the country. At about the same time, his wife and children also secretly left the family home. On reaching the Isle of Man (outside the British government's jurisdiction) they started a new life.

Despite his shameful conduct, neither his son Thomas, nor Dickens's father, lost their jobs in the Navy Pay Office. This may well have been due to the intervention of another relative, Sir John Barrow, who held the highly influential post of Second Secretary of the Admiralty.

With Barrow a fugitive, his family found themselves in a precarious financial position. While Elizabeth was married and

Thomas in work, their eldest daughter, Mary, twenty-one, was not yet married, nor was her sister, Sarah. Frederick, the oldest son, who was eighteen, was either studying, or unable to support himself. The five remaining children were all dependants. While the children's uncle, John Barrow, surely helped, the main responsibility rested on the shoulders of Thomas Barrow and John Dickens.

John Dickens's background was far from exalted. His parents met while they were in service in London. His mother, Elizabeth Ball, was a housemaid for the Marquis of Blandford, in Grosvenor Square, Mayfair, and his father, William Dickens, was a footman employed by the Crewe family, nearby at 18 Lower Grosvenor Street. John Crewe was the Whig MP for Chester, and his family owned a considerable amount of land in Cheshire. In the early part of the nineteenth century, he became Lord Crewe. His wife, Frances, was a noted beauty and extremely popular in London's social circles.

In 1781, John Dickens's parents were married at St George's, Hanover Square, only a few minutes' walk from the Blandfords' residence. There was a marked age difference between the two: she was thirty-six; her husband was in his sixties. Following the wedding, William Dickens was promoted to the position of butler or steward by the Crewes. His wife was employed as a servant. They had two sons, the older William, and John, who was born on 21 August 1785. A month before both boys were baptized, their father died.

Following the death of her husband, Elizabeth Dickens was appointed housekeeper at Crewe Hall. She remained in this role for the next thirty-five years, retiring at the age of seventy-five. During her time of service, the Crewes both took a personal interest in the welfare of William and John. They paid for their education and then helped William set up his business in London – a coffee shop in Oxford Street – and were instrumental in securing John's position at Somerset House.

Mrs Dickens, as remembered by Lord Crewe's three grandchildren, would entertain them on a winter's evening around the fire in her room, with fairy stories, historic tales, and personal anecdotes. After she had retired and was living in lodgings in Oxford Street, she would repeat these various narratives, including, no doubt, accounts of life at Crewe Hall, to her eagerly attentive grandson, Charles.

The imprint of his upbringing was apparent in John Dickens's personality and actions. He was a man of refined tastes and culture: evidenced by his unusually large collection of books, essays, plays, and novels, which were to prove invaluable to his son. John was always well dressed, enjoyed entertaining his friends lavishly, and was prone to a rather pompous style of speech. One Dickens family visitor tellingly observed that he sensed something of the "ghost of gentility hovering in their company". Those who knew John would doubtless have been shocked to learn of his humble beginnings.

Before leaving the Crewes and their influence upon the Dickens family, further inferences can be drawn from the pages of *Bleak House*. Written between 1851 and 1853, Elizabeth Dickens appears as Mrs Rouncewell, the long-serving housekeeper of the Dedlock family at Chesney Wold. John Dickens is the housekeeper's younger, errant son, George. Ill-advisedly borrowing money, he fails to repay it, thereby causing a friend, as the loan guarantor, financial hardship. John Dickens did exactly the same thing. The writer's uncle, William Dickens, features as Rouncewell, the Ironmaster.

The appearance of these three characters is not the only link between the novel and Dickens's family history. There are also marked similarities between the Dedlocks' ancestral home, Chesney Wold, and Crewe Hall and between Sir Leicester Dedlock and Lord Crewe. There is also something deeper and darker that can be drawn from the novel regarding the writer's perception of the relationship between his grandmother, his father, and the Crewes. One of the narrative's central plot devices is that of illegitimacy: Lady Dedlock and her former lover, Captain Hawden, have a daughter, Esther Summerson. The devious lawyer, Tulkinghorn, discovers Lady Dedlock's secret, attempts to blackmail her, and is subsequently murdered by her maid, Hortense.

Eight months before Charles started to write *Bleak House*, John Dickens died. In the process of coming to terms with his loss,

Dickens may have used the narrative to give form to an internalized suspicion that his father had been the illegitimate son of John Crewe or someone else connected with his household.

There is one further circumstance that merits consideration. When Elizabeth Dickens died, at the age of seventy-nine, she left an estate worth £950. Around £50,000 today, this was a large sum, particularly for someone who had only been earning eight guineas a year during the last twenty years of her working life. Added to this, she had already given her older son £750 some years before. How could a retired housekeeper have accumulated what was a small fortune at that time? It may well have been the case that the Crewes were extremely generous employers, who took an active interest in the well-being of their faithful servants, and the sum was a retirement gift. Conversely, it could indicate some clandestine act on their behalf.

We come now to the last of the three names that appears on Dickens's baptismal record, Huffham. This was the surname of his godfather. John Dickens had met Christopher Huffam during the course of his work. Huffam was the head of a well-known, established firm, which provided rigging to the Navy, and John hoped that he would prove to be an influential friend to Charles in later life. It was even rumoured that Huffam had some connection with the royal family. In Dickens's novel, *Dombey and Son*, Mrs Chick confirms John Dickens's aspirations: "Godfathers, of course, are important in point of connexion and influence." It would appear that Huffam was negligent in the performance of his duties towards his godson. When he died on 6 May 1839, Charles made no reference to the event in any of his correspondence. Despite this, there does appear a brief reference to Huffam in a short 1853 *Household Words* autobiographical piece, "Gone Astray".

While Huffam may have neglected his responsibilities as a godfather, he made a sizeable deposit in the bank of his godson's creative resources. When visiting his home in Church Row, Limehouse, near the Thames, Dickens was given access to his nautical manufactory warehouse at Limehouse Hole, where his acquisitive imagination ran riot. The fictional legacy of these visits is most apparent in *Dombey and Son*.

THE WORKHOUSE, THE
THEATRE, AND ROYALTY

Four months after Dickens was born, the family moved. By the time the author had reached his sixteenth birthday, he would have done so again fourteen times. Some of these moves were to do with work, as Navy pay clerks were liable to be transferred to various naval locations at short notice, but others, as in this case, were due to financial constraints. The new property, 16 Hawke Street, Portsea, was some £15 a year cheaper to rent.

John Dickens has been depicted as having an over-optimistic and improvident approach to money, both through his fictional self, Wilkins Micawber (*David Copperfield*), and in the numerous biographies of his famous son's life. Though commended for his conscientiousness as a father, husband, and employee, he seemed unable to live within his means. He had a penchant for lavish entertaining and expensive tastes.

Although his imprudence probably did contribute to the move, it may well have not been the only reason. His wages had to go beyond his own family, as we have seen, even though it appears his career was prospering. At the time, he had been working as pay clerk for the Navy Pay Office for seven years (the last five in Portsmouth) and he had progressed well. Just as a friend of the Crewe family had secured him his first position, so another, Richard Brinsley Sheridan, Canning's successor as "Treasurer of the Navy" (1807–12), is likely to have assisted in his subsequent promotion. Not just an administrator, he was also responsible for visiting Navy ships and distributing the crews' pay in person.

By the time he arrived in Portsmouth in November 1807, he had risen from his original post of temporary clerk to Fifteenth Assistant Clerk for the General Business in Pay Branch. This resulted in a pay increase of around £30 per year. The following year he was promoted again to Twelfth Assistant Clerk, and in the year of his marriage (1809) his salary was approximately £180 per annum. Four years into his career, his income had more than doubled. Bob Cratchit, Scrooge's long-suffering clerk in *A Christmas Carol*, was forced to provide for a family twice the size on just £40 a year. But clearly this was not enough for John Dickens.

The new family home was around a mile from their first home, and a reasonable walking distance from John's work. Though its location was not as desirable as Mile End Terrace, it was still considered perfectly respectable, with naval officers frequently housed in the street. Although a little cramped, once old enough, Charles, with his older sister, would play happily in the small back garden, under the watchful eye of the maid. The family remained at 16 Hawke Street for eighteen months, leaving on Christmas Day, 1813. At the time, Elizabeth Dickens was around six months pregnant with her third child.

The third, and final, Dickens family home in Portsmouth was 39 Wish Street. Within a mile or so of their two previous residences, the house was situated in a very pleasant, small street, in the new extension of the town, Southsea. The favourable nature of the move, both in location and accommodation, was reflected by the rental being roughly twice that of 16 Hawke Street. They moved in on Boxing Day and remained until Christmas Day of the following year. During this stay, two significant family events occurred.

First of all, Elizabeth Dickens's older sister, Mary (affectionately known as Aunt Fanny), came to live with them. She had been recently widowed: her husband, Thomas Allen, a Royal Marine Officer, had died in Brazil. She was to become a great favourite with the children and to remain part of the family for the next eight years. With the addition of Mary's £50 a year pension and John's further promotion to Eleventh Assistant Clerk in June, the household finances were in a much healthier state.

On Monday, 28 March 1814, Dickens's younger brother, Alfred Allen – his middle name was given in honour of his aunt – was born. On this occasion, John Dickens chose to place a birth announcement in the leading Whig London newspaper, *The Morning Chronicle*. Around twenty years later, his oldest son would be one of the paper's leading parliamentary reporters, and its pages would contain a collection of his early work. Six months later, baby Alfred was dead. He was to be one of two siblings to die in childhood.

In December, due to the partial defeat of Napoleon and the end of the war in America, John Dickens, was recalled to London at very short notice. Around Christmas Day, 1814, the Dickens family left the naval town for the last time. Charles, not yet three, would always remember that it had been snowing. In *David Copperfield*, the author refers to both the perceptiveness and longevity of childhood memories: "I think the memory of most of us can go farther back into such times than many of us suppose, just as I believe the power of observation in numbers of very young children to be quite wonderful for its closeness and accuracy." In a second passage, he writes: "If it should appear from anything I may set down in this narrative that I was a child of close observation, or that as a man I have a strong memory of my childhood. I undoubtedly lay claim to both of these characteristics."

Dickens had a remarkable memory which, in his own words, "possessed the qualities of a sensitive photographic plate". In later life, his ability to draw on images, characters, events, and impressions from his childhood enriched his writing. In two of his *Household Words* articles, he drew directly upon his Portsmouth memories. His early childhood days in the town vindicated one of his favourite theories about life, which he liberally expressed in his fiction: *the smallness of the world*. Throughout his lifetime, he would refer to the remarkable coincidence of one of the ushers from Wellington House Academy (the final school he attended) becoming tutor to the son of his acting friend, William Macready, to justify this belief. In his writing, these coincidences more closely resemble providential appointments. Oliver's meeting with Mr Brownlow outside a Clerkenwell bookshop in *Oliver Twist* is a good example of this.

John Dickens's transfer to London resulted in an actual salary reduction of £47. This was due to a system whereby employees working away from London in various ports were granted an "Outport Allowance". The household budget was once again stretched, especially through supporting Elizabeth's family. Dickens's family, including Mary Allen (Aunt Fanny) and a servant, moved into 10 Norfolk Street, a central London first-floor property above a grocery shop owned by their landlord John Dodd. On 23 April 1816, a second daughter, Letitia Mary, was born. Baptized the following month, at St Mary-le-Bone Church, Westminster, she was to be the longest lived of all Charles's siblings, reaching the age of eighty-three.

Financially, the family struggled at this time. In 1824, when John Dickens was arrested for debt, John Dodd was named as one of his creditors – this could have been for either rent arrears, or an unpaid shop bill. Despite this, the relationship between the two must have remained civil, as the Dickens family were to return to the property for a second time between 1829 and 1831. The property was significantly situated, for only nine doors away stood the Strand Union Workhouse – possibly an inspiration for *Oliver Twist*.

The Dickens family were not in Norfolk Street for long and soon moved to another naval town, Sheerness, on the Isle of Sheppey, Kent. Leaving Norfolk Street around Christmas Day, 1816, they moved into "Blue Town" until 4 April 1817. Blue Town, which gained its distinctive name from the practice of its earliest residents of painting their primitive wooden homes with blue paint, "borrowed" from their employers in the naval dockyard, was effectively a suburb of the main town.

Whereas the Norfolk Street workhouse may have provided some material for his writing, the theatre, on the corner of Victory Street and the High Street, next door to the family home, inspired a passion and interest that engaged Dickens throughout his life.

From performing comic songs for his father's friends, producing and writing his own plays, watching plays and pantomimes in London and Rochester, and dreaming of becoming an actor, the theatre, as will be seen, played a key role in his creative and imaginative development.

In later life, John Dickens, with reference to the family's stay in Sheerness, would amuse his listeners with anecdotes of how, on an evening, he would sit in his room and hear what was going on on stage. His personal highlight occurred when he was able to join in with the singing of "God Save the King" and "Rule, Britannia!".

On the 25 March 1817, the *Kentish Chronicle* reported that the number of clerks employed in the Sheerness and Chatham dockyards was to be reduced, with seven being discharged at Sheerness. Based on the timing of the family's departure, ten days after the article appeared, it seems likely that John Dickens's next transfer to Chatham was due to this restructuring. On this occasion, the disruption of moving was reduced, since the two towns were only twelve miles apart. The family were to remain in the town for the next five years.

When the 27-year-old writer was working on his third novel, *Nicholas Nickleby*, he travelled to Portsmouth, with his friend and future biographer, John Forster. Forster would later remember standing with Dickens, watching a military parade and being astounded at his ability to describe the shape and formation of those taking part, based on a memory from his Wish Street days when, as a two-year-old, he stood in the exact same spot. His capacity to remember details from the past is noteworthy and serves as an excellent metaphor: the participants in the parade represent the perceptions, images, events, and people of Dickens's childhood years, and the shape they formed reflects the writer's impressive ability to marshal, enliven, and embed these memories within the pages of his work.

3

THE HAPPY DREAM OF CHILDHOOD

Dickens's Chatham childhood days, the happiest of his life, were key to his imaginative and creative development as a writer. The author's friend and biographer, John Forster, described the town as "the birthplace of his fancy", and it was here that he first dreamt of being an author. The family's stay in the bustling military town was spent at two separate addresses: 2 Ordnance Terrace and 18 St Mary's Place. Here Charles began his formal education; developed his love of reading, performing, and the theatre; took his first tentative steps as a writer; and gazed upon his fairy-tale castle, which he would one day own and in which he would eventually die. It was also where the first seeds of religious experience and perception were sown.

They moved at some point in April 1817. The new house, 2 Ordnance Terrace, was set well back from the road. With two hawthorn trees, the front garden was enclosed by tall iron railings. This pleasant, comfortable leased property was to be the home of not only the existing family (John, Elizabeth, Charles, Fanny, Letitia, Aunt Fanny, and two servants), but an additional two children, yet to be born, Harriet and Frederick.

Situated in a decidedly middle-class, respectable location, with a hayfield to the front, its setting was not dissimilar to Mile End Terrace. The two servants, Jane Bonny (kitchen maid) and Mary Weller (the thirteen-year-old nursemaid) were based in the basement, next to the cellar and large kitchen; John and Elizabeth's bedroom and the parlour were on the first floor; while, in keeping with the normal practice of the period, the children were all together in one of the attic bedrooms. Aunt Fanny had the other.

The view from the front attic bedroom, which may well have been Dickens's, was particularly impressive. Through the wide sash window, he would have been able to see over the rooftops of the lower town, into the harbour and dockyard, with its tall chimneys. Beyond this stretched the marshes and the Medway valley, with its verdant Kentish hop and corn fields and orchards. Such was his lofty vantage point, he would even have been able to see the "Chatham lines", where the residential regiments were constantly drilling and taking part in mock battles. Dickens would soon also be in the position to enjoy the occasions when, with his father, he sailed along the Medway to Sheerness, aboard the Navy pay yacht, *Chatham*. Trips in the high-sterned cutter were to become one of his happiest pastimes and would inspire his imagination.

It is likely, due to the relative quietness and isolation of Sheerness (the town's population was around 800 people, only a fraction of Chatham's 24,000), that it took the Dickens family a little time to acclimatize themselves to their new surroundings. In contrast to the peaceful, well-ordered surroundings of Ordnance Terrace, the town itself was vibrant and prosperous. As well as the busy Saturday weekly market, there were numerous fairs, processions, and celebrations. In May, there was the first of two annual three-day fairs, the second being in September. On the first of May, the local chimney sweeps paraded through the town, an event the author wrote about in his 1836 sketch, "A Little Talk About Spring and Sweeps". On the next day, it was the turn of the milkmaids.

For two days in August, the town came to a virtual standstill, as huge numbers of people gathered for the annual horse-racing event up at the "Chatham Lines". On St Clement's Eve (22 November), the blacksmiths' apprentices would march along the streets. As they progressed, singing, making speeches, reading rhymes, and dancing, they would collect money from those watching, to fund a celebratory supper in the evening. In Chapter 12 of *Great Expectations*, Joe

Gargery, Orlick, and their apprentice Pip, sing a song to St Clement, the patron saint of blacksmiths. Two days later, on St Catherine's Eve, it was the turn of the ropemakers' apprentices, another thriving trade reliant on the naval dockyard.

Dickens's happiest childhood days and the nurturing of his creativity did not solely take place within the precincts of Chatham. It is a "*tale of two towns*", with the second being Rochester. With their Ordnance Terrace home lying close to the blurred boundary between the two, the Dickens family could have reasonably considered themselves to have been residents of the more respectable, quiet twin town.

Imperceptibly merging with Chatham, Rochester provided the young writer with a very different perspective. Situated around the meandering Medway river, the ancient market town, with its cathedral, formidable castle, and Guildhall (which the young Dickens believed was the model for the palace the Genii of the Lamp built for Aladdin) had various other sixteenth- and seventeenth-century buildings. Whereas Chatham was very much centred on the here and now, Rochester instilled in the boy a reflective appreciation of the past, which was to become a feature of his writing.

During these blissful childhood days, father and son would often be seen walking hand in hand together. On Sunday afternoons, after church, these walks developed into lengthy excursions into the surrounding countryside. One of their favourite routes involved crossing Rochester Bridge and climbing up to Gad's Hill, through Cobham Woods, part of Lord Darnley's estate – a distance of around two miles. On reaching the main Gravesend to Rochester road at Higham, they would continue on to picturesque hamlets, such as Chalk (Dickens was to spent his honeymoon there, at Mrs Nash's cottage, in 1836), Shorne, where the author expressed a wish to be buried, Cobham, Frindsbury, and Snawridge Bottom. The love of this area, and of walking, would remain with him throughout his life.

Pausing close to the John Falstaff Inn and, almost certainly, relating to his son the humorous details of Shakespeare's account of Falstaff's unsuccessful robbery in the selfsame location (*Henry IV, Part 1*), John Dickens spotted an opportunity to pass on some words of wisdom to his impressionable five-year-old son. Pointing to a nearby impressive rose-brick, ivy-fronted detached property, which to the boy took on the form of a wonderful mansion, his father explained that if he were willing to work very hard, one day he could own such a house. According to Dickens, the sentiment was often repeated. Perhaps it was as much an acknowledgment of the speaker's frustrated social expectations as an encouragement to his son. These aspirational words were etched deeply into the child's memory.

On how many occasions, the then owner, the Reverend Linton, Rector of Higham, saw the boy dreamingly gazing in, is not known; but the child would make regular pilgrimages up to the house, as though he was committing to memory every detail of his longed-for home.

Some thirty years later, the successful 43-year-old writer, walking through the snow on his return from his birthday celebration in Gravesend, paused outside the house. Noticing it was for sale, he instructed his solicitor to commence negotiations immediately. Having started off at £1,500, he eventually paid £1,700, plus an additional £90 for a shrubbery across the road.

After having lived in the house for three years, Dickens, in his *All the Year Round* piece, "Travelling Abroad" (April 1860), includes a passage in which he travels back in time thirty-nine years to meet himself at Gad's Hill. As well as providing autobiographical information, the excerpt reveals his perception of his childhood self, expresses the importance he placed on the property, and demonstrates the vivid connectedness he maintained with his past. It also illustrates how he perceived Gad's Hill Place as being a point of convergence between his past, present, and future.

The neighbours at Ordnance Terrace provide an excellent example of how, as a boy, Charles subconsciously accumulated material for his future writing. As a result of his highly retentive memory and his ability to discern the characters and foibles of those around him (an attribute inherited from his mother), he was able to weave these impressions into his first book.

At about the same time as the Dickens family arrived, another family, the Stroughills, moved into the terrace. They had three children: George, aged twelve, Mary, nine, and Lucy, seven. Although George, seven years older than Charles, was his closest friend during those Ordnance Terrace days, Lucy occupied a far more precious place in his young heart. Mary Weller (the nursemaid) would later recall how the "blue-eyed, golden-haired fairy" was the special favourite and little sweetheart of Charles. In later life, he confessed that he had fallen in love with the constant companion of his Ordnance Terrace days.

At the beginning of *Sketches of Young Couples* (1840) Dickens, thinking about himself and Lucy, writes of two children, aged between six and eight, "he, all love and attention, and she all blushes and fondness" and how "they have dreamt of each other in their quiet dreams". Twenty years later, in "Dullborough Town", the narrator reflects on his lost childhood sweetheart, Miss Lucy Green. These two references reveal something of the heartache that the nine-year-old boy must have felt when, in the spring of 1821, his relationship with Lucy and her brother came to a sudden end. The sentimental reunion that takes place between the narrator, Lucy, and her husband, an old school friend of his and now a doctor, at the end of "Dullborough Town", bears no relation to reality. Lucy Stroughill had married Joseph Large, a shipwright, and subsequently died following childbirth four years before *Sketches of Young Couples* was written.

Next door to the Dickens family, at 3 Ordnance Terrace, lived a very colourful, obdurate individual, Duncan Calder. Bellicose by nature, he took it upon himself to challenge the parish authorities over the rateable value of his house. He was so persistent that not only were his rates reduced, but so too were those of all the other properties in the terrace.

Mr and Mrs Dickens's closest friends were the elderly couple, Richard and Mary Ellen Newnham, at number 4. Sixty-six-years-old when the family moved in, Mr Newnham, an affable, kind man, was a retired tailor, and his wife, three years younger than her husband, was a generous, warm-hearted lady, who frequently invited Fanny and Letitia for tea.

Such was the strength of the relationship between the two families that three months before the death of Richard Newnham (June 1827), John and Elizabeth named their final child Augustus Newnham. Letitia, the Newnhams' special favourite, was named as a beneficiary in Mr Newnham's will; both Fanny and Letitia were also beneficiaries of Mrs Newnham's will. Of all the Ordnance Terrace residents, Mrs Newnham is by far the most significant.

In "Our Parish", the opening section of Dickens's first book, *Sketches By Boz* (1836), Ordnance Terrace appears as Gordon Place, "a neat row of houses, in the most airy and pleasant part of the parish". The residents of Gordon Place are clearly based on Dickens's neighbours: the "Half-Pay Captain" (Duncan Calder), who opposes the parish authorities at every turn and generally makes a nuisance of himself as the leader of the opposition party, and "The Old Lady" (Mary Ellen Newnham).

The similarity between Mary Ellen Newnham and her fictional counterpart is undeniable: both are widows; both have an only son living in India and a servant called Sarah; both delight in entertaining their neighbours' children, including the two girls from number 2 (Fanny and Letitia); both are financially independent; and, just as Mary Ellen Newnham lived next door to Duncan Calder, so "The Old Lady" lives next door to the "Half-Pay Captain".

In reading about "The Old Lady", we learn that the Dickens family regularly attended church at St Mary the Virgin and that they accompanied Mrs Newnham: "She walks home with the family next door but one, and talks about the sermon all the way, invariably opening the conversation by asking the youngest boy [Charles] where the text was." The author also remembers Mrs Newnham's charitable disposition and regular acts of kindness: "Her name always heads the list of any benevolent subscriptions and hers are always the most liberal donations to the Winter Coal and Soup Distribution Society." Additionally, on returning from Chatham's Saturday market, she distributes money to various elderly people, who call at her home.

It is also notable that in the evenings it is "The Old Lady's" regular practice to listen to her maid, Sarah Bourne, read from the Bible. Dickens concludes:

> *Thus, with the annual variation of a trip to some quiet place on the sea-coast, passes the old lady's life. It has rolled on in the same unvarying and benevolent course for many years now, and must at no distant period be brought to a final close. She looks forward to its termination, with calmness and without apprehension. She has everything to hope for and nothing to fear.*

Mary Ellen Newnham died eight years later in 1843, at the age of eighty-nine.

This close representation clearly demonstrates Dickens's ability, even as a boy, to recognize within individuals the qualities he would later associate with his interpretation of what constituted true religion. The highly respected old lady acts as a counterpoint to another Gordon Place resident, the eldest Miss Willis, who exhibits the ill-temperedness that was to typify his fictional representation of false religion.

Dickens's creative development during this time was not solely due to the stimulation of his surroundings. It was also greatly enhanced by visits to the theatre, pantomimes, family-based theatricals, and storytelling. The Theatre Royal in Rochester was rather narrow, uncomfortable, and shabby but, to the wide-eyed child, it must have proved magical. The Royal featured a mixture of Shakespeare, pantomime, and variety. Despite its distinctly provincial nature, Edward Keen, one of the leading tragedians of the period, and the great comic actor, Charles Mathews, whom Dickens would seek to emulate, both performed there. As a direct result of these theatre visits, he began writing his own plays, which, according to the writer, were received "with great applause from overflowing nurseries". Although none of them survived, something is known of one of them: *Misnar, The Sultan of India*. Closely based on "The Enchantress", one of James Ridley's *Tales of the Genii* (1764), it features a gracious and young prince (no doubt Dickens himself), who counters the threat of demons and monsters through the utterance of wise thoughts.

At this point, his writing endeavours and interest in the stage were greatly encouraged by James Lamert. Somewhat older, James was the son of the man who was to become Aunt Fanny's second husband. He befriended Dickens and, during the breaks from his Sandhurst education, would not only take him to Rochester theatre, but would involve him in his various homegrown plays, including Mrs Inchbald's *Collection of Farces*. These were performed at Ordnance Terrace and Ordnance Hospital, where James's father, an army surgeon, had his quarters. He also built Charles his own toy theatre, which further contributed to his creative output.

Of all the various forms of theatrical entertainment, nothing appealed to Dickens more than pantomime. The undoubted highlight of his childhood theatrical experience came in 1819 and 1820, when his father, for two consecutive Christmases, took him to Sadler Wells Theatre, London, to see the celebrated clown, Joseph Grimaldi, appear in pantomime. These two occasions were special moments in a golden time in Dickens's childhood. Eighteen years later, he would edit Grimaldi's memoirs with his father's help.

Dickens was a performer. The man who, in later life, was to captivate tens of thousands of people with his dramatic reading performances was the same boy who stood upon the table at the Mitre Inn, Chatham and entertained his father's friends, and others, with a medley of comic and sea songs. With the enthusiastic encouragement of his proud father, the sound of the boy's clear, unabashed treble singing voice became a regular feature of the family's social calendar.

With an already impressive repertoire, his favourites being Charles Dibdin's sea songs, he would perform alone, or with his sister, Fanny, at birthday and Twelfth Night parties, for his father's guests, family, friends, relatives, whoever came to visit, achieving quite a reputation as he did so. Not content with just singing other people's compositions, he set about writing his own comic songs, one of which was called "Sweet Betty Ogle". What with Fanny practising and developing her piano playing and singing, with the encouragement of her mother, Ordnance Terrace was quite a musical home.

Dickens's boyhood performances also included recitation and comic acting. The positive affirmation he received from these musical and acting performances helped to establish within him an inner sense of his own ability, a self-belief that would sustain him through the darker times that were approaching.

Storytelling also played an important part in Charles's time at Ordnance Terrace. Even though John Dickens took great pleasure in entertaining his children with the occasional tale, it was the female members of the household – Mrs Dickens, Aunt Fanny, Mary Weller, and occasionally John Dickens's mother – who regularly stoked the developing fires of Charles's imagination. Of these, it was the vivid bedtime stories of the young maid, Mary Weller which were indelibly etched upon his memory.

Forty years later, in *Nurse Stories* (*All the Year Round*, September 1860), he reproduced three of them: firstly "Captain Murderer", a man who married young brides, killed them, and put them in pies; the one that involved a supernaturally large, glaring-eyed cat, which prowled the world at night stealing the breath from sleeping children (she led Charles to believe that the cat had a particular thirst for his); and, finally, a story about Chips, the shipwright, who is plagued by rats which eventually eat him. To accentuate the impact of these stories, she would always precede them "with a long hollow groan and a clawing of the air with both hands". If this were not bad enough, she also had the habit of connecting these accounts with people she knew. On many occasions, Dickens was left lying on his bed terrified and unable to sleep.

When she was not scaring her young charge, she would soothingly sing or hum Dr William Fuller's "Evening Hymn" to settle him to sleep:

Now, now that the sun hath veil'd his light
And bid the world goodnight;
To the soft bed my body I dispose.

But where shall my soul repose?
Dear, dear God, even in thy arms.
And can there be any so sweet security!
Then to thy rest, O my soul!
And singing, Praise the mercy
That prolongs thy days.

Hallelujah!

The threatening clouds of financial hardship were once again gathering over the family. On 14 August 1819, John Dickens was forced to borrow the substantial sum of £200 (the same amount as his annual salary at that time) from a James Millbourne of Kennington Green, Surrey. Around the same period, he also borrowed an undisclosed amount from his good friend and neighbour, Richard Newnham.

Unable, shortly after, to meet the annual payment of £26, the settlement of the loan fell upon the guarantor, his brother-in-law, Thomas Barrow, who paid off the debt on 26 May 1821. The incident, quite understandably, caused considerable tension between the two families. Thirty-six years later, at the time of his death, Barrow still had not been repaid.

Why Dickens's father was forced to take out this loan is not known. It did not help that naval clerks at that time were paid quarterly. Certainly the family costs had increased, following the birth of two more children: Harriet Ellen (born August/September 1819) and Frederick William (born 14 July 1820). It seems more likely though that the extra money was needed to further support Elizabeth's family; Thomas Barrow's willingness to act as guarantor seems to support this.

In the spring of 1821, after four happy years, Dickens looked across the hayfield opposite the terrace for the last time. Following their belongings down the hill, they were never to see the two hawthorn trees blossom in their front garden again. For the nine-year-old Charles, the move, caused by the family's financial problems, was particularly difficult. He not only had to leave behind a wealth of happy memories, but also his cherished friends, Lucy and George.

4

THE READER, THE WATCHER, AND THE LEARNER

Although, undeniably, a downward move, both literally and figuratively, the new Dickens family home at 18 St Mary's Place (also known as The Brook) was by no means drastically inferior to Ordnance Terrace. The white plaster-fronted, modest semi-detached property, while lacking the meadow view, provided, with its six rooms, only marginally less space than they had before. Though not quite as desirable as their previous spacious location, it was, nonetheless, the preferred location for most of the non-residential officers attached to the nearby naval dockyard. The house, opportunely situated next door to the aptly named Providence Baptist Chapel, and overlooking St Mary's Church, was to be the setting for the development of Charles's religious beliefs, love of reading, and education.

During the first year or so of the family's time at Ordnance Terrace, his mother, with the occasional help of her sister, Mary, taught Charles and Fanny daily. These lessons provided them with an excellent rudimentary education. Many years later, Dickens confided to John Forster that he was convinced "she had taught him thoroughly well".

Around the age of six, Dickens, along with his sister Fanny, was sent to school for the first time in nearby Rome Lane. The elderly female teacher was apparently something of a tyrant. Charles would exact his revenge by reproducing her likeness in his *Dombey and Son* characterization of Mrs Pipchin: "the excellent ogress... a bitter, ill-favoured, ill-conditioned old lady of a stooping figure, with a mottled face, like bad marble, a hook nose, and a hard grey eye, that looked as if it might have been hammered out on an anvil without sustaining any injury".

Dickens may not have derived any educational benefit from his time at Rome Lane, the same cannot be said of his next school.

Just before leaving the house each morning, Dickens would proudly adjust his white, woollen beaver hat, a familiar sight to the residents in "The Brook", being the uniform of William Giles's school. The impressively named "Classical, Mathematical and Commercial School" was situated in a former almshouse on the corner of Rhode Street and Best Street. Within a short walk of Charles's home, the school's pupils mainly comprised children of army and naval officers posted in the town.

William Giles, the son of the Baptist minister responsible for the chapel next door to the Dickens family, was the antithesis of Charles's Rome Lane teacher. Twenty-three-years old when he started the school, William had been educated at St Aldate's School, Oxford, went on to become a master there, and then attended university in the city. As well as having had an excellent education, he had the reputation for being a cultivated reader and elocutionist. In addition, he was also an ordained Baptist minister.

If any of his neighbours, or those whom he regularly passed on the way to school, looked carefully at Charles, they would have noticed, over time, the increased confidence of his step. This positive change was attributable to his schoolmaster recognizing his pupil's enormous potential. The double encore he received following his first year's examination recitation from the Humourist Miscellany stayed in his memory throughout his life. Unquestionably, the two-year period that he spent at the school under the tutelage of William Giles contributed to his knowledge and educational development, especially with regard to his writing.

In the same way that Ordnance Terrace was connected with the theatrical aspect of Dickens's childhood, so St Mary's Place was the home of his reading. In the whole of the house, there was one small room adjoining Dickens's attic bedroom that was neglected by the whole family. To him it was a veritable Aladdin's Cave. As a young man, his father had acquired an eclectic collection of eighteenth-century books, essays, plays, and novels. Under normal circumstances, the son of servants could not possibly afford such an expensive luxury, but, as we have seen, he had them nonetheless.

Mary Weller, commenting on the amount of time Dickens spent closeted away upstairs, described him as being "a terrible boy to read". These protracted periods of reading, while inspiring and cultivating his imagination, also served another important purpose. At this time, Dickens was unsettled. The Ordnance Terrace move and the reasons behind it, along with the impending break-up of the household circle, due to his Aunt Fanny's forthcoming December marriage to Dr Lamert, were preying on his mind. His reading provided him with a welcome escape from these concerns and brought with it a sense of "picturesqueness and sunshine and hope beyond place and time".

It was during this time that Dickens began to suffer from violent, painful spasms in his side, which lasted for several years. Although undiagnosed at the time, they may have been caused by a kidney stone, which would have proved excruciating. Such attacks prevented him from joining in the active games of his friends. Instead, he would occupy his time looking on and reading. These episodes, though obviously distressing for both himself and his family, did increase his appetite for reading and gave him more time to observe the world around him.

Dickens was a contemplative child who loved to watch. Whether at night, standing hand in hand with Fanny, gazing up at their favourite stars, or looking out as the local children played in the churchyard, St Mary's Place proved an excellent vantage point from which to do so. Through the autobiographical voice of David Copperfield, Dickens reveals both his childhood familiarity with St Mary's and its churchyard, and its close link with his reading: "every stone in the church, and every foot of the churchyard, had some association of its own, in my mind, connected with these books, and stood for some locality made famous in them." In the same way, the images, events, people, objects, and buildings that he closely observed at this time were to become associated with his writing.

In addition to the bedroom window view, The Brook, due to its location, also afforded the opportunity for Charles to experience the sights, sounds, and smells of the busy naval dockyard. He would regularly observe the actual construction of ships. One of the eminent shipbuilders there was Gabriel Snodgrass. Dickens was to use both his surname and Christian name in *The Pickwick Papers* (Augustus Snodgrass and Gabriel Grubb). Of particular interest to him were the convicts, who provided forced labour for the Navy. At the end of each day, he would watch them file through the town with great numbers on their backs. Each night they would return to their prison hulks moored just beyond the dockyard.[1] He also recalled prisoners arriving on the top of stagecoaches from London and the feeling of unease it caused among their fellow passengers. These convict recollections found expression within the pages of *Great Expectations*.

The family's stay at St Mary's Place was a relatively short one. In the summer of 1822, around sixteen months after moving in, John Dickens was, once again recalled, probably at short notice, to London. Three months earlier he had been transferred from the "Pay Branch" to the "Branch for the Inspection of Seaman's Wills and Control of Licensed Agents". His salary at this time was £350, and it would remain at this figure until his early retirement on medical grounds three years later.

The make-up of the household at the time of this forced move had undergone several changes. Following her marriage to Dr Lamert, Aunt Fanny, along with the family's maid, Jane Bonny, had moved to Ireland. Dr Lamert's son, James, came to live at St Mary's Place, and, exactly three months after the wedding, Elizabeth Dickens gave birth to Alfred Lamert Dickens. He was given the same name as Dickens's baby brother, who had died in Portsmouth (see Chapter 2).

---

1 Prison hulks were decommissioned ships used as floating prisons in the eighteenth and nineteenth centuries.

Mary Weller, now eighteen, having formed a strong attachment with a local shipwright, Thomas Gibson, decided not to go to London. She was replaced by a young orphan girl from Chatham workhouse.

In spite of the financial storm clouds and family changes, The Brook had been a reasonably happy home for the young Dickens. Along with the reading and watching, he, along with his siblings, had often enjoyed visits to Fort Pitt Fields with their beloved Aunt Fanny and Dr Lamert. There had been parties, dancing, rowing on the river in the summer, and skating in the winter.

The inevitable sense of sadness and disruption felt by the ten-year-old was, on this occasion, short-lived. At the last minute, it was announced that an alternative arrangement had been made for Charles. He was to remain behind with the Giles family. So, in the company of his schoolteacher, he watched as his family clambered aboard the stagecoach bound for London.

Charles's stay with the Giles's family (June–September 1822) and the relationship he had with them proved important in the development of his Christian faith. There can be no question that they made a favourable and lasting impression upon the boy, and helped shape his emergent religious views. The two youngest Giles boys, John and Samuel, though slightly older than Dickens, were his great friends. In a speech many years later, the author alluded to Samuel as being "almost his daily companion" and remembered their "rambling together through the same Kentish Fields" with his brother. Twenty-one years after leaving Chatham, on visiting Manchester for a fundraising dinner, Dickens met up with John Giles, who had followed his oldest brother and father into the ministry.

According to Fanny, the Dickens children were "brought up in the Church of England", as their parents had been before them. This did not, however, preclude the family from attending the Baptist chapel next door. The main reason for their quite frequent visits was to hear the Reverend Giles (senior) preach. While John and Elizabeth Dickens were by no means devout, they, nevertheless, encouraged personal religious observance among their children.

Charles remembers his mother reading him Bible stories as a young child. Evidence of this exists in an amusing family anecdote involving his insistence on walking the same route every day with Mary Weller. When admonished by his mother, the young boy cheekily replied: "Mamma, does not the Bible say we must walk in the same path all the days of our life?" This was a loose reference to Proverbs 22:6. Also, in Chapter 2 of *David Copperfield*, there is an autobiographical reference to St Mary's:

One Sunday night my mother reads to Peggotty and me in there (the best parlour) how Lazarus was raised from the dead (John Chapter XI). And I am so frightened that they were afterwards obliged to take me out of bed, and show me the quiet churchyard out of the bedroom window, with the dead lying in their graves at rest, below the solemn moon.

A close study of his writing reveals a wealth of biblical references and allusions, as well as a detailed knowledge of the *Book of Common Prayer*. Both, in part, were attributable to the religious observation of his childhood and youth. It is also likely that his lifelong practice of prayer started as a result of his mother's encouragement.

The development of Dickens's religious views during his formative years, and beyond, had very little, if anything, to do with quality of the services he attended. Forster, specifically referring to his time at St Mary's Place and with the Giles family, described how the boy "had an intuitive understanding of the character and weakness of the grown-up people around him". What was to become apparent in his adult life, but was equally true of his childhood, was that the definition and example of faith was to be learned through observing others.

On an early autumn day, the ten-year-old Dickens stopped for a moment to look for the last time at his school and temporary home. Having done so, he turned towards his destination, Timpson's coaching office. As teacher and pupil walked beside each other, there was a tangible sense of their mutual sadness regarding their impending separation.

In contrast to the bustling departure of his family a few months earlier, the boy was the only inside passenger in the firm's Blue-Eyed Maid London coach. Having waved goodbye to William Giles, the boy settled back into his seat, as the coach slowly pulled away, ending his happy five-year association with the twin towns of Chatham and Rochester. In his hand, he clutched a copy of Oliver Goldsmith's *Bee*, a last-minute farewell gift from William Giles. Putting the book aside for a moment, he reached inside a nearby bag and pulled out his white beaver school hat. Teary-eyed, he placed it upon his head, keeping it there until he arrived at his London destination.

5

Disturbing Shadows of Debt and Despair

If, to borrow from the opening lines of Dickens's *A Tale of Two Cities*, his Chatham days could be described as the best of times, the next three years were to be the worst of times. Had Charles known of the dark days that lay before him, he would probably have asked William Giles to allow him to stay. Difficult and disturbing as they were to prove, they, nonetheless, contributed to the development of his steely determination, which was to play a key role in his future success. Be that as it may the memories of this period were to cast a shadow over the rest of his life. Perhaps he actively chose to harness their effect, or they exerted some control over him. There can be no doubt, however, that the extraordinary energy and drive he exhibited throughout his career was fuelled by the deeply ingrained images of this time.

Crossing the newly built Queen Street Bridge at Southwark, his thirty-mile journey ended in the courtyard of the Cross Keys, one of the City of London's postal inns, situated in Wood Street, Cheapside. Waiting for him, as the Blue-Eyed Maid pulled in, was his father who, on finishing work at 4.00 p.m, had walked the mile and a half from Somerset House to meet him. As was their frequent habit in Chatham, the two set off side by side to walk to their Camden Town home. After walking for around an hour, Dickens was doubtlessly relieved to leave behind the smoke and stench of the city streets and enjoy the peace and quiet of the fields that separated Camden Town from the rest of London. In 1791, Lord Camden had leased out land for the purpose of building around 1,400 houses, and the area tended to attract the better off poor and shabby genteel, of whom the Dickens family were a typical example. In those pre-railway days, Camden Town had a distinctive semi-rural feel. Fields formed a boundary with Somers Town; Kentish Town was little more than a collection of cottages, market gardens, and the occasional impressive house; Chalk Farm was just a farm; and to the north were the woods of Highgate.

Bayham Street, a row of around forty houses, near to the Fleet River and backing on to hayfields, was one of only a few roads in the area at that time. Number 16, a three-storey, narrow terraced Georgian house, was smaller than either of the Chatham properties, having only four proper rooms. Space must have been tight for the three adults (James Lamert was still with them), six children, and the Chatham workhouse servant. Claustrophobic by modern standards, it was not considered so among Victorian lower middle-class families. To the poor it would have seemed great comfort.

Such was Dickens's unhappiness during this time that it was to drastically prejudice his description of both the area and the house. To the fifty-year-old adult, brooding over the darkest days of his childhood, Camden Town had transmogrified into a "shabby, dingy, damp and mean a neighbourhood, as one would desire to see", and his house had become "a mean small tenement with a wretched little back garden abutting on a squalid court".[2]

In "The Haunted House" (*All the Year Round*, Christmas 1859), Dickens, reflecting on his early experiences of Bayham Street, writes: "I was taken home, and there was Debt at home as well as Death." The death to which he refers would certainly have been that of his beloved Aunt Fanny, who, within months of marrying and moving to Ireland, had died at the age of thirty-four. The funeral took place in Cork on 25 September 1822, and the shocking news of the sudden bereavement must have closely coincided with his arrival. It is also

---

2   A tenement was a house that had been divided up, where several families lived in separate rooms.

possible that the reference could relate to a second family tragedy that may have taken place around the same time. As alluded to in the previous chapter, records regarding his youngest sister, Harriet, are for some reason vague. It has been suggested by other biographers that she died of smallpox around this time.

Having been away for three months, Dickens had been insulated from the family's worsening financial predicament. On his return, he was quickly exposed to its grim reality. John Dickens had lost his £90 a year Out Port allowance, but was still receiving a generous salary of £350. Yet even though the rent on the house was only £22 a year and the rates below £4, they were in arrears. He had run up various unpaid bills with local shopkeepers and tradespeople, and was moving closer to the debtors' prison. His creditors, however, had satisfied themselves with the imposition of a "Deed" – essentially, an agreement between John Dickens and those to whom he owed money. The Deed, in the young author's imagination, took on a far more sinister form. The insecurity it caused was by no means quieted by the forced sale of some of the family's belongings or people arriving at the house to assess the value of various objects of furniture, including Dickens's own bed.

Death and debt were not the only dark clouds assailing him. What grieved him most was that his parents made no attempt to arrange for his return to school. The sense of neglect and pain he strongly felt was immeasurably heightened by the success of his older sister, Fanny. Seven months after his arrival, on 9 April 1823, she was awarded, at the age of twelve, a prestigious pupil-boarder scholarship, to study piano and singing at the Royal Academy of Music, situated in Tenterden Street, Hanover Square. Taught piano by the great Ignaz Moscheles, a pupil of Beethoven, and singing by the great Crivelli, she went on to perform in public concerts and teach at the Academy for seven years. Whereas his parents were willing to fund his sister's musical education and allow her to develop her talents, it appeared to him that his ambitions and dreams were of no consequence. His absence from school was to last three years.

Deprived of an education and companionless, he would often leave the house and walk along the road to the nearby almshouses. Once there, he gazed at the dome of St Paul's in the distance, as it rose above the smoke-filled air of the city. On these occasions, and when he was able to snatch moments of privacy in his attic bedroom, his thoughts would drift back to Giles's school, his friends the Stroughills, and their imaginary games in the Ordnance Terrace hayfield. Finally, Gad's Hill Place would rise and eclipse the shadows.

During his time at Bayham Street, a potentially catastrophic incident took place. On being taken into London on a sightseeing tour, probably with his father or James Lamert, Dickens found himself lost and alone. After looking around the impressive Palladian-style church, St Giles-in-the-Field, they had made their way down to the western end of the Strand to see Northumberland House. As the ten-year-old was looking up at the much-admired Percy Lion, the two lost sight of each other and became separated. Seemingly oblivious to the very real dangers that could so easily have beset him, Charles spent the rest of the day wandering the streets and visiting various landmarks.

In his autobiographical *Household Words* account of the event, "Gone Astray", written some thirty years later, he describes how, on recovering his composure, he sat down on a step and planned out his future. What form these plans took is not known, but they may well have involved him becoming either a writer or actor.

Dickens, who must have had some knowledge of the area, decided to embark on a Dick Whittingtonesque imaginary adventure, which took him from the Strand to the Guildhall, passing Templar's Bar, St Dunstan's, and St Paul's. He was intrigued by the close-up view of the cathedral that he had often seen at a distance. In the article, he also recalls staring in at the kitchen window of the Mansion House and being driven off by one of the cooks. On reaching the Guildhall, he spent some time carefully studying the gigantic twin statues, Magog and Gog, which were to feature in his *Master Humphrey's Clock*. After this, he used some money from his godfather, Christopher Huffam, to buy a theatre ticket in Goodman's Fields, off Whitechapel Road. By the time he left, it was evening, and at this point the reality of his situation finally hit home. Finding a watchman, he was eventually safely reunited with his extremely worried father.

The poignancy of this episode, taking place as it did when he was feeling neglected at home, is reflected in the following observation he made to John Forster: "I knew that, but for the mercy of God, I might easily have been, for any care that was taken of me, a little robber, or a little vagabond." The experiences of that day, Bayham Street and beyond, helped develop within Charles an empathy with the disadvantaged and, more importantly, a fervent desire to improve their situation.

One of the only few bright spots, in what was otherwise a desultory stage in his life, was the toy theatre, brought from Chatham, and various visits to his uncle, Thomas Barrow, Christopher Huffam, and, occasionally, his grandmother. Even though tension existed between his father and uncle, no such constraints existed between Barrow and his sister, Elizabeth, or his favourite nephew, Charles. In 1814, at the age of twenty-one, Barrow had fallen from a carriage, while working for the Navy Pay Office, and broken his leg. A subsequent fall resulted in a second break in the exact same place. When it failed to heal, it was decided that the leg had to be amputated. It was during Thomas's convalescence that Dickens became his "little companion and nurse". At that time, Barrow was living above a bookshop in Gerrard Street, Soho. The recently widowed owner, Mrs Manson, took a liking to Charles and would regularly lend him books.

Not only did he benefit from witnessing his uncle's fortitude and determination in successfully overcoming his disability, he also discovered that he was a man of some culture. He would also have overheard the conversations that took place when visitors arrived. One such visitor was Charles Wentworth Dilke, a work colleague of both John Dickens and Barrow, and a friend of the recently deceased poet, John Keats. Around fifteen years later, on a cold February day, Dilke, sitting in the editor's office of the *Athenaeum*, opened a package containing a copy of a recently published book, *Sketches By Boz*. Swiftly reading through the attached handwritten note, he paused as he studied the signature and recognized the writer as the boy he had met in his friend's room all those years ago.

Charles also enjoyed visiting his godfather's home in Church Row, Limehouse, around four-and-a-half miles along the Thames from central London. He was often called upon by Huffam to perform the comic songs of his Chatham days. Hugely appreciated by his host and his various guests, the enthusiastic applause and attention he received was in marked contrast to the dreary hours he spent each day at home. Less frequently, there were also visits to his grandmother's home in Oxford Street. While there, he would listen attentively to her stories about his father's childhood and her recollections of life at Crewe Hall. On one occasion, she gave him a generous gift of a silver pocket watch.

Added to these most welcome excursions, Dickens, as well as reading, channelled his creative energies into his toy theatre. He would painstakingly cut out the costumed characters, paste them onto cardboard, and glue them to sticks. After patiently training his younger brother, Frederick, to move the little players on the stage, Charles would narrate all the plays himself. Among these were *The Miller and His Men* and *Elizabeth, or The Exile of Siberia*. His love of these productions continued throughout his adult life. When, many years later and living at Gad's Hill Place, his son received a toy theatre, Dickens could not resist personally putting on a performance of *The Elephant of Siam*.

The unhappiness of his Bayham Street days did not prevent him from writing. The first sketch involved Thomas Barrow's eccentric barber, who was rumoured to have been the father of the famous artist Turner. He would regularly call in and shave Dickens's uncle. This was accompanied by a piece about his family's aged, deaf kitchen helper. Regrettably, not only has neither sketch survived, but the author, although proud of both, allowed no one to read them.

Towards the end of 1823, Charles's mother came up with what she believed to be the solution to the family's financial difficulties:

she would open a school. To enable this to happen they needed a larger property, closer to the centre of London. On Boxing Day, the eleven-year-old Dickens, along with his family, left Bayham Street for the last time.

Elizabeth Dickens's plan, though risky, was by no means completely reckless. She was an educated woman, who had taught her own children well. She had enlisted the help of Christopher Huffam who, through his work, had both the influence and contacts to recommend the school to naval families and employees of the East Indian Company. The ambitious property chosen for this venture was 4 Gower Street North, Camden Town. Closer to the city centre, the newly built house was situated in a neighbourhood inhabited by professionals and gentry. The relative affluence of the area and the comfort of the six-room house was reflected in the annual rent of £50 per year – over twice that of Bayham Street and the same as the Dickens's first family home at Mile End Terrace. With the double-window front rooms and large basement kitchen, it would have appeared a grand home for all the children, including Charles.

Very soon after moving in, Elizabeth Dickens proudly supervised the erection of a large brass plate on the front door. It read "Mrs Dickens's Establishment". Charles was sent out into the surrounding area to deliver circulars announcing the presence of the school and its virtues. Unfortunately, around the time the school opened, Christopher Huffam was declared bankrupt, due to a severe economic downturn. Years later, Dickens ruefully recalled, "Nobody ever came to the school, nor do I recollect that anybody ever proposed to come, or that the least preparation was made to receive anybody." The brass door plate was duly removed.

On Monday, 9 February 1824, John Dickens left the house for work at the normal time. Beside him, dressed in a pale suit, was his son. Having celebrated his twelfth birthday only two days earlier, it was his first day at work. Walking down Tottenham Court Road towards the Strand on that winter's morning, Charles was still struggling to come to terms with his parents' willingness to deprive him of an education.

When James Lamert, who had moved out from Bayham Street a few months before, came to visit the Dickens family in their new home, Charles had been delighted to see him again. By the time he left, he wished he had never come. It transpired that rather than taking up his army commission, Lamert had joined his brother-in-law, William Edward Woodd, in an exciting business venture based at 30 Hungerford Stairs, The Strand. Hearing of his close friends' financial predicament, he had come to offer their son a job. His parents, much to the young author's horror, enthusiastically accepted.

Over twenty years later, in his "autobiographical fragment", Dickens wrote of his bewilderment over their decision:

> *It is wonderful to me how I could have been so easily cast away at such an age. It is wonderful to me that, even after my descent into the poor little drudge I had been since we came to London, no one had compassion enough on me to suggest that something might have been spared, as certainly it might have been, to place me at any common school. My mother and father were quite satisfied. They could hardly have been more so, if I had been twenty years of age, distinguished at a grammar school and going to Cambridge.*

Towards the end of their mile walk, as they reached the Strand, Dickens caught sight of Warren's Blacking Warehouse, his place of employment. The last building on the left-hand side of Hungerford Stairs, it was nothing more than a semi-derelict, rambling old house, situated next to the Thames. With rotten floors and staircases, a stench of dirt and decay, and full of rats, it was difficult to perceive how anyone would wish to work there. It is inconceivable that the lost boy of the previous year, who sat on the steps near to Northumberland House to plan his future, would ever have imagined he would find himself in such place.

In spite of the dilapidated state of the building, the blacking (shoe polish) business in London was thriving. Charles Day, the owner of one of Warren's competitors, Day and Martin, left the colossal sum of £350,000 following his death. Another large concern was Warren's Blacking. This had originally been owned by two brothers, Robert and Jonathan. In 1821, the latter, following an argument, set up his rival firm, also called Warrens, as close to his brother's as possible. Robert Warren's was 30 the Strand, while Jonathan Warren's was at 30 Hungerford Stairs, the Strand. The Hungerford Stairs business was in turn bought by Lamert's brother-in-law, William Woodd.

On arriving, Dickens was met by James Lamert and taken to the first-floor office, which overlooked the river. As an act of kindness, rather than working with the other employees, room was set aside for him in the office. After a short while, Bob Fagin, one of the boys from downstairs, came and showed him what to do. Following the demonstration, Charles, equipped with string, scissors, paste, and blue paper, sat at his small work-table and proceeded to stick the labels on jars of shoe polish. For ten hours a day, six days a week, for around a year, this mundane task became his sole occupation.

There was nothing unusual about his situation – children were frequently employed at this time. The majority of them generally started their working lives at the age of seven or eight. Under the terms of the First Factory Act of 1819, the under sixteens were permitted to work up to twelve hours a day. Indeed, with a lunch hour, half an hour for tea, a starting salary of six shillings a week, and the goodwill of James Lamert, he was far better off than the vast proportion of his contemporaries. But to the bright, intelligent Dickens, who, even then, had a sense of his own potential, it was a soul-destroying experience.

THE PRISONER AND THE PUPIL

On Friday, 20 February 1824, having completed his eleventh day at Warrens Blacking Warehouse, Dickens set off for home. During the course of his three-mile walk through the dark, but by now familiar streets, whatever thoughts filled his mind, none could prepare him for the hammer blow that awaited him on his return to Gower Street North. The patience of one of his father's creditors, James Karr, had run out; John Dickens had been arrested for debt. He was not alone. In 1837, the year his son was writing *Oliver Twist*, 35,000 people suffered the same fate.

Initially, Dickens's father was detained in a nearby sponging-house (these houses represented the debtors last chance to avoid imprisonment). Throughout the Friday evening, and all weekend, Mrs Dickens made frantic, but ultimately fruitless efforts to secure the necessary money. Meanwhile, Charles acted as a go-between between his detained, broken down father and his mother. On Monday, 23 February, the 39-year-old John Dickens was taken to the Marshalsea Prison in Southwark. Charles was heartbroken.

The next month or so was especially difficult for Charles. As well as having to contend with the drudgery and frustration of Warrens, he was forced to act as his mother's agent, as she sold and pawned various items of furniture, household and personal effects. He was also forced to dispose of his beloved books. On an almost daily basis the house was emptying. By mid-March only a few chairs remained, and the family was confined to the two parlour rooms. The only brief respite occurred on a Saturday evening, when he would use two pennies from his week's pay to buy a copy of *The Portfolio*: a collection of horror stories, fables, disasters, murders, and sketches of London life. Not only did Dickens derive enormous pleasure from its pages, but it was to impact positively upon his future writing.

On Lady's Day (25 March), Elizabeth Dickens handed over the key to 4 Gower Street North to the landlord. As had been previously decided, she, along with Letitia, Frederick, and Alfred, joined John Dickens in the Marshalsea. Still receiving his salary, the family income of around £6 a week allowed them to live quite a comfortable life. Waited upon by their Chatham workhouse servant during the day – nearby lodgings outside the prison were provided for her at night – they had a pleasant enough room, plenty to eat and drink, and were no longer being harangued by their creditors. Ironically, they were better off than they had been for some time.

Arrangements had been made for their son to stay with an old friend of the family, Elizabeth Roylance, who lived at 37 Little College Street, Camden Town, near to Bayham Street. Fourteen years earlier, she had kindly sheltered Charles Barrow for several months at her Brighton home, while he was on the run from the authorities.[3] The last time she had seen Charles he had been only two years old. He and Fanny had stayed with her for two weeks while their mother was visiting her exiled family on the Isle of Man. Along with the Rome Lane School teacher, Elizabeth Roylance also served as a model for the severe Mrs Pipchin in *Dombey and Son*.

Already feeling neglected, because he was forced to work at Warrens, Charles felt the isolation and separation from his family deeply: "I was out at the blacking warehouse all day and had to support myself upon that money all week, I certainly had no other assistance whatsoever (the making of my clothes, I think, excepted) from Monday morning until Saturday night. No advice, no counsel, no encouragement, no consolation, no support, from anyone that I can call to mind."

For around a month, this unbearable drudgery, loneliness, and weekly separation from his family continued. Then, during one of his

3   See Chapter 1.

Sunday visits, the normally reserved, stoic boy could contain his sense of injustice no longer. It was the first occasion he had revealed the true extent of his feelings. By the time he had completed his heartfelt plea, his father had determined to intervene on his son's behalf.

Very soon after his outburst, on 2 May, he moved into 1 Lant Street, The Borough, only a few minutes' walk from the Marshalsea. He was now able to breakfast with his family before work and to spend his evenings with them. His landlord, Archibald Russell, an agent in the Insolvency Court, his elderly wife, and grown-up lame son, were very kind to Charles. On one occasion, Mr and Mrs Russell stayed up all night to nurse him through a bout of his kidney illness. Though still faced with the ordeal of Warrens and deprived of an education, the move, nonetheless, brought some welcome relief.

If there was a compensation in John Dickens's imprisonment, it would be in providing his son with a wealth of material for his future writing career. Mr Pickwick is imprisoned in the Fleet Debtors' Prison (*The Pickwick Papers*), the Dorrit family in the Marshalsea (*Little Dorrit*), and Mr and Mrs Micawber, modelled on Charles's parents, end up in the King's Bench Debtors' Prison (*David Copperfield*). The King's Bench is also linked to Walter Bray in *Nicholas Nickleby*.

On an evening, Dickens would eagerly listen to his mother's perceptive descriptions of various prisoners and their histories. One specific incident impressed itself upon him. His father, due to his oratory powers, had been elected Chairman of the Debtors' Governing Committee; they had decided to draw up a petition to raise funds to enable the prisoners to toast King George IV's forthcoming birthday. Securing a seat in the common room, Charles watched as the prisoners filed in to sign the petition. Looking back on the scene some years later, he recorded:

> *I sincerely believe I made out my own little character and story for every man who put his name to the sheet of paper, their different peculiarities of dress, of face, of manner, were written indelibly upon my memory. I would rather have seen it than the best play ever played. And I thought about it afterwards, over the pots of paste-blacking often and often.*

Unlike their sensitive, contemplative son, Charles's parents possessed a remarkable resilience and ability to quickly recover their spirits: his father compared himself to a cork bobbing along the river of life. Within days of his imprisonment, he had come up with a plan: he would retire from work on medical grounds and apply for a pension. On 2 March 1824 he wrote to W. M. Huskisson, the Treasurer of the Navy, enclosing a medical certificate, signed by two doctors, detailing that he was suffering from a chronic urinary infection to support his request. It would take a year for his application to be granted. In the meantime, on 28 May 1824, after three months in prison, he was released. At the end of April his mother had died and he had been unable to attend the funeral service at St George's Hanover Square due to his imprisonment.

On leaving the Marshalsea, the Dickens family, along with Charles, went to stay with Mrs Roylance. The Chatham workhouse servant girl did not join them, and no more is known about her. Due to the severe lack of space, it was only a temporary arrangement. At this point, Dickens's father returned to work. Each morning, Charles left the house to walk with him, fervently hoping it would be the last day at Warrens. Much to his dismay, not a single word was uttered on the subject.

Meanwhile, Mrs Dickens was busily looking out for alternative accommodation for her family. Four weeks after their release, the family moved into their new home, 29 Johnson Street, Somers Town. Built around 1796, the street was typical of the new residential development that had sprung up within this predominantly rural location. Overlooking the fields that bordered Camden Town, the inhabitants of the area tended to be mainly shopkeepers and clerks, very much in keeping with the Dickens family status at that time. Number 29, backing on to Rhode fields, with its six rooms on three floors, as well as a roomy attic, and a washroom in the back garden, was somewhat larger than their nearby former Bayham Street home.

One feature of Johnson Street that suited Charles's mood at this time was the extreme darkness that engulfed the area at night. Three days after moving in, he was forced to endure a painful situation which highlighted his own sense of disappointment and hopelessness. On 29 June, with his proud parents, he attended a public concert organized by the Royal Academy of Music. During the course of the evening, his sister Fanny's performance received enthusiastic applause, and later she received a prize and silver medal from King George IV's sister, Augusta. Years later, revisiting the still painful memory of that night, Dickens wrote: "I could not bear to think of myself beyond the reach of all such honourable emulation and success. The tears ran down my face. I felt as if my heart were rent. I prayed, when I went to bed that night, to be lifted out of the humiliation and neglect in which I was. I had never suffered so much before."

Days, weeks, months passed and still not a word was uttered about his resuming his education. Torn between a belief in his own capabilities and potential and "the secret agony of my soul [as I] felt my early hopes of growing up to be a learned and distinguished man, crushed in my breast", the dreary course of his life continued.

On moving to Johnson Street, Dickens was relieved to find that he could make friends among the neighbouring children. Almost directly opposite lived the Mitton family, who had moved in around six months earlier. Especially friendly with Mary Ann, who was his own age, he also made the acquaintance of her brother, Thomas Mitton.

At some point, Woodd decided to relocate the business to improved, larger premises. This must have come as a welcome relief to all the employees at Warrens. The new address was on the corner of Bedford Street and Chandos Street, Covent Garden, just to the north of the Strand. On a lunchtime, Dickens would call in at the nearby White Swan Tavern. The site where the tavern once stood was acquired in 1970 by one of London's long-standing publishing houses, J. M. Dent & Sons Ltd. Established in 1888, the company, along with many others, was to publish numerous collections of his work.

The new location had several windows overlooking the street, and it was decided that it would be a good idea to have a couple of the quicker boys on show: Dickens and Bob Fagin. This decision was to prove Charles's salvation. Such was their dexterity, they would often attract a group of onlookers. On one occasion, Somerset House being reasonably close, Dickens's father and Charles Dilke were passing. Seeing him in the window, they stopped. John was not without family pride, and the sight of his son put on show in a shop window filled him with indignation. The next day, when his son arrived at work, he handed James Lamert a letter written by his father. Although James was always kind to Charles, it was obvious from his reaction that its contents had upset him. In spite of Charles's mother's attempts to persuade Lamert to take him back – something her son bitterly resented – the rift between the two men was irreconcilable. After around thirteen months, the darkest chapter of Dickens's life to date came to an end.

The trauma that he felt while at Warrens cannot be overstated; his own wife and children knew nothing about his being there until after his death. In adult life, the author would avoid Hungerford Stairs, Chandos Street, and Bedford Street. Yet allusions to Warrens were to appear in no fewer than eleven of his fifteen novels. The whole experience, however, did help to create, in both the child and the man, an indomitable will to succeed. Thinking back to his time there, Dickens stated: "I do not write resentfully or angrily, for I know that all these things have worked together to make me what I am."

On 10 March 1825, just prior to his son leaving Warrens Blacking Warehouse, John Dickens, after twenty years' service, was granted early retirement on medical grounds and awarded an annual pension of £145. With a mixture of relief and sadness, for he had enjoyed his work and had some success in it, he looked around for alternative employment. Though careless at times about the family finances, he was nonetheless hardworking. Having painstakingly taught himself shorthand, and with the help of his brother-in-law, John Barrow, who was a journalist on *The Times*, John Dickens started working as a journalist for *The British Press*, a daily newspaper established in 1803. Some years before, in 1820, an article he wrote on the Chatham Fire had been published in both the *Kentish Gazette* and *The Times*. His choice of new career was to prove highly influential for his son's future.

At 7 a.m. on a spring morning, Charles, wearing a jacket and trousers of mixed black and white material, left the house. The neighbours, and those who had regularly watched him walk to work, would have noticed not only a difference in his clothing, but also in his whole demeanour. Instead of walking the length of Hampstead Road, he turned off, and at the corner of Granby Street entered a large wooden building, grandly named Wellington House Classical and Commercial Academy. The school, also referred to as Mr Jones's Classical Academy, was far from perfect, despite its reputation for being one of the best in the area. The owner and head teacher, a Welshman, William Jones, was little more than a sadistic tyrant, who frequently beat the boys with his mahogany ruler. Dickens described him as being both "ignorant and brutal". Elements of Jones's character can be seen in two of Dickens's notorious fictional head teachers: Wackford Squeers (*Nicholas Nickleby*) and Mr Creakle (*David Copperfield*).

Nevertheless, Mr Jones did have the good sense to employ proficient teachers, and the school did provide a reasonable education for the non-boarders, like Dickens, who were spared Jones's brutality, in case their parents heard of it. In addition to the standard subjects of the period, which included Latin (in which he won a prize), history, arithmetic, geography, English, and French, pupils were also taught the hornpipe and dancing. For a short time, Charles also had violin lessons, perhaps hoping to emulate Fanny's musical accomplishments. On making little progress, he wisely gave up. But it was not the formal teaching that was to prove especially beneficial; rather it was his involvement in extracurricular activities and being able to enjoy the company of friends.

While at Wellington House he, along with a friend, John Bowden, produced a light-hearted weekly newspaper, which they lent out among the boys in return for marbles, pieces of slate pencil, and toffees. Simultaneously, Charles was also taking his first tentative steps into the world of journalism, contributing penny a line notices to his father's newspaper. He also belonged to a literary club, whose members lent each other various Saturday and weekly magazines; also, occasionally, he would write and circulate his own tales. One area in which the school did excel – though Jones, and his staff, could take no credit for it – was in the boys' theatrical productions. While Dickens was writing and organizing various plays, a fellow pupil, William Beverley, who went on to become a celebrated theatrical painter, would design and paint wonderful scenery. As well as productions put on for the pupils and staff, there were also informal affairs in pupils' homes.

Then, around a month after his fifteenth birthday, the Dickens family's finances once again intervened in his education. At the end of October 1826, *The British Press* newspaper fell victim to the economic recession that was gripping the country, and John Dickens lost his job as a parliamentary and marine insurance reporter. With the £450 he had received from his mother having been largely used to pay off two debt instalments, money was once again extremely tight.

Evicted from 29 Johnson Street for the non-payment of rates, the Dickens family, including their newly born sixth child, Augustus Newnham, took up temporary lodgings just around the corner in one of the thirty-two houses that made up the Polygon, Clarendon Square. So named because of the fifteen sided, three-storey design, it was actually considered to be a more respectable area than Johnson Street.

Whereas Frederick (seven) and Alfred (five) were allowed to remain at Dr Dawson's school in Brunswick Square, the fifteen-year-old Charles was under no illusion about his own fate. In spring 1827, his two years at Wellington House Academy and his formal education came to an abrupt end.

Before joining the young clerk on his first day at the offices of Ellis and Blackmore; it is worth considering the factors which had shaped him up to this point. First, and foremost, his parents had exerted the greatest influence upon him. Apart from his resentment regarding the neglect of his education, Dickens enjoyed an excellent relationship with his father. In later life, he wrote: "I know my father to be as kind-hearted and generous a man as ever lived in the world. Everything that I can remember of his conduct to his wife, or children, or friends, in sickness and affliction, is beyond praise. By me, as a sick child, he has watched night and day, unweariedly and patiently." Chatty, good hearted, and jolly, the two, despite John Dickens's occasional financial lapses, were to remain on good terms throughout the rest of their lives.

His relationship with his mother was more complex. Resembling her greatly in his later years, many of the traits of his genius can be traced back to her. There appears to have been a sense in which Dickens felt he had to strive continually to gain his mother's approval, and her pride in her oldest son was not always apparent. This feeling may have been linked to a sense that she favoured Fanny over himself; the encouragement of his sister's musical talents and the funding of her academy place, while he languished at home, or worked at Warrens, would have reinforced this.

By the standards of the day, Dickens had received an adequate, if not good education. Even ten years after he left Wellington House Academy, 79 per cent of boys around his age could not read, and 67 per cent could neither read nor write. Added to this, his literary abilities had been greatly enhanced by his reading.

The fifteen-year-old had also developed a sense of religious awareness that went beyond simply attending church. By this stage, he had already developed the daily habit of prayer, which was to continue throughout his life. He had a good knowledge of both the Bible and *Book of Common Prayer*. Though there is less information on his attendance at services after Chatham, he, along with his family, regularly went to church on Sundays. We also know that when living in Johnson Street, he occasionally attended the Dissenting chapel, in nearby Seymour Street.

I BEGIN LIFE ON MY ACCOUNT[4]

The transformation from schoolboy to office boy was complete in a matter of weeks. Dickens's mother, anticipating her son's impending premature departure from Wellington House Academy, had already taken steps to find him a suitable position. Her aunt, Elizabeth Charlton, kept a lodging house in Berners Street (off Oxford Street), and it was to one of her guests, Edward Blackmore, a junior partner in a nearby legal firm, that she applied. On meeting Dickens and finding him to be "a clever, good-looking youth", he happily agreed to take him on. So it was, that on the following Monday morning, in May 1827, the fifteen-year-old who, by now, took a great deal of care over his appearance, left his home in the Polygon and set off for the Gray's Inn offices of Ellis and Blackmore.

Uncertain of his final destination, he was, nonetheless, on the road to what he firmly believed to be a bright future. If nothing else, his starting salary of ten shillings a week, an increase of four shillings from his last employment, promised a degree of self-indulgence. On being introduced to his fellow clerks, he was overjoyed to discover (in line with what was to become a firmly held belief in the smallness of the world) that among their number was an old school friend from Wellington House Academy, Daniel Tobin.

Much of Dickens's time was taken up carrying legal documents to and from the legion of public offices (around 150) that were to be found in London at that time. One can only imagine how his highly creative mind conjured with such names as the "Alienation Office",

---

4   Heading of *David Copperfield*, Chapter 11.

the "Prothonotaries Office", and the "Six Penny Receivers Office". He also made regular visits to the law stationers off Chancery Lane, ushered clients into the solicitors' offices and, from January to March 1828, took responsibility for keeping the petty-cash book. Whether consciously, or not, he was constantly accruing material for his future writing career. Edward Ellis, the senior partner, was to appear as Mr Pickwick's legal adviser, Mr Perker, in *The Pickwick Papers*, three names from the petty-cash book (Bardell, Corney, and Rudge) were adopted for characters, and he also encountered the originals for Miss Flite (*Bleak House*) and Newman Noggs (*Nicholas Nickleby*) while there.

At the end of 1827, the firm, which specialized in working with provincial solicitors, moved to a new address in Gray's Inn. The relocation resulted in the clerks having a second-floor office overlooking Holborn. The mischievous Dickens would relieve the boredom by dropping cherry stones onto the hats of passers-by below. On the occasions when people came up to complain, he would treat them with such innocence and politeness that they would leave perfectly happy. In addition, he brought a great deal of comic relief into the office: his mimicry of an elderly, snuff-taking laundress in nearby Holborn Court was a particular favourite with his workmates.

In spite of these brighter moments, and a subsequent pay increase to fifteen shillings a week, Dickens found the law, and his work tedious. Edward Blackmore believed that he disliked the drudgery of legal life. Added to this, Charles must have felt stifled and frustrated. Yet he was to consider a legal career for some time. In 1834, he wrote to the Steward of New Inn, stating his intention to "enter at the bar, as soon as circumstances will enable me to do so". Five years later, having already written two novels, he entered his name at the Middle Temple.

Dickens's eighteen months at Ellis and Blackmore, which was to come to an end in November 1828, proved to be a significant period in his life. While there, he wrote a comic play entitled *The Strategies of Rowena*. Essentially an abridgment of Carlo Goldoni's 1748 work, *The Cunning Widow*, a fragment of the original still survives today.

Also, during this time, no doubt inspired by his father, he took it upon himself to learn shorthand – a must for anyone seeking to embark on a career in journalism. Using a week's salary, he purchased a copy of Gurney's textbook, *Brachygraphy* (ironically subtitled: *An Easy and Compendious System of Shorthand*), which, at the time, was considered the most celebrated manual on the subject. Showing commendable tenacity and commitment, and with the help of his father and uncle, John Henry Barrow, he achieved, in a matter of months, what an average person would take three years to accomplish. His proficiency in shorthand was not only to provide him with a source of income for the next eight years, it was also to prove invaluable in his future writing career and public readings.

By the time he had left the legal firm, his encyclopaedic knowledge of the highways and byways of London, which was to inspire an inexhaustible supply of material for his first sketches, was just about complete. More importantly, it was not just the streets, taverns, theatres, and shops he knew so well, but also the people. According to his friend George Lear, "He could imitate, in a manner that I never heard equalled, the low population of the streets of London in all their varieties, whether mere loafers or sellers of fruit, vegetables, or anything else."

Following his departure from Ellis and Blackmore, the sixteen-year-old immediately took up a similar position with a solicitor by the name of Charles Molloy, who had an office in Lincoln's Inn Fields. He was to remain there for only three months, until his seventeenth birthday. This decision, in view of his general dislike of the law, and the role of clerk in particular, seems an odd one. However, at this time, he had not quite completed his shorthand studies, and the firm may have offered him some extra money. Added to this, his friend from his Johnson Street days, Thomas Mitton, who was to act as his solicitor in the future, also worked there.

Now confident in his shorthand ability, Dickens left Molloy's employment and, indeed, legal work altogether. Too young to find a position as a parliamentary reporter, he once again turned to the Charltons for help. His great-uncle, Charles, was a senior clerk at the Doctors' Commons. He also had a young relation, Thomas Charlton, who worked there as a freelance shorthand writer. On the recommendation of his great-uncle, Charles took up a similar position. Dating back to the sixteenth century, or perhaps even earlier, Doctors' Commons was effectively a college of lawyers, who were granted exclusive rights to practise civil law, essentially in matters relating to Ecclesiastical and Admiralty law. The college also exercised jurisdiction over matters relating to wills and probate for most of southern England and Wales. Within the confines of the Commons courtyard stood the Prerogative Office, where wills were recorded and stored. Members of the public, by paying one shilling, could search for the wills of those who had died.

When Dickens first entered the courtyard, through the archway, leading from Knightrider Street, next to St Paul's Cathedral, the architecture and general appearance must have reminded him of the fairy tales he was so fond of reading as a child. The absurdity of Doctors' Commons lay not in its archaic forms and appearance, but in the fact that the four different courts – Admiralty Court, Prerogative Court (which dealt with testamentary issues within various dioceses), the Court of Arches (the provincial court of the Archbishop of Canterbury), and the Consistory Court (the diocesan court of the Bishop of London) – were all held in the one building and presided over by the same people. Beyond the pantomime of role and robe swapping, the extremely insular nature of the Commons, as explained by Mr Spenlow in *David Copperfield*, afforded a very good living for all those involved. It is little wonder that in *Bleak House* the legal system is depicted as being convoluted, overly complex, and designed to benefit those within it, rather than those who used it.

In the spring of 1829, Dickens began his four-year career at Doctors' Commons by taking notes on evidence and judgments for the firm of proctors for whom his great-uncle worked. Proving his competence, he quickly established himself as a freelancer and co-rented a reporter's box in the court with Thomas Charlton. Although mainly working within the Consistory Court, a copy of one judgment, dated November 1830, for the Court of Arches, has been preserved. The case itself may well have been used in the author's "Doctors' Commons" sketch six years later. Even though it was tedious at times, the issues raised in these two Ecclesiastical courts would have proved of interest to Dickens. In later life, he exhibited a simple faith, allied with a strong aversion to matters relating to disputes about doctrine and forms of religion. Perhaps he witnessed too many petty squabbles at this time.

Financially, working at Doctors' Commons presented the young Dickens with two drawbacks: the lack of a consistent income, due to his reliance on commissions rather than a fixed salary, and the lengthy termly holidays taken by the proctors and doctors. Soon after starting the job, he took to working as a reporter in various Metropolitan Police courts to supplement his income. In addition, he took the step of acquiring business cards to further promote his services: "Charles Dickens/Shorthand Writer/10 Norfolk Street, Fitzroy Square".

Just prior to his eighteenth birthday, on 7 February 1830, while still living in Norfolk Street, Dickens once again called in to Berners Street to see his great-aunt and uncle. His purpose, on this occasion, was to enlist Charlton's help in supporting his application for a reading ticket at the Library of the British Museum. Having obtained it, he completed the application process, and shortly afterwards Charles joined his father as a reader. He was to renew the annual ticket on at least four occasions.

Charles's determination to secure a place in the Reading Room at the youngest possible age shows his passionate commitment to self-improvement through education. Whilst by the lower middle-class standards of the period, his formal education was by no means neglected, it was a woefully inadequate preparation for a sparkling writing career. This was confirmed by Henry Danson, an old school friend from Dickens's Wellington House Academy days: "Depend on it, he was quite a self-made man and his wonderful knowledge and command of the English language must have been acquired by long and patient study after leaving his last school." When John Dickens was asked where his son was educated, he replied: "He may be said to have educated himself."

In 1831, the nineteen-year-old Dickens felt sufficiently secure to take on the expense of sharing an office with a proctor, Charles Fenton. Situated close to Doctors' Commons, at 5 Bell's Yard, it provided him with a convenient location for writing up his notes. Had he checked the official Law List register at this time, his personal entry would have caused him a degree of emotional turmoil. Whereas the address had been entered correctly, his name had been misspelt. This, in itself, would not have caused him any great concern, after all "Dickins" had also mistakenly appeared on his parents' marriage certificate. But it was almost the same dismissively grating name, Dickin, by which Maria Beadnell's mother continuously addressed him.

When the incorrect register entry occurred, Dickens had already been in love with the petite and pretty Maria for around a year. The youngest of three daughters, she lived in the City of London, at 2 Lombard Street, and her parents often hosted evening parties. Charles had first met her in 1829, via his sister Fanny. She was nineteen, two years older than him. For the next four years, his infatuation, and the frustrations that their relationship produced determined his decisions and honed his character. The emotional pain and disappointment also fuelled his determination to succeed.

Capricious and flirtatious, Maria, who had other admirers, enjoyed Charles's obviously increasing devotion to her. He was a handsome young man, with a depth of character and resourcefulness she had not noticed before in others. She liked his company and appreciated his clever conversation and creativity. Her scrapbook, the richest surviving source of his early writings, contains numerous entries, including six poems. One of these, entitled, "Bill of Fare", is a cleverly constructed acrostic of her name.

In those heady, early days of his relationship with Maria, all seemed sweetness and light, but Dickens had failed to fully take into account one important overriding factor: his relative social inferiority, which was linked to his seemingly limited career prospects. Neither was his case helped by the lower middle-class status of his own parents. A visual reminder of this harsh reality confronted him each time he visited Maria's home. Next door to their house was a branch of Smith, Payne, and Smith's Bank, where George Beadnell held a relatively senior position.

In view of this, and Mrs Beadnell's sense of class consciousness, it was unlikely that they would encourage or consent to Maria forming a strong attachment to a shorthand writer and part-time police court reporter. In some ways, the situation was not drastically different from that which had confronted his own father, when he had courted Dickens's socially superior mother. But whereas Elizabeth's parents stopped short of actively discouraging their daughter, it was not to be long before the Beadnells did so.

On one occasion, at least, during the early stages of their romance, marriage was discussed. Walking out together, close to Lombard Street, the couple sought shelter in the nearby church, St Michael's Queenhithe, to escape the rain. At some point during their time there, Dickens turned to Maria and said, "Let the blessed event occur at no altar but this!" He went on to claim that she consented "that it should be so". The hopes he so sincerely held in his heart were soon to be crushed.

At some point, after their daughter Margaret's wedding, in March 1831, Mr and Mrs Beadnell intervened decisively. Maria, under the partial pretence of completing her education, was sent to Paris. Dickens was devastated. She was away for around a year. On her return, while the young author's devotion remained unchanged, he sensed a decided shift in her attitude towards him. Tensions between the two were accentuated by the involvement of Maria's best friend, Marianne Leigh.

The relationship was still fraught by the time of Dickens's twenty-first birthday celebration, on 11 February 1833. The party itself, which took place at 18 Bentinck Street, near Portland Place, was quite a grand affair considering the limited resources available. Waiters were hired to serve refreshments, and the room was made ready for music and dancing. Try as he might, his attempts to secure a private conversation with Maria were frustrated. Towards the end of the evening, he did manage to secure a brief interview, but this proved to be far from satisfactory. Finding the strain unbearable, Charles wrote to Maria on 18 March, informing her of his decision to end their relationship.

Although her reply temporarily renewed his hopes, they were quickly quashed by the cold, detached demeanour she exhibited at the amateur home-based theatrical evening he had organized on Saturday, 27 April. Dickens played four separate parts and was the driving force behind the whole evening, including the numerous rehearsals. Throwing himself wholeheartedly into a project to cope with emotional pain was to become a feature of his adult life.

The great love affair had ended. Confused and emotionally exhausted, he retired to lick his wounds. The experience of the last four years had imparted within him one essential quality: the desire to succeed and overcome any obstacle that lay in his path. If George Beadnell had taken the time to look into the eyes of his daughter's rejected suitor at this point, he might well have seen the glowing embers of self-belief, fuelled by a sense of destiny. The young man of restricted prospects was three years away from literary greatness and public adulation.

Even though the broken relationship had left deep scars, Dickens did maintain a degree of contact with the family. Six years afterwards, following the death of Maria's brother, Alfred (a lieutenant in the army who was killed in India), Charles wrote a compassionate and sincere letter of comfort and condolence to George Beadnell. More significantly, twenty-two years later, on Saturday, 10 February 1855, Dickens received a letter from Maria. Whether this was the first time they had corresponded since their youthful love affair had ended is not known. However, the note certainly aroused his curiosity and, no doubt, stirred up memories of the past. It had arrived, ironically, just prior to his planned visit to Paris.

Whatever his romanticized thoughts or expectations surrounding the meeting, they were quickly dispelled by Maria's appearance. Having married a Finsbury sawmill manager ten years earlier, the 45-year-old Mrs Henry Winter bore little resemblance to Charles's idealized image of his youthful love. It was not just the loss of her beauty, her alluring little laugh, engaging trivial chatter, and charming, quiet voice that troubled him. All these had been replaced by a silly giggle, muddled conversation, and a jarring loudness of speech. What was worse, on the two occasions they met (the second involving her and her husband dining with Dickens and his wife ten days later), Maria implied, through her mannerisms and general conduct, that some secret confidence still existed between them. When she attempted to arrange further meetings, Charles took steps to disappoint her. She eventually understood that he had no intention of resuming any sort of relationship with her.

As was often the case, an important event was reproduced within the pages of Dickens's fiction. The idolized Maria of his youth appears in *David Copperfield* as Dora Spenlow, David's first wife. Modelled on his young love, even down to her annoying little dog and the completion of her education in Paris, she is portrayed as being pretty, adorable, capricious, and completely impractical. With her death and David's subsequent marriage to Agnes Wickfield, one senses an autobiographical description of his romantic affiliation shifting from Maria Beadnell to his wife, Catherine Hogarth. In May 1855, a few months after Maria's surprise reappearance, Dickens started his eleventh novel, *Little Dorrit*. Here she takes the form of Christopher Casby's widowed daughter, Flora Finching, a foolish middle-aged woman, who insists on playing out some pretence that Arthur Clennam, her childhood sweetheart, was seeking to rekindle their affection.

8

THE ACTOR, THE REPORTER, AND THE WRITER

While his relationship with Maria Beadnell still hung in the balance, Dickens very nearly abandoned the path he had started on. At one point he planned to emigrate to the West Indies, but this idea got no further than a lengthy conversation with one of his relatives. However, his ambition to become an actor was pursued far more rigorously.

As we have seen, from a young age, Dickens had been fascinated with all things theatrical, and this heartfelt interest was to continue throughout his life. When he worked at Ellis and Blackmore he, and another clerk, Thomas Potter, would attend the theatre most nights. The young author's favourite was the veteran comic actor, Charles Mathews, whom he had first seen when he was a child at the Theatre Royal, Rochester. During the actor's six-year season at the Adelphi Theatre (1828–34), Dickens would attend as regularly as his commitments would allow. What especially interested him was Mathews's "monopolylogues", a one-man show, in which he would play a variety of parts, usually characters drawn from the lower urban classes. Transfixed, he would go home and quickly learn the performances by heart.

The young author's attachment to the theatre had been further strengthened by his sister, Fanny. On completing her four years at the Royal Academy of Music, she had already taken her first tentative steps in establishing her theatrical singing career. Often, as in their childhood, she would accompany Charles on the piano as he entertained her musical friends with a medley of comic songs.

Sitting in his small Bell Yard office, Dickens came to a momentous decision. Either from a determination to prove Maria's parents wrong about his prospects, or as an antidote to his despair over her being sent to Paris, he sent a letter to George Bartley, stage manager of Covent Garden Theatre. It was essentially a request for an audition. Bartley was very interested, and a date was arranged. What especially pleased Dickens was Bartley's request that his audition piece "should be anything of Charles Mathews I pleased". The only person who knew of the plan was Fanny. In the strictest confidence, he had asked her to come along and play for him as he sang.

On the morning of his appointment, Charles was struck down with a debilitating cold. His face was inflamed, his ears ached, and his voice was severely affected. He was forced to cancel. Even though in his apology note he stated his intention to try again the following season, it was never followed up. This proved to be a key moment in Dickens's life. Had he been successful – the testimony regarding his remarkable powers of comic mimicry while at Ellis and Blackmore, and the later comments of William Macready, one of the leading actors of his generation, would indicate that this would have been the case – the whole course of his life could have changed. He was two years away from writing his first published sketch and, had he become completely absorbed in his fledgling acting career, this might never have been written. Crucially, within what may have only been a matter of weeks, he was about to embark upon the final stage of his journey towards authorship.

The black ink of newspaper print was as much part of Dickens's DNA as it was his father's, who, following the collapse of *The British Press*, had taken up the position of parliamentary reporter at the *Mirror of Parliament*. A few years later, he was joined by his son. Founded in January 1828, the *Mirror* was a weekly periodical entirely devoted to recording parliamentary speeches and debates. Charles had other strong family links to this publication: Two of his uncles, Edward and John Barrow – the latter being the proprietor and editor – also worked there. It was the most obvious place for Dickens to start his political reporting career. Originally helping out on an informal basis, it wasn't long before John Barrow came to appreciate the abilities of his nephew. In recognition of this, he was formally employed as a parliamentary reporter.

Whereas Charles's proposed entry into acting would have done little to improve his suitability in the eyes of Maria's parents, his new role certainly would. Attracting many university graduates, it was commonly viewed as a stepping-stone to developing a promising career. Interestingly, three leading literary figures – Joseph Addison, Richard Steele, and Samuel Johnson – all previously held the same position.

In order to record the debates, Dickens, and his fellow eighty to ninety reporters, had to squeeze into the Public Gallery in St Stephens Chapel. In cramped conditions and forced to sit in the back row, it was often hard for them to hear what was going on, let alone record it. Added to this, it was stuffy and poorly lit. Following the late-night debates, he, and his fellow reporters, would go to a little tavern in the Old Palace Yard and write up their copy. Despite these less than helpful conditions and exhausting, unsociable hours, Dickens quickly established a positive reputation among his fellow reporters. James Grant, of the *Morning Advertiser*, stated that he "occupied the very highest rank, not merely for accuracy in reporting, but for marvellous quickness in transcript". This admiration was not just restricted to his colleagues.

In 1833, during the course of the second reading of the Irish Coercion Bill, the future Prime Minister, Edward Stanley, delivered a speech lasting over six hours. Such was its length, John Barrow allocated eight reporters, including his nephew, to cover it. When it eventually appeared, Stanley found that, with the exception of the first and last part, it was littered with errors. As a consequence, he requested that the individual responsible for the correct sections be entrusted with the important task of amending the whole speech. One can only imagine the pride that John Dickens must have felt when he was dispatched by Barrow to collect his son from the country to attend a meeting with the Stanley. On first meeting, the boyish-looking 21-year-old was reported he have said, "I beg your pardon, but I hoped to see the gentleman who had reported part of my speech." On completing the task, Dickens received a highly complimentary letter of gratitude. Three years later, the leading politician, no doubt remembering with a smile their original meeting, was to receive a copy of the young reporter's first book.

The drive, determination, and energy that was to sustain him throughout his writing career had by now become evident. Not content with his demanding post at the *Mirror of Parliament*, or his occasional work at Doctors' Commons, Dickens took up a third position. On 5 March 1832, a new seven-penny evening newspaper, the *True Sun*, was launched. Taking a radical, reforming political stance, it quickly proved popular with the lower social classes, so much so that when it faced financial difficulties in the autumn around 3,000 working people gathered at a London tavern to raise money to keep it going.

Dickens, employed as a general reporter (this avoided a clash of interest with his political work at the *Mirror of Parliament*), was on the staff for the very first edition. The management took particular pride in the newspaper's ability to circulate parliamentary news rapidly across the country. An article detailing an important debate that ended in the House of Lords at 7 p.m. on 18 April 1832 was available to be read in Sheffield twelve hours later. But with his increased responsibilities at his uncle's newspaper, where he had been given a subeditor's role, he was only able to stay at the *True Sun* for four months.

Despite the short-lived nature of his appointment, it was still to prove significant for his future writing career. At around the same time Dickens started the newspaper employed a new drama critic. On seeing Charles on the office stairs, he was immediately struck by his "keen animation of look". The critic, John Forster, only two months younger than the writer, was to become a lifelong friend and one of his most trusted advisers. Godfather to Charles's daughter, Mary, executor of his will, he also went on to be his first biographer.

The commencement of Dickens's parliamentary reporting career coincided with the closing stages of one of the most important, controversial political debates of the nineteenth century: the 1832 Reform Bill. Such was the public interest in the proposed ground-breaking Bill, that every morning paper was forced to engage at least ten reporters to cover it. In the provinces, starved of news, cheap London newspapers, such as the *True Sun*, priced at 7d, were snapped up for the inflated price of a shilling. Essentially, the Bill was designed to bring about electoral reform. In 1831, about only one in fourteen of the entire male population were entitled to vote.

Tensions throughout the country were running high. On 27 April 1831, following the House of Lords rejection of the first Bill, Londoners responded with the "Great Illumination". Supporters of reform placed candles and lamps in their windows, and the capital was soon ablaze with light. Six months later, when the second version of the Bill was again defeated in the Lords, there were riots in Derby, Nottingham, and Bristol. On 4 June 1832, the Bill was finally passed.

Dickens was not overly enthusiastic. He believed that the changes introduced would do very little to benefit working-class people: only those who held property of a certain rateable value could vote, and most people owned no property at all. Nor did he have much time for the archaic practices of the House. The extent of his antipathy towards the political system can be seen in his highly satirical *Household Words* piece, "The Thousand and One Humbugs" (1855). It is also apparent in his less than flattering depiction of his various fictional MPs, such as Cornelius Brook-Dingwall, "the typical member who has a great like of his own abilities, which must be a great comfort to him as no else had" (*Sketches By Boz*).

On the evening of 27 July 1833, Dickens found himself once again dining at the home of John Barrow. Since his uncle had left his wife and set up home in Norwood with his mistress, Lucina Pocock, Charles had become an increasingly frequent visitor. On this occasion, the three were joined by a very important guest. Aware of his nephew's ambition to further his journalistic career by joining one of the top London daily newspapers, Barrow had invited John Payne Collier. Formerly of *The Times*, Collier, in his role as subeditor, was responsible for parliamentary reporting at the *Morning Chronicle*. Established in 1769, by the early 1830s it had a daily circulation of around 1,000. Stamp duty – which was high – was applied to newspapers, so they were relatively expensive. Consequently, there was considerable competition among the various titles to attract the small numbers of readers who could afford to pay such a price on a daily basis.

Although the evening ended on a high note, with Charles performing one of his favourite comic songs, "The Dandy Dogs'-Meat Man", and his own composition, "Sweet Betsy Ogle", the anticipated job offer was not forthcoming. Unbeknown to both uncle and nephew, William Clement, who had brought the *Chronicle* in 1821, had recently sold it for £17,000. The new owners, led by the abrasive John Easthope, a former Whig (Liberal) MP, who had made his fortune on the Stock Exchange, planned to use the newspaper to champion reform and represent the views of the Whig party. In spite of the inevitable ensuing changes, Collier did put in a good word for Charles, but at the time his recommendation was ignored.

A few months later, in the fading light of an autumn evening, after leaving the *Mirror of Parliament* building, Dickens set off purposefully in the direction of Fleet Street. On approaching his planned destination, Johnson Court, he hesitated. Deliberately timing his arrival to ensure that there would be no one present at the office, he furtively posted a large envelope through the door. Having done so, he quickly left.

The next morning, Captain Holland, the new owner and editor, who had just purchased the *Monthly Magazine*, arrived at work. Handed the post by his clerk, he sat down and sorted through it. Accustomed to receiving potential contributions from prospective writers, he placed the envelope to one side, planning to read it later. No doubt, if he had appreciated the singular importance of its contents, he would have acted with far more urgency. When he did finally come around to reading the piece, entitled "A Dinner at Poplar Walk", he was suitably impressed and wrote a few lines to the author to tell him so. Unfortunately, for some reason, the note failed to reach Dickens prior to the appearance of the magazine's next edition.

Consequently, when Dickens bought the next copy, he had no idea whether his sketch had been included or not. Having done so, he hurriedly made his way to Westminster Hall, preferring its relative privacy to that of the surrounding busy streets. Once there, he eagerly scanned the pages of the publication. Unaware that the editor had actually changed his original title to "Mr Minns and His Cousin", he at first thought that his sketch had been rejected. On closer examination, however, he eventually found it.

After reading through the nine-page sketch, he confided to his close friend Henry Kolle, in a letter dated 3 December 1833, that "my eyes were so dimmed with joy and pride, that they could not bear the street, and were not fit to be seen there". Soon after, he was to receive Holland's polite and flattering note, in which he not only confirmed his favourable opinion of the author's work, but requested that he submit further papers. Dickens was to write five more sketches for the magazine prior to leaving the *Mirror of Parliament*.

Focusing on the Buddens's attempts to further their son's prospects by ingratiating themselves to his wealthy godfather, Augustus Minns, this first sketch is little more than a parody of social aspiration. Sandwiched between weighty articles on subjects such as "The Phenomena of Magnetism" and "The Operation of Monopolies", there was little to suggest that its writer, for the next thirty-five years or so, would use his writing to campaign for the rights of the poor.

The following year, in an attempt to stage a serious challenge to the Tory-based *Times* – the highest selling newspaper in Europe – the management of the *Morning Chronicle* decided to recruit more political reporters. This strategy of staff expansion and restructuring saw the newspaper's circulation dramatically increase by 5,000 in two years. One of the newly recruited reporters, Thomas Beard (whom Charles had first met at the Beadnells' home), when asked by his employers to recommend a colleague, had no hesitation in naming his close friend as being "the fastest and most accurate man in the gallery". This, and Collier's previous endorsement, proved sufficient. At the end of August 1834, having resigned from the *Mirror of Parliament*, Dickens achieved his ambition and took up his new position at the *Morning Chronicle*.

His opening assignment involved travelling by steamboat to cover Earl Grey's celebratory banquet in Edinburgh. During the course of the voyage, he noticed that one of his fellow passengers, a travelling salesman, was reading to himself his fourth *Monthly Magazine* sketch, "A Bloomsbury Christening". Watching, he was overjoyed to observe that he was laughing in appreciation of the sketch's comic content.

Responsible for pushing through the historic Reform Bill of 1832, the ex-Prime Minister Earl Grey was especially popular in Scotland (they had particularly benefited from the introduced changes to the voting system). Dickens's first eleven-column article, describing the events surrounding the "Grey Festival", appeared at the top of the middle page on 17 September. Nine days later, "Omnibuses", the first of his five *Street Sketches* appeared in the paper. This was an important step for his fledgling writing career. With a circulation of around 6,000, the readership of the *Chronicle* was ten times that of the *Monthly Magazine*.

Two of the pieces – "Shops and Their Tenants" (October) and the final one, "Brokers' and Marine-Store Shops" (December) – represent Dickens's original attempts to expose his readers to the distressing realities confronting the poor. In the first, the narrator describes the various occupants of a shop situated on the Surrey side of the Thames, just beyond Marsh gate. The first business having failed, the premises are leased by a widower and his family. With the father forced to work elsewhere, the eldest daughter is left in charge of both the shop and her three young siblings. By degrees, it becomes apparent that the shop is failing, as is the health of the girl. The younger children, although clean, are forced to wear threadbare and shabby clothes. Unable to let the rooms above the shop, the rent is unpaid. The daughter is forced to work into the early hours making objects to sell. The sad narrative concludes:

"We believe the girl is past all suffering, and beyond all sorrow. God help her! We hope she is."

This sketch is also important as it is the first used by Dickens to attack the false motives of those, who, in the guise of charity, sought to interfere in the lives of the poor for their own gratification. This was to become a recurring theme and culminated in his vilification of Mrs Pardiggle and her dealings with the brick-maker and his family in *Bleak House*. In detailing the sad plight of the eldest daughter, he writes:

> *We often thought, as her pale face looked more sad and pensive in the dim candle-light, that if those thoughtless females who interfere with the miserable market for poor creatures such as these knew but one-half of the misery they suffer, and the bitter privations they endure, in their honourable attempts to earn a scanty subsistence, they would, perhaps, resign even opportunities for the gratification of vanity, and an immodest love of self-display, rather than drive them to a last dreadful resource, which it would shock the delicate feelings of these charitable ladies to hear named.*

He continues the theme in a later *Monthly Magazine* sketch, "A Passage in the Life of Mr Watkins Tottle" (January 1835). On hearing the curate, Mr Timson, asking Miss Lillerton to make a donation to the church's soap, coals, and blanket distribution society, the forthright Gabriel Parsons scathingly interjects:

> *I'll tell you what, it's my private opinion, Timson, that your distribution society is rather a humbug. What on earth is the use of giving a man coals who has nothing to cook, or giving him blankets when he hasn't a bed, and giving him soup when he requires substantial food? Why not give 'em a trifle of money as I do, when I think they deserve it, and let them purchase what they think best? Why? – because your subscribers wouldn't see their names flourishing in print on the church door – that's the reason.*

"Brokers and Marine-Store Shops" focuses on the plight of those consigned to debtors' prisons – in this case, the King's Bench – and the "Rules" (this term relates to those debtors who were permitted to live in the immediate vicinity of the prison). Using the metaphor of decay and contamination to represent the prison and those confined within it, Dickens uses the objects for sale in the nearby shops to paint a picture of the desperation and destitution of those prisoners forced to sell all their possessions.

John Black, the long-serving, highly respected editor of the *Morning Chronicle*, quickly came to recognize Charles's abilities and potential. Indeed, it was Black, many years later who provided an excellent anecdote that was to bridge three distinct stages of Dickens's life. Walking through Hungerford Stairs Market on one occasion, he was struck by the singular behaviour and kindness of his young colleague. In front of them was a small, poorly dressed boy, being carried by his father. As they followed father and son through the market, Dickens managed to feed the boy a whole bag of cherries, without his parent knowing. No doubt, as he secretly fed the boy, he remembered himself as poor child, sticking labels on polish bottles within a few hundred yards from where he stood. The fifteen-year-old office boy, who used to drop cherry stones on people's hats from his Ellis and Blackmore office window, had found a far more compassionate way of utilizing cherries. The successful reporter and emerging writer still remembered his past.

Dickens's editor was not the only person to appreciate his talent. Shortly after reading the *Street Sketches*, William Harrison Ainsworth visited the newspaper's offices to enquire about the author's identity. Harrison was the author of *Rookwood*, a fictionalization of the lives of the celebrity criminals, Dick Turpin and Jack Sheppard, which had achieved a great deal of success. On his being pointed out, Ainsworth quickly set out to establish a friendship with the young political reporter. He quickly recognized his potential and took him under his wing. From that time on, Charles was a regular visitor at the author's Harrow Road home.

Whereas his introduction to reporting for the *Morning Chronicle* was exciting and enjoyable, events in Parliament were soon to lead to a period of frantic activity. Three months after he started, King William IV asked the ageing Whig Prime Minister, Lord Melbourne, to resign. This was to be the last time in British history that a reigning monarch would exercise their constitutional right in this way. Dickens expressed his strong sense of indignation over the affair with his satirical piece, "The Story Without a Beginning", which appeared in the *Morning Chronicle* a week before Christmas. When the even older Duke of Wellington refused to take his place, the moderate Conservative, Robert Peel, was appointed. As a result, Parliament was dissolved on 29 December. The general election took place in the January and February.

On 31 January 1835, the *Evening Chronicle* was launched, a sister newspaper to the *Morning Chronicle*. Appearing three times a week, it was primarily aimed at the provincial towns surrounding London. To boost initial sales, Dickens was commissioned to write a series of twenty pieces entitled *Sketches of London*. The first, "Hackney-Coach Stands", featured in the paper's opening edition, and the last, "The Ladies' Societies", appeared in August. While he received no extra pay for his five *Street Sketches*, his weekly salary was now increased by two guineas a week.

"Gin Shops" (February 1835) and "The Pawnbroker's Shop" (June 1835) are worthy of special note. Both are set in a particular deprived area of Drury Lane, known as "The Rookery": "The filthy and miserable appearance of this part of London can hardly be imagined by those (and there are many such who have not witnessed it.)" Dickens then goes on in "Gin Shops" to expose the overcrowding and squalor associated with such locations:

Wretched houses with broken windows patched with rags and paper: every room let out to a different family, and in many instances to two or even three – fruit and "sweet-stuff" manufacturers in the cellar, barbers and red-herring vendors in the front parlours, cobblers in the back; a bird fancier in the first floor, three families on the second, starvation in the attics, Irishness in the passage, a musician in the front kitchen, and a charwoman and five hungry children in the back one – filth everywhere – a gutter before the house a drain behind – clothes drying and slops emptying from the windows; girls of fourteen or fifteen, with matted hair, walking about barefoot, and in white great-coats, almost their only covering; boys of all ages, in coats of all sizes and no coats at all; men and women, in every variety of scanty and dirty apparel, lounging, scolding, drinking, smoking, squabbling, fighting and swearing.

Having detailed the reality of living in such conditions, he then challenges the commonly held preconceptions about the social evil of drunkenness:

Gin drinking is a great vice in England, but wretchedness and dirt are greater and until you improve the homes of the poor, or persuade a half-famished wretch not to seek relief in the temporary oblivion of his own misery, with the pittance which, divided among his family, would furnish a morsel of bread for each, gin-shops will increase in number and splendour.

Throughout his career, the author would argue passionately that the spiritual redemption of the destitute depended upon improving the physical aspects of their lives and providing them with an education. In expounding this view, he did, at times, face opposition from those within the Church, who believed that the poor suffered due to their depraved spiritual state: improving their welfare was unnecessary, what mattered was their Christianization.

"The Pawnbroker's Shop" explores the inextricably linked fate of three women at different stages of the same doomed journey. Dickens concludes by asking his readers: "How many females have terminated the same wretched course, in the same wretched manner?" Throughout these early sketches, and beyond, there is a constant emphasis on the poor being unable to escape their fate: their only hope of redemption rested with those willing to fulfil their Christian responsibility towards their neighbours.

George Hogarth, the newly appointed editor of the *Morning Chronicle* (he had previously been its music critic), greatly admired Dickens's writing. Charles soon warmed to the intelligent, affable, fatherly fifty-year-old Scotsman, whose credibility soared when it was discovered that he had published a book called *Musical History, Biography and Criticism.*

Within a month, just after his twenty-third birthday, Dickens was invited to the Hogarths' home, 18 York Place, just off the Fulham Road. Having left Scotland in 1830, the family, after spending a short time in both Halifax and Exeter, had settled in London. Three of the daughters – Catherine, who was nineteen when Dickens met her, Mary, who was fifteen, and Georgina, who was seven – were all to play a significant role in his life. Catherine, though not possessing the sparkling beauty of Maria, was nonetheless pretty. With attractive bright blue eyes and long glossy black hair, she spoke with a charming Scottish accent. Lacking Maria Beadnell's silly and flirtatious nature, Catherine was an engaging, pleasant young woman. While one suspects that the Beadnells had spoilt their daughter, Catherine had clearly benefited from a well-balanced upbringing. Her mother, some ten years younger than her husband, had ensured that her children were affable, cultivated, uncomplicated, and well brought up.

Another marked difference between Maria and Catherine was the way Dickens was perceived by the two families. While the Hogarths, in common with the Beadnells, occupied a higher social position than the Dickens family, they clearly understood that their potential son-in-law was an exceptional young man. George Beadnell, with his banking background, interpreted prospects in purely financial terms, but Catherine's father placed far more weight on Charles's literary potential. In the Hogarth household, music, literature, and culture were seen as important, and anyone who was gifted in these areas was highly valued.

Dickens was accepted with open arms and genuinely felt part of the family. The relationship between him and Catherine quickly flourished, and they were engaged within three months. One important part of their courtship was the presence of Catherine's sister, Mary, as chaperone. During this time, and over the next two years, Dickens would develop a deep, sincere love for her.

In June, he took up residence at 11 Selwood Place, just around the corner from the Hogarths' York Place home. Prior to this, he had been living alone at 13 Furnivals Inn, Holborn.

In September, Dickens's writing career moved forward, with the publication of "Seven Dials" in the journal *Bell's Life in London*. The first of twelve sketches in a series entitled *Scenes and Characters*, it occupied a prime position on the front of the popular metropolitan weekly journal owned by William Clement, the former proprietor of the *Morning Chronicle*. As well as raising his profile and earning more money, the writer attracted a new London-based audience for his work. Within a month of its appearance, Dickens met with the publisher, John Macrone, in his St James's Square office, to negotiate a contract for a collection of his work to be published in a book. Initially introduced through their mutual friend, William Harrison Ainsworth, it was agreed that for the sum of £150 Dickens would produce thirty-five sketches to be sold in two volumes. In a bid to boost sales it was also agreed that George Cruikshank, the well-known caricaturist would act as illustrator. The book, which is to be the subject of the next chapter, did not appear until February of the following year.

"Seven Dials", "The Prisoners' Van" (November 1835), and "The Streets at Night" (January 1836) provide excellent examples of Dickens's ground-breaking work. Never before had someone specifically set out to write about the realities of life within the deprived areas of London. It was this, and his remarkable acuteness and accuracy of observation, that differentiated his writing from that of most of his contemporaries. He was able to take his predominantly middle-class readers into a hidden world and awaken their social consciences, revealing the despair and hopelessness of that world's inhabitants.

"Seven Dials" focuses on the St Giles's area of West-Central London, which had developed a notorious reputation. Densely populated, impoverished, and containing a large criminal element, it was a place that no respectable person would dare to visit. Designed in the late seventeenth century by Thomas Neale, the then Master of the Royal of Mint, it comprised seven converging streets in the middle of which was a seven-sided stone undial. Despite its genteel beginnings, it had become little more than a honeycomb of slum dwellings, squalid courts, and blind alleys.

Once there, there was little hope of escape. Adopting a light-hearted narrative tone, Dickens takes his readers along the streets, carefully pointing out the gin shops; the drunken women fighting; the general indolence of its residents; and its chronic overcrowding. The sketch ends with a description of various tenants who share one house: the carpet-beater who "extends his professional pursuits to his wife; the Irishman who comes home drunk every other night, and attacks everybody and the two families who assault each other".

"The Prisoners' Van" is used to fix in his audience's mind the causal link between poverty and crime in the lives of children and young people. In the sketch, the narrator arrives outside Bow Street Police Office just in time to witness convicted prisoners being loaded into a van. They are to be taken to the Middlesex House of Correction in Cold Bath Fields – punishment there would have included the treadmill (a large 24-spoke paddle wheel that prisoners were forced to climb). The primary focus of the story is on two sisters: Emily, aged sixteen, and Bella, not yet fourteen. The elder, having suffered "two additional years of depravity" has become hardened, brash, and criminalized. Contrastingly, her sister has still retained her sense of shame and some remnants of decency and innocence. Both have been sentenced to six weeks' hard labour. While it is Bella's first offence, her sister is no stranger to prison. In addition to the two sisters, the reader's attention is drawn to the other prisoners, which include "boys of ten, as hardened in vice as men of fifty".

As was to be often the case, Dickens seamlessly switches from his role as documentarist to that of the impassioned advocate of social reform:

> *These two girls had been thrown upon London streets, their vices and debauchery, by a sordid and rapacious mother. What the younger girl was then, the elder had been once; and what the elder then was, the youngest must soon become. A melancholy prospect, but how surely to be realized; a tragic drama, but how often acted... These things pass before our eyes, day after day, and hour after hour – they have become such matters of course, that they are utterly disregarded. The progress of these girls in crime will be as rapid as the flight of pestilence, resembling it too in its baneful influence and widespread infection. Step by step, how many wretched females, within the sphere of every man's observation, have become involved in a career of vice, frightful to contemplate; hopeless at its commencement; loathsome and repulsive in its course; friendless, forlorn, and unpitied at its miserable conclusion.*

In painting this inevitable downward cycle towards depravity and misery, Dickens plants in the reader's mind the sense that they are the passive observers of these daily events. Society looks on, but chooses to do nothing. The readers look on and choose to do nothing. Throughout his career he would constantly reveal the plight of the poor, and ask "What can be done?" and "Why should we do it?" His clearly expressed solution to these two questions was that individuals should intervene on behalf of the poor: it was their Christian responsibility to do so.

The final sketch of *Scenes and Characters*, "The Streets at Night" (January 1836), demonstrates his remarkable ability to transform what is essentially a gentle light-hearted piece of writing into a hard-hitting appeal on behalf of the poor. One minute three neighbours are busily ordering muffins in a small suburban street, the next, the harsh reality of poverty is set before the reader.

That wretched woman with infant in her arms, round whose meagre form the remnant of her scanty shawl is carefully wrapped has been attempting to sing some popular ballad, in the hope of wringing in a few pence from the compassionate passer-by. A brutal laugh at her weak voice is all she has gained. The tears fall thick and fast down her own pale face; the child is cold and hungry, and its low half-stifled wailing adds to the misery of the wretched mother, as she moans aloud, and sinks despairingly down, on a cold damp doorstep. Singing! How few of those who pass such a miserable creature as this, think of the anguish of heart, the sinking of soul and spirit, which every effort of singing produces. Bitter mockery! Disease, neglect, and starvation, faintly articulating the words of the joyish ditty, that has enlivened your hours of feasting and merriment. God knows how often! The weak tremulous voice tells a fearful tale of want and famishing; and the feeble singer of this roaring song may turn away, only to die of cold and hunger.

In this passage the writer evokes two redemptive images: the compassionate passer-by and the desire to share relative wealth with the destitute. With the biblical imperative, "love thy neighbour as thyself" always before him, Dickens sought to mobilize those he influenced through his work to fulfil what he believed to be their divine commission.

By the time "Seven Dials" appeared, Charles, and his friend Thomas Beard had already established themselves as the *Morning Chronicle's* star political journalists. As such, they were given the assignments deemed to be of special importance. One such occasion was a speech by the Home Secretary, Lord John Russell, at a by-election dinner in Bristol, on 7 November 1835. The fierce rivalry between the Whig *Morning Chronicle* and the Tory *Times* manifested itself in the competition to outdo each other when it came to the speed with which they could publish political speeches and events. On Dickens's first assignment, *The Times*, at a cost of £270, had managed to print the Lord Grey Edinburgh Banquet speeches the very next morning, a day before his report appeared.

Determined to win, Dickens and Beard planned their Russell speech campaign with military precision. Having taken down the speech in shorthand, they hired a gig, one driving while the other transcribed his work, and sped to the Waggon and Horses Inn near Marlborough (on the main London road). From there it was taken on by a rider. It appeared in the next morning's edition of the *Morning Chronicle* on page three. It was a major triumph for the paper. The following month, John Black gave Dickens the additional role of writing theatre reviews.

Sketches By Boz and Sparks on Sunday

On 8 February 1836, the day after his twenty-fourth birthday, Dickens's first book *Sketches By Boz: Illustrative of Every-day Life, and Every-day People* went on sale. With his remarkable ability to vividly reproduce the reality of life in London's conveniently overlooked areas, the sketches proved popular with both critics and readers alike. Both *The Satirist* and *Morning Post* reviewers described his work as being inimitable. Within six months John Macrone had published a second edition. At this point, the name of the author was still being kept secret. It was not until five months later that an advertisement in the *Athenaeum* revealed Boz's true identity. Dickens first used the *nom de plume* at the end of his *Monthly Magazine* sketch "The Boarding House" (August 1834), and it was often used throughout his early writing career. It was inspired by his younger brother Augustus's mispronunciation of Moses, the pet name that Charles had given him.[5] Due to his nasal tone, Moses became Boses, which in turn became Boz.

While this is an amusing family anecdote, the use of the name Moses has symbolic significance within the context of his passionate crusade for social justice. As a prophetic voice for the disadvantaged and forgotten, Dickens sought to expose the suffering endured by the poor, believing they were just as trapped as the people of Israel had

---

5   Moses was the name of Dr Primrose's son in one of the author's favourite books, *The Vicar of Wakefield*, by Oliver Goldsmith.

been in Egypt. The same God who heard the cries of the Israelites heard the cries of those sinking in the mire of poverty. Dickens set out to awaken the spiritual conscience of a nation through his writing.

The seven pieces which formed "Our Parish", the opening section of *Sketches By Boz*, with the exception of "Our Next-Door Neighbour", originally appeared in the *Evening Chronicle Sketches of London* series. Within its pages, the author exposes the abject failure and inadequacies of the existing Poor Law system; questions the charitable motives of those helping the needy; highlights the depravation endured by those trapped within the downward spiral of poverty; and provides an initial glimpse into the religious themes which were to occupy his future writing.

At the time, each parish effectively operated in the same way as local government does today. It had rate-raising powers and responsibility for implementing the Poor Law and overseeing the provision of lighting, pavements, sewage, policing, and a fire service. The day to day management of the parish affairs rested with a body called the "select vestry". Chaired by the local clergyman, it was made up of two churchwardens and overseers, whose particular responsibility was to supervise the provision of the Poor Law. There was also a paid vestry clerk to advice on legal matters. The "select vestry" in turn was elected by the "vestry": the homeowners of the parish who paid £50 or more in rates.[6] The term "vestry" derived from the small room where vestments for use in church services were kept, and this is where these meetings took place. As parishes grew, due to substantial population increases, new, purpose-built halls were constructed to house the meetings, but the term "vestry" was retained.

Although there were monthly meetings and committees set up to deal with especially pressing issues, it was the annual meeting of the vestry members that generated the most interest and often caused controversy. The annual poor rate was set at this meeting. Far too

---

6 Individuals who had more than one property within the parish were entitled to multiple votes, up to a maximum of six.

frequently, those who looked to the parish for help suffered from the self-interest of those relatively wealthy members of the vestry who sought to minimize their contributions. Added to this, the overseers on the "select vestry" (often referred to as the board), constantly sought ways to reduce spending. As a result, the poor were often neglected.

As Dickens understood only too well, a profound contradiction lay at the heart of the parish system: the tension between its spiritual and temporal function. The care of the poor was not, in his view, a civil responsibility, but a Christian one. Those individuals who regularly attended church on Sundays, including the overseers, made up a significant portion of the vestry, yet when it came to applying Christ's teaching they acted selfishly. The writer was not alone in recognizing the failure of individuals to apply their faith in practical ways. The leading Victorian churchman, E. B. Pusey, in a clever parody of Matthew 25:35–40 wrote:

> *I did not give to the poor: but I paid what I was compelled to the poor rate of the height of which I complained. I did not take in little children in Thy name, but they were provided for; they were sent severed indeed from father and mother to the poorhouse, political economy forbade it… I did not visit Thee when sick, but the parish doctor looked in on his ill paid rounds.*

Faced with what he believed was the church's wholesale abdication of its responsibilities towards the poor, the author first set about exposing the woeful inadequacies and cruelty of the parish administration. In Chapter 4, "The Election for Beadle", Dickens describes the adversarial nature of vestry politics: "Our parish, which like all other parishes is a little world of its own, has long been divided into two parties, whose contentions, slumbering for a while, have never failed to burst forth with unabated vigour, on any occasion in which they could possibly be renewed."

He then goes on to describe how: "They divided the vestry fourteen times on a motion for heating the church with warm water instead of coals and also had a violent disagreement over the recipe for the pauper's soup served in the workhouse." His representation of vestries as being a forum for pointless squabbling is repeated in another sketch, "Doctors' Commons" (October 1836). Here he describes them as being the "Great Parochial British Joint Bank of Balderdash".

Next, he focuses on those employed by the vestry to administer the parish's poor relief. The Master of the Workhouse is described as being "a tall, thin bony man", who "eyes you, as you pass his parlour-window, as if he wished you were a pauper, just to give a specimen of his power. He is an admirable specimen of a small tyrant: morose, brutish, ill-tempered; bullying to his inferiors, cringing to his superiors." In contrast, the Parish Schoolmaster, in charge of the education of the workhouse children, is a sad figure. Unable to effectively teach those in his care, he is himself only one step away from becoming a pauper. The children of the poor are brutalized within the workhouse and failed in the classroom. The readers are asked to consider what hope there is for them.

The parish official that was to most symbolize the author's animosity towards the Poor Law provision was the beadle. Officious and pompous, their sartorial splendour of cocked hat, gold-laced coat (normally red), and large headed staff was in stark contrast to the menial nature of their duties, which included removing homeless vagrants from the streets; helping to collect the poor rate; and keeping the workhouse children in order during church services.

Simmons, the "Our Parish" beadle, who savagely canes a workhouse child in church for dropping his collection on the floor, is the antecedent of several such parish officers, most notably Mr Bumble in *Oliver Twist*. They all share one common description: overweight beadles in charge of half-starved workhouse inmates. This was not a new idea: in 1795, Lewis Walpole, in his *Vestry Dinner* caricature, depicts an emaciated pauper looking on as corpulent members of the vestry gorge themselves on an abundance of food. Robert Seymour, whom Dickens was to briefly work with on *The Pickwick Papers*, also produced a series of illustrations, *Heaven and Earth* and *The New Poor Laws*, on the same theme. In *Oliver Twist*, he was to extend the motif to include the members of the parish board.

Having highlighted the callousness, incompetence, and selfishness of those responsible for the implementation of the parish's Poor Law provision, Dickens turns his attention to the woeful inadequacies of the system itself. In the opening passage, which charts the downward cycle of "a poor man", and his family, his readers are left in no doubt as to the dysfunctionality of the existing structure and its failure to help those in need:

How much is conveyed in these two short words – "The Parish!" And with how many tales of distress and misery of broken fortune and ruined hopes, too often of unrelieved wretchedness and successful knavery, are they associated! A poor man, with small earnings, and a large family, just manages to live from day to day; he has barely sufficient to satisfy the present cravings of nature, and can take no heed of the future… His taxes are in arrears, quarter-day passes by, another quarter-day arrives: he can procure no more quarter for himself, and is summoned by – the parish. His goods are distrained, his children are crying with cold and hunger, and the very bed in which his sick wife is lying is dragged from beneath her. What can he do? To whom is he to apply for relief? To private charity? To benevolent individuals? Certainly not – there is his parish. There are the parish vestry, the parish infirmary, the parish surgeon, the parish officers, the parish beadles. Excellent institutions, and gentle, kind-hearted men. The woman dies – she is buried by the parish. The children have no protector – they are taken care of by the parish. The man first neglects, and afterwards cannot obtain work – he is relieved by the parish; and when distress and drunkenness have done their work upon him, he is maintained, a harmless babbling idiot, in the parish asylum.

This was representative of the fate of literally tens of thousands of families in London at that time. Dickens exposes the absurdity of a system in which those prosecuted by the parish for non-payment of rates are forced to seek help from the selfsame institution when they are unable to pay. Central government made no direct attempt to assist the poor, choosing to leave the implementation of the Poor Law to individual parishes, and London-based charities did not begin to proliferate until the 1850s.

Dickens, perhaps inspired by his childhood memories of Chatham and Rochester, chose suburban locations to show the stark social inequalities that existed in the parishes in and around London at that time. The wealthier residents of "Our Parish" all live in the extremely pleasant residential area of Gordon Place, based upon Ordnance Terrace; while the destitute family live in the rundown area of George's Yard.

Far from discouraging such divisions between the rich and the poor, the seating arrangements of parish churches during the first half of the nineteenth century actually reinforced them. The existence of pew rents (paying for seats) meant that the wealthier members of the congregation were seated in prime locations; whereas the poor were assigned pews in the least desirable areas – the side aisles or the gallery. Dickens accentuated this segregation by describing how the churchwardens and overseers had their own curtained pews. Thus, even in church, the needy were reminded of their lowly social position and need to defer to their superiors. In certain churches social deferment also applied to the distribution of communion – a complete departure from the teachings of the New Testament.

In "The Broker's Man" (Chapter 5), Dickens again returns to the subject of poverty, taking his readers by the hand to George's Yard, "a dirty little court at the back of the gas works".

Within the ground-floor room of a two-room house – the top floor occupied by a separate family – four or five children grovel about listlessly on the sand-covered floor; a neglected baby lies constantly crying in the backyard. A few weeks previously, the husband and father had been transported, probably for some petty offence. The family's rent is six months overdue and they are about to be evicted. The old woman, a grandparent, is taken to the parish infirmary where she very soon dies. The mother, who up to this point had been a hardworking woman, is driven wild by her misery and, after several visits to the house of correction, bursts a blood vessel and dies. The children, separated from their mother, are placed in the workhouse.

Dickens, here, and throughout his writing career, was to constantly pose the question: "Who will break this cycle of despair?" Although primarily using his sketches to promote the welfare of the poor by appealing to the consciences of his readers, he also introduced a further spiritual principle which was to preoccupy him throughout his career. The author fervently believed that true faith was not a matter of formal religious practice, but was best expressed through the practical demonstration of Christ-like qualities in an individual's life.

At the end of June 1836, four months after *Sketches of Boz* first appeared, Chapman and Hall produced a strongly worded pamphlet, complete with three illustrations by Hablot K. Browne (Phiz), passionately attacking the proposed changes to the laws governing Sundays. Entitled *Sunday Under Three Heads*, it attracted a glowing review from *The Weekly Dispatch*: "We will be bold to say that there is more sound philosophy; ay, and more true Christianity, in this little book than all the sermons and pamphlets that have been published against Sabbath breaking."

It was written under the pseudonym Timothy Sparks, and very few of its readers, if any, would have realized that its author was Boz. The fact that the recently married 24-year-old, who was struggling to juggle his journalistic and writing responsibilities, found time to write it, emphasizes the importance he placed upon the issues concerned.

It is extremely difficult for us today to comprehend just how important matters relating to religion were within Victorian society. In 1838, Parliament received more petitions regarding Sunday legislation than any other single issue, with the exception of slavery. No fewer than eight major Bills were debated on the subject in the House of Commons between 1833 and 1838. Around ten years later, Lord Ashley's proposed Bill to ban Sunday post was supported by a staggering 4,419 petitions, bearing more than 650,000 signatures.

Sunday Under Three Heads represented Dickens's angry response to the Bill for the "Better Observance of Sunday", which was progressing towards its second reading in Parliament. Founded in 1831, the Lord's Day Observance Society had realized that the most effective means of introducing Sunday legislation lay in influencing the political process. The following year, the Scottish Whig MP, Sir Andrew Agnew, became the organization's parliamentary figurehead. Dickens was to refer to him as the "Lord's Day Baronet".

Witnessing at first-hand the parliamentary debates surrounding the Bill, Dickens railed against what he believed to be the hypocrisy and puritanical nature of the Sabbatarians. The proposed legislation would penalize the disadvantaged members of society, while the more affluent would be virtually unaffected. Those proposing the restrictions that would effectively curtail the only leisure time available to the lower classes did not have the slightest idea of the misery they would cause. Nor did they appreciate the benefits and opportunities that an unrestricted Sunday provided for ordinary people.

Sunday Under Three Heads begins with a hard-hitting "dedication" to C. J. Blomfield, the then Bishop of London, and a supporter of the proposed legislation. Dickens severely criticizes him for his ill-informed views regarding the leisure activities of the lower classes. How, he argues, can someone from such an "elevated rank" and in receipt of such a "princely income" possibly understand the hardships and challenges confronting the less fortunate, or appreciate the importance of being able to have a break from six days of drudgery?

Divided into three parts, the pamphlet begins by describing the various innocent pastimes that take place on Sundays: visits to tea gardens, river excursions, trips to the country, families sharing a proper cooked meal, everyone enjoying a much-needed day of rest. Dickens wanted to counter the Sabbatarian images of drunken excesses and debauchery, which, in part, were used to justify these new proposals.

Having favourably represented the current state of affairs, he attacked the proposed legislation and laid out its potential negative impact. Central to his argument was the social injustice of the Bill: banning public transport would prevent the poor and labouring classes from travelling, while the rich had their own private carriages. The disadvantaged had no ovens, so relied on the bakehouses to cook their food; these would be closed, but the wealthy would be served hot meals at home. Shops, coffee houses, tea gardens, theatres, and museums would also be shut. No one was to work on Sundays, but this ban would not extend to servants employed in the houses of the rich. In *Nicholas Nickleby*, his third novel, with reference to an advertisement for a cook, placed by the aptly named MP, Mr Gallanbile, he returned to this point: "no victuals whatever, cooked on the Lord's Day, with the exception of dinner for Mr and Mrs Gallanbile, which, being a work of piety and necessity is expected."

The pamphlet ends with Dickens's visionary expectation of what Sundays could become. Set in a village in the south-west of England, the day begins with an excellent, well-attended service in the parish church. The narrator is especially impressed by the elderly clergyman's compassion and friendliness towards his parishioners. During the course of an evening walk, he comes across a group of villagers playing cricket. Watching with some pleasure, he suddenly sees the clergyman approaching and anticipates a display of displeasure regarding their playing sport on a Sunday. Much to his surprise, the elderly gentleman takes up a suitable vantage point and enjoys the game. We later learn that it was the clergyman himself who purchased the equipment and was instrumental in providing the actual cricket pitch.

Dickens uses this idyllic scene to express the view that Christian observance and relaxation on a Sunday were not mutually exclusive, but complementary. He develops this idea further by suggesting that the British Museum, National Gallery, and other public exhibitions should also be open on a Sunday.

For Dickens, Christianity had to be practical to be effective. It was not acceptable that the churches largely neglected the vast numbers of destitute people living in London and other urban locations. Having been personally affected by debt and poverty, he had made it his business to familiarize himself with its awful realities and was determined to make its dreadful images known to those who lived in complete ignorance of the appalling suffering of the poor. He was motivated, as we have seen, by a heart for social justice, a living practical faith and an unshakeable belief in God's desire for the Church to help the destitute.

10

CHARITABLE ANGELS AND THE
INVISIBLE WORLD OF POVERTY

Four days after the publication of *Sketches By Boz*, Dickens expectantly awaited the arrival of William Hall, the junior partner of the publishers Chapman and Hall. Over Christmas, they had achieved considerable success with a coffee-table volume entitled *The Squib Annual*. Robert Seymour, its illustrator, had approached the publishers with the idea of producing a book that depicted the comic sporting adventures of the Nimrod Club. In need of a writer to produce the text to go along with his plates, the partners, having been impressed by *Sketches By Boz*, decided to approach Dickens. As a result of his meeting with William Hall, he agreed to provide twenty-four pages of text for each instalment, for a fee of £14 3s 6d per number. The new venture was to involve a considerable increase in his writing output: The total combined length of four of his sketches was around 8,000 words, the same as just one monthly issue of *The Pickwick Papers*.

Even though he had to fit his writing around his work at the *Morning Chronicle*, Dickens still managed to complete the opening number by 20 February. The very next day, both Edward Chapman and William Hall visited his new home to read through what he had written. Both were more than satisfied with his work. By the time the first instalment appeared, Dickens had already influenced and shaped the novel's content and direction. Under the terms of the original contract, his role was simply to provide accompanying text on the theme of "manners and life in the country" for Seymour's four monthly illustrations. However, within six days of his initial February meeting, he had already determined both the title and the identity of the main character, Samuel Pickwick.

Advertisements for *The Pickwick Papers*, edited by Boz, appeared on 26 March 1836, in the *Athenaeum* and *The Times*. Five days later, the first green paper-wrapped, one shilling monthly number appeared. Despite Dickens's high expectations, neither the public nor the reviewers showed any great enthusiasm. Selling only 400 of the 1,000 printed, it was, in comparison with *Sketches By Boz*, a disappointment. Consequently, Chapman and Hall decided to produce only 500 for the next number. This did little to alleviate the writer's sense of unease.

On Saturday, 2 April 1836, Dickens and Catherine were married at St Luke's Church, Chelsea. It was a relatively small family affair. Thomas Beard, his long-standing friend and colleague, acted as best man, and the guests adjourned to 18 York Place for the wedding breakfast. The happy couple, revisiting the scene of Charles's long Chatham country walks with his father, honeymooned for a week at Mrs Craddock's little slated cottage in the small village of Chalk. The newlyweds were to share their first matrimonial home with Charles's brother, Frederick, and Catherine's sister, Mary. It had been decided that as well as helping out the Hogarths, who still had nine children at home, Mary would provide excellent companionship for Mrs Dickens.

Within a fortnight of Dickens completing the second instalment of *The Pickwick Papers* on his honeymoon, a catastrophic event took place that not only threatened the future of the work, but the writer's whole career. On 20 April, three days after his only meeting with Dickens, Robert Seymour went out into the garden of his Islington home and shot himself through the heart. The writer's response was characteristically energetic and robust. With the project hanging in the balance, he came forward with an alternative proposal. For a £6 per instalment pay rise, he would increase his monthly contribution from twenty-four pages to thirty-two. As a result, the number of illustrations would be reduced to two. Chapman and Hall, on the basis of the continued popularity of *Sketches By Boz* and their considerable investment already in the project, agreed. The success, or otherwise, of *The Pickwick Papers* now rested solely in the hands of the author.

Initially, the publishers had ample reason to question the wisdom of their decision. The sales of the next two numbers proved no better than the first, even though they had returned to the original print run of 1,000 copies for the new third instalment. In an attempt to boost their exclusively London-based monthly sales, they distributed 1,500 copies, on a sale or return basis, throughout numerous provincial towns. All but fifty came back unsold. Added to this, their attempts to find a suitable replacement for Seymour were proving frustrating. On discovering that George Cruikshank was too busy, they considered three others: the future author William Thackeray, who was turned down by Dickens; John Leech, who was to later illustrate *A Christmas Carol*; and Robert William Buss. The latter, despite having no experience of book illustration, was offered the position. Although he provided the two illustrations for the third instalment, neither he, nor the publishers, were happy with what he had produced. He resigned after only three weeks.

Following this disastrous appointment, Hablot K. Browne, also known, as we have seen, as Phiz, was appointed. He was currently employed on their periodical, *The Library of Fiction*. It was to mark the beginning of his productive relationship with Dickens.

The appearance of the fourth number of *The Pickwick Papers* on 30 June 1836 marked a crucial point in Dickens's life. The first indication he received of the dramatic turnaround in Pickwick's fortunes was a congratulatory letter from the editor of the influential *Literary Gazette*. He had been especially impressed by the introduction of a new character, Sam Weller, as were many others. The subject of Phiz's illustration, Weller first appears cleaning visitors' boots in the yard of the White Hart Inn. Subsequently employed by Mr Pickwick, his lively Cockney wisdom was to provide a constant source of amusement during the course of his master's misadventures.

By August, the monthly sales had increased a hundredfold to 40,000 copies, and Dickens's commission to £25 per instalment. By

November, it had reached 50,000. The unprecedented popularity of Pickwick was remarkable. It appealed to a broad cross-section of society: doctors visiting patients in their carriages; judges seated in court; children; and even labourers. Although unable to afford a shilling to buy a monthly number, this last group would club together to join a library, so that one of them could borrow a copy to read to his fellow-workers. Dickens had captured the nation's imagination. It was a defining moment.

His meteoric success, though most welcome, nonetheless presented the writer with a thorny problem. In May, delighted with the success of *Sketches By Boz*, John Macrone agreed with Dickens that he would write a three-volume novel by November of the following year. In return, he would receive £200 and a 50 per cent share in the profits of all sales above 1,000 copies.

Four months later, the author also signed a £1,000 contract with Richard Bentley to produce two novels, one of which was to be *Oliver Twist*. The agreement, shortly afterwards, was extended to include the editorship of a new monthly journal, *Bentley's Miscellany*, due to be launched in the January of the following year. The proposed salary of twenty guineas a month was very attractive.

Following the public acclaim for the fourth instalment of *The Pickwick Papers*, Macrone saw his opportunity to capitalize on the author's dazzling popularity: He would republish the Sketches in monthly parts. Dickens was incensed. Believing it would damage the sales of Pickwick, he enlisted the help of John Forster and Thomas Mitton, his legal adviser, in an attempt to buy back the copyright, which he had previously sold to Macrone. By now the value of the writer's work had dramatically increased, so much so that Macrone was now asking for £2,250. Fortunately, Chapman and Hall came to his aid and paid the full amount. After *The Pickwick Papers*, they sold it in instalments. It was a sobering lesson, which Dickens was to remember for some time.

Between the age of fifteen and twenty-four, Dickens had demonstrated a remarkable degree of energy, determination, and ambition. Not content with society's expectation of a lower middle-class boy, whose father had been imprisoned for debt, he raised himself to a position of financial security and found success and admiration within his chosen profession. Virtually irreplaceable at the *Morning Chronicle*, his long-term journalistic career guaranteed, he had exceeded the limited prospects set out for him. But he was not finished. By now he realized his chance of greatness rested not with newspaper print, but within the pages of books, his books. Just as he used his time as a lowly office clerk to learn shorthand, so, too, his four years in journalism provided him with an opportunity to learn and practise the art of writing.

Fittingly, on 5 November 1836, John Easthope, reluctantly and with a degree of animosity, accepted Dickens's resignation. With the exception of a few brief weeks as editor of *The Daily News* ten years later, this was to be the end of his journalistic career. From now on, he was determined, come what may, to fulfil his destiny as a writer. Society could no longer judge him based on his social status: his writing alone would define him now. The touch paper had been lit, and for the next twenty years, or so, the nineteenth-century skies were to be transformed by the exploding fireworks of his creative genius.

The Pickwick Papers was the launch-pad for Dickens's remarkable career. The popularity, goodwill, and self-belief it generated were to sustain him for many years to come and enable him to capture the public imagination and establish a real rapport with his readers. It effectively represented the foundation upon which all his future work would rest. In view of this, it is important to appreciate just how close he came to not writing it. Prior to meeting with him, the publishers had already contacted two other writers, both of whom turned down the opportunity. Dickens was effectively their third choice. Secondly, at the outset, the success of the book was seen to depend on the reputation of Robert Seymour, and with sales already below what was expected at the time of his suicide, the future of the book was in serious doubt. Yet it was to be a triumph.

Dickens was a visionary: he saw both the appalling suffering of the poor and the complete ineffectiveness of the existing agencies to address it. In the absence of central government intervention, neither the woefully inadequate, antiquated Poor Law parish system, nor the Church possessed the necessary resources to stem the overwhelming tide of human suffering. Engulfed by the twin social forces of burgeoning population growth and mass urban migration, the existing structures could no longer meet the crippling demands placed upon them. As early as 1818, before these factors really took hold, the annual cost of poor relief was already estimated to be £8 million.

When the first official census took place in 1801, the population of the United Kingdom was estimated to be around 16 million. By the time Dickens had completed *The Pickwick Papers* (1837), it had increased to 25 million – an average annual rise of 250,000.

This vast population increase was, in itself, sufficient to seriously undermine the traditional means of administering relief to the poor, but it was combined with the hugely significant shift towards urbanization: by 1851, more than half the capital's population, aged over twenty, had not been born in London. The reality of the truly dreadful conditions endured by those living in the city's slums at the time is reflected in the Public Health records of the period: in 1847, 500,000 – one in four of the population of London – suffered from typhus fever, and over the next two years, 70,000 died of cholera.

With the introduction of the Poor Law Amendment Act of 1834, the poor had to go to the workhouses to find help. This, in effect, meant that the Church, and the agencies it supported, represented the only hope of the disadvantaged. Lacking the necessary physical resources to meet the overwhelming need, the clergy adopted a strategy, whereby they sought to instil a sense of responsibility for the well-being of the poor within the hearts and minds of their predominantly middle-class congregations. Although the Church was powerless to introduce ambitious large-scale projects aimed at alleviating poverty, it did, nonetheless, prove effective in mobilizing its members to take action on behalf of those who were unable to help themselves.

Dickens was at the forefront of this initiative to awaken the social conscience of his predominantly middle-class readers. This he sought to achieve through the creation of his "charitable angels", characters in his books that lived out his belief that the compassionate intervention of individuals could transform the lives of the poor. If those who professed to belong to the Christian faith practically applied the teachings of the Bible, then a genuine attempt to combat the unacceptable spectre of poverty could take place. While in his first three novels, *The Pickwick Papers*, *Oliver Twist*, and *Nicholas Nickleby*, there are several characters who show kindness to the poor, the author confers angelic status on only one specific character per novel.

His original charitable angel is "the benevolent gentleman", Samuel Pickwick. In Chapter 16, on arriving at Bury St Edmunds, he stays at the Angel Hotel. Later on in the narrative (Chapter 45), Samuel Weller refers to his employer as being "an angel in tights and gaiters" and "a reg'lar thoroughbred angel". Mr Brownlow (*Oliver Twist*) and Charles Cheeryble (*Nicholas Nickleby*) are Dickens's two other charitable angels.

These three, socially and financially, were best placed to make a difference. In each case, their kindness, benevolence, and willingness to intervene brought about a dramatic change in the lives of those they helped. The author firmly believed that his readers, following their example, could do likewise, and, as a result, the seemingly inevitable downward cycle of poverty that entrapped countless thousands of people could be broken.

Samuel Pickwick is the writer's most exuberant, energetic charitable angel. Fittingly beginning his two-year adventure at the Golden Cross Hotel, Charing Cross, he positively exudes cheerful benevolence. Reflecting both the prevalent materialism of the period and the experience of many readers, Mr Pickwick, at the end of the book, expresses how "nearly the whole of his previous life has been devoted to business and the pursuit of wealth". As a result of his experiences, however, he has been exposed to "numerous scenes of which he had no previous conception": in particular, his coach journey through one of London's most deprived areas, Whitechapel, and his time within the debtors' prison. In the same way, Dickens's readers were compelled to consider the previously unseen harsh daily routines endured by those less fortunate than themselves.

In his Preface to the first Cheap Edition of *The Pickwick Papers* (1847), Dickens states: "Fiction is vindicated by its promotion of important social improvements." In relation to Mr Pickwick's imprisonment in the Fleet Debtors' Prison, this point is well illustrated. The author used two-and-a-half instalments (six chapters) to highlight what actually went on within these prisons. The year *The Pickwick Papers* was published, around 40,000 people were arrested for debt. Dickens's description of the "poor side" of the Fleet in Chapter 52 proves an excellent example of this approach. The prison episode also showed the extent of Mr Pickwick's generosity and kindness. On his departure, such is his popularity that the prisoners gather to bid him farewell:

> At three o'clock that afternoon, Mr Pickwick took a last look at his little room, and made his way, as well as he could, through the throng of debtors, who passed eagerly forward to shake him by the hand, until he reached the lodge steps. He turned here to look about him, and his eye lightened as he did so. In all the crowd of wan, emaciate faces, he saw not one which was not happier for his sympathy and charity.

Fittingly, his final words to the prisoners were, "God bless you, my friends."

To reinforce this sense of general philanthropy, Dickens also details specific acts of charity to certain prisoners: Pickwick's compassion for a husband, woman, and young child; his kindness to the Cobbler and the Chancery Prisoner; and his gracious payment of Mrs Bardell's £150 legal fees, despite the fact that she was responsible for his being imprisoned in the first place. In doing so, she and her son Tommy, were released from the prison. In the final paragraph of the book, it becomes clear that, even after his retirement to Dulwich, he continued in his charitable activities: "He is known by all the poor people about, who never fail to take their hats off, as he passes, with great respect. The children idolise him, and so indeed does the whole neighbourhood."

Embodying the principle of the effectiveness of individual charitable intervention, Samuel Pickwick is also used by the author to demonstrate the practical Christ-like quality of grace. From the moment he first appears in Chapter 2, the travelling actor, Alfred Jingle, exposes Mr Pickwick and his companions to a series of misadventures. Attaching himself to them, he takes full advantage of their hospitality and then accompanies them to Dingley Dell. While there, he elopes with Rachael Wardle. Tracked down by her brother and Mr Pickwick, Jingle agrees to let her return home for a payment of £120 – having earlier conned Tracy Tupman out of £10 for the marriage licence. Later, he turns up under the assumed identity of Captain Fitz-Marshall. Pursued as far as Bury St Edmunds, he and his mischievous servant, Job Trotter, set a trap for Mr Pickwick at "Westgate House Establishment for Young Ladies". As well as being placed in a highly compromising situation, Mr Pickwick also contracts a severe case of rheumatic fever. Finally, in seeking to frustrate another of Jingle's cunning plans, he is arrested in Ipswich on suspicion of seeking to conduct a duel.

The next time he comes across Alfred Jingle and Job Trotter, he finds them struggling to survive in the poor side of the Fleet Debtors' Prison. On the first occasion of their meeting in the prison, Dickens encourages his readers to consider all that Mr Pickwick has suffered at their hands and to assume his reaction:

"Here, Job; where is that fellow?"…

"Here Sir," cried Job.

"Come here, sir", said Mr Pickwick trying to look stern, with four large tears running down his waistcoat. "Take that, sir."

… In the ordinary acceptation of such language, it should have been a blow. As the world runs it ought to have been a sound, hearty cuff; for Mr Pickwick had been duped, deceived, and wronged by the destitute outcast who was now wholly in his power. Must we tell the

truth? It was something from Mr Pickwick's waistcoat-pocket, which clinked as it was given into Job's hand, and the giving of which, somehow, or other imparted a sprinkle to the eye, and a swelling to the heart, of our excellent old friend as he hurried away.

From that point on, Mr Pickwick takes it upon himself to provide for both Alfred Jingle and Job Trotter. Looking into their affairs, he arranges their release from prison by paying off their debts. More than this, knowing it has always been Jingle's ambition to emigrate to the West Indies, he funds both their passages to Demerara and uses his previous business contacts to secure them both work on a plantation. Importantly, Dickens also makes the point that, following his angel's gracious charitable intervention, both men are reformed characters and have become "worthy members of society".

11

OLIVER TWIST: THE PARABLE OF THE GOOD SAMARITAN AND FEMALE ANGELS

On 1 January 1837, there was a double celebration at Richard Bentley's New Burlington Street office. Not only was it New Year's Day, but the first number of the *Miscellany* had gone on sale. Those reading the correspondence page would have noted that the editor referred to himself as the Inimitable Boz. This was the name that William Giles, his old schoolteacher from Chatham, had inscribed on the silver snuff-box that he had sent his former pupil to celebrate the success of *The Pickwick Papers*.

Five days later, on Epiphany, Dickens's first child, Charles Culliford[7] Boz was born. As with his father, he was born on a Friday. For the opening number, probably due to time pressure and the impending arrival of the baby, the author produced a comic piece, not too dissimilar to his sketches, though longer. At the conclusion of "The Public Life of Mr Tulrumble", he makes reference to writing some further Mudfog Chronicles. In the next monthly issue, he began the story of a boy born in Mudfog workhouse. Originally based on an idea that he had at the time of writing "Mr Minns and His Cousin", *The Adventures of Oliver Twist*, which was to appear in twenty-four monthly instalments (February 1837–March 1839), was to become one of his best-known books.

---

7   His grandmother's maiden name.

By the time the third number appeared in March, the popularity of *Bentley's Miscellany* was such that the writer was able to renegotiate the original terms of his agreement. As a result, he was offered an extra £10 per month for the first additional 1,000 copies sold and £5 for each subsequent 500 increase. The extra income was to prove most useful. The same month Dickens had placed an offer on 48 Doughty Street, Bloomsbury. Leased for a period of three years at £80 per annum, the solid brick, twelve-roomed Georgian house was a tangible reminder of his literary success. This sense of achievement was reinforced by the fact that people wishing to call upon the Dickens's could only enter the "broad wholesome street" by passing through two sets of impressive gates, one at the Johnson Street end and the other at the junction of Guildford Street. One can imagine the pride he must have felt when, on the first occasion that his family visited his home, they were ushered into Doughty Street by a porter, wearing a gold-laced hat and mulberry-coloured coat, complete with the Doughty arms on the buttons.

Within a month of moving in, a family tragedy occurred that was to profoundly affect the rest of Dickens's life. During their courtship days, as we have seen, Mary Hogarth had acted as Catherine's chaperone. She was devoted to them both. Now seventeen, she had become a constant support to her sister, especially following the birth of Charley. Happy, lively, understanding, and amiable, she had developed a genuine sisterly love for her brother-in-law. By the spring of 1837, such a bond of friendship existed between them that she had become essential to his domestic happiness. It was not, however, until her untimely death that the true extent of his feelings was revealed.

On the evening of Saturday, 7 May, Dickens accompanied Catherine and Mary to St James's Theatre to see a production of his one-act farce, *Is She His Wife? Or Something Singular*. This was not the only reason for their visit. On the same bill were two musical dramas in which the lead parts were sung by Fanny Dickens's fiancé, Henry Burnett. Arriving home, Mary retired to bed around 1.00 a.m. Shortly afterwards she was taken ill and the family doctor was sent for. At this point, there was seemingly no cause for alarm. In the morning, her condition worsened, and her mother, and sister, Georgina, were sent for. On the Sunday afternoon, at 3.00 p.m, she died in Dickens's arms. The same day, the undertaker called and her coffin was placed in the bedroom overlooking the garden. Before her burial, Charles removed a lock of her hair and placed her ring upon his finger.

Dickens was overcome with grief. Both forthcoming instalments of *The Pickwick Papers* and *Oliver Twist* were postponed. This was to be the only time throughout his career that he was not to fulfil a writing commitment. He arranged and paid for the funeral, which took place five days after her death, on Friday, 13 May. Etched upon her headstone at the new Kensal Green Cemetery, Harrow Road, was his own epitaph: "Young, beautiful and good, God in his mercy numbered her among the angels at the early age of seventeen." Following the ceremony, he left a note with William Harrison Ainsworth, asking that he arrange for a rose tree to be planted on the grave. This request was to prove significant, for when Dickens returned to writing *Oliver Twist*, Mary Hogarth was to inspire the first of his female angels: Rose Maylie.

Shortly after the funeral, with the added trauma of Catherine having suffered a miscarriage, the family went to stay for a fortnight at Collins's Farm, North End, Hampstead. The strength of Dickens's attachment to his sister-in-law became apparent in his determination to be buried next to her. It was only the death of her brother, George, four years later, that persuaded him to relinquish his claim. Also, he was to have recurring dreams about her almost every night for four months. Although becoming less frequent, they were to continue for several years. She also appeared to him, in what Dickens was later to describe as a vision, in 1844, while he was working on *The Chimes* in Genoa. According to the author, Mary spoke to him about the nature of true religion.

On a happier family note, in the summer both of his sisters married: Fanny to Henry Burnett, with whom she had studied at the Royal Academy of Music, and Letitia, to his long-term friend, Henry Austin, now an architect and engineer. The writer admired both men and was delighted for them both. Also, two of his brothers had taken their first steps in securing long-term careers: Frederick within the Treasury Department and Alfred as a trainee civil engineer on the railway. In September, John Macrone died suddenly at the age of only twenty-eight. Despite their previous disagreement, Dickens, although struggling under an enormous workload, produced a book, *The Picnic Papers*. This collection of entertaining pieces raised around £450 for the publisher's widow and two children.

A couple of months later, on 18 November, Chapman and Hall organized a banquet at the Prince of Wales Tavern in Leicester Square to celebrate the completion of *The Pickwick Papers*. Much to his relief, the final two numbers, nineteen and twenty, appeared that month, as did the first edition of the book. During the course of the evening he was presented with a cheque for £750. This brought his total income from the book up to around £2,500. His publishers could afford to be generous: their total profit for the venture was around £14,000.

Oliver Twist was the first of his books to be published under his own name. In it, Dickens uses the parable of the Good Samaritan from the Gospel of Luke, chapter 10, as a framework, both to evoke compassion for the poor and to show the means by which they could be helped. During the course of his conversation with the parish undertaker, Sowerberry (Chapter 4), Mr Bumble draws his attention to "a very elegant button" on the gilt-edged lapel of his official beadle's coat. In doing so, he points out that "the die is the same as the parochial seal – the Good Samaritan healing the sick and bruised man." The man, who was lying by the roadside, after having been robbed, is replaced by the workhouse orphan, Oliver, who, following his trial, is left lying senseless on the pavement. In the writer's representation, the parish and the law, both of which neglect the boy, correspond with the role of the priest and Levite. The part of the Good Samaritan is played by the author's second charitable angel, Mr Brownlow. This is confirmed by George Cruikshank's illustration, "Oliver Recovering from Fever", in which he is depicted gazing intently upon a painting of the Good Samaritan.

Described as having heart "large enough for six ordinary gentlemen of humane disposition", Mr Brownlow is far less exuberant than Mr Pickwick. Whereas his predecessor liberally showers his kindness and charity upon all those who come within the sphere of his influence, Brownlow is far more focused in his generosity. This is due to his more reserved, serious nature. As a young man, he suffered terrible heartbreak, when his bride-to-be died on their wedding day. In Chapter 11, during the course of Oliver's sham trial, Dickens writes of "angels blind with weeping". Shortly afterwards, Mr Brownlow weeps over Oliver's plight. On rescuing the boy, they travel home by carriage and, en route, just before reaching his Pentonville home, they pass the Angel at Islington (the Angel Inn). There is also a deeper, theological clue to his angelic identity, which his religiously knowledgeable readers would have readily understood. Oliver, despite Fagin's efforts to corrupt him, retains his innocence. In so doing, he is identified with those whom God has chosen to enter heaven. The biblical book of Hebrews, in its first chapter, describes how angels have a specific responsibility towards such people.

When, seven years prior to starting the novel, Dickens registered as a reader at the British Museum, he gave his address as 10 Norfolk Street (North London). Nine doors away was a workhouse. Even after many years, the haunting neighbourhood story of the heavily pregnant woman still lingered. Having been denied access to the workhouse, she was forced to give birth in the street, and her newly born baby died. This took root in his imagination, along with the daily sight of the starving and destitute inmates being marched up and down the street; the frequent sight of coffins coming and going; and the piercing screams of the insane.

Oliver Twist was born in the workhouse, and his unmarried mother, Agnes Fleming, died shortly after giving birth to him. He endures a loveless, miserable existence for the first eight years of his life in the "farm", a branch of the workhouse where young children were kept. On the occasion of his ninth birthday, he is collected by the beadle, Mr Bumble and presented to the "Board". Limbkins, the chairman, briskly informs the bewildered child: "Well! You have come here to be educated and taught a useful trade, so you'll begin to pick oakum to-morrow at six o'clock." This involved disentangling individual fibres from huge coils of thick rope used in ships. It was just one of the mind-numbing tasks assigned to those in the workhouse; another, as witnessed by Dickens in his Norfolk Street days, was breaking up blocks of granite for road repairs. Workhouse children were also used as cheap labour in factories and cotton mills. The parish authorities turned a blind eye to the atrocious conditions they suffered.

When Oliver commits the unforgivable sin of asking for more food, the horrified members of the "Board", convinced of his wickedness, attempt to apprentice him to the despicable chimney-sweep, Gamfield. Being unsuccessful, they then, in the hope of his being flogged to death, think about sending him away to sea as a cabin boy. Eventually, he ends up being apprenticed to the parish undertaker, Sowerberry. Treated no better than a dog and forced to sleep among the coffins, he decides to run away to London.

Within these opening seven chapters, Dickens attacks the ideology of the Poor Law policymakers and their introduction of the Poor Law Amendment Act of 1834, which, as we have seen, marked a fundamental shift away from outdoor relief (helping the poor to remain in their own homes, usually by subsidizing their low wages) to indoor relief: imprisoning them within the workhouse. Children were separated from their parents, husbands from their wives; and these draconian measures were also ruthlessly applied to the elderly. Moreover, before the Act, the poor remained in their local parish; post legislation, large-scale Union workhouses were set up, resulting in people being removed from their own communities.

At the centre of the Amendment Act was an ideology, loosely based on the philosopher Jeremy Bentham's utilitarian theory, which held that the poor enjoyed being poor. Therefore, if their experience within the workhouse could be made as dreadful as possible, they would make the decision to abandon poverty and improve themselves. When Oliver appears before the "Board" on his ninth birthday, Dickens provides a wonderful parody of the absurdity and cruelty of this position:

> *The members of this board were very sage, deep philosophical men; and when they came to turn their attention to the workhouse, they found out at once what ordinary folks would never have discovered – the poor people liked it! It was a regular place of public entertainment for the poorer classes… "Oho!" said the board, looking very knowing; "we are the fellows to set this to rights; we'll stop it all in no time." So, they established the rule that all poor people should have an alternative (for they should compel nobody, not they) of being starved by a gradual process in the house, or by a quick one out of it.*

The writer also makes clear that the Church itself was, at times, complicit in the neglect of the poor. In Chapter 5, Oliver, in the course of his undertaker apprenticeship role, attends a pauper's funeral. The burial, which takes place in an obscure corner of the churchyard overgrown with stinging-nettles, is delayed by an hour. When the clergyman at last arrives, he indecently rushes through the service and spends a mere four minutes by the graveside. Having done so, he hands his surplice to the clerk, completely ignores the two mourners, and walks off. Meanwhile, the sexton fills in the grave: "it was not a difficult task; for the grave was so full that the uppermost coffin was within a few feet of the surface."

Marcus Stone remembers that following the publication of the book, his friend received a stern letter from a correspondent angered by the fact that he had dared to suggest that a Church of England minister would act in such a shameful fashion. Ironically, unbeknown to the clergyman that had written Dickens had based the scene on a funeral he had actually seen conducted by the very same individual in the village of Cooling in Kent. In response, the author directly quoted the words of the prophet Nathan to King David (2 Samuel 12): "thou art the man."

After detailing the abject failings and negligence of the parish, Dickens moves on in the novel to expose the gross injustice of the legal system. On arriving in London, Oliver, having unwittingly fallen in with Fagin and his gang of young criminals, finds himself falsely accused of stealing Mr Brownlow's pocket watch. While the actual perpetrators Jack Dawkins (the Artful Dodger) and Charley Bates escape, he is arrested and taken to the nearest police magistrates' court. Just prior to writing the court scene, the author, with the help of a former journalistic colleague, Thomas Haines, managed to observe at first-hand the notorious magistrate, Allan Stuart Laing, who was based at the Hatton Garden Police Court. At the time, members of the public were banned from the police courts, and the only information as to what went on was to be found in newspaper reports. Fang was the fictional representation of the judge Dickens saw that morning.

Dazed, bewildered, and having been roughly mistreated, the boy has no hope of being treated fairly. Before his case is heard, one of the officers refers to Oliver as "young gallows". This carefully chosen phrase conveys the barbaric nature of sentences handed down to juvenile offenders. It was not until 1847 that Parliament passed the Juvenile Offenders Act, which raised the minimum age of adult criminality to fourteen, and it was nine years after this that the Penal Servitude Act replaced transportation with prison sentences – too late to save the Artful Dodger.

When Oliver is first brought before the magistrate, Fang is

reading a leading article in a newspaper of the morning, referring to some recent decision of his, and commending him, for the three hundred and fiftieth time, to the special and particular notice of the Secretary of State for the Home Department. He was out of temper; and looks up with an angry scowl.

Despite Mr Brownlow's persistent appeals for leniency, Fang informs the clerk of the court he will deal with the "young vagabond" and "hardened scoundrel" summarily. In deciding on sentencing Oliver, who, at this point, is in a precarious state of health, to three months' hard labour, he is effectively signing his death warrant. Only as a result of the late intervention of the bookstall keeper, who witnessed the whole affair, is the boy grudgingly acquitted. On leaving the courtroom, Mr Brownlow finds Oliver collapsed on the pavement.

There he lay. A helpless victim of the parish and the law, robbed of his dignity, health, and hope. Alongside him were the thousands upon thousands of neglected, forgotten children, invisible to all, except to those who, like the author, sought them out. At this point, Dickens imaginatively rewrites the parable. Rather than there being a religious, cultural gulf between the person in need and the Good Samaritan, he switches it to one of social class. In so doing, he sought to directly challenge one of the early Victorian Church's deeply held beliefs: God had ordained the social order and each individual should be content with their lot. A divinely commissioned hierarchy existed which should not be interfered with. This was not a view to which the author subscribed.

Queen Victoria's chaplain, Reverend Henry Melvill, insisted that poverty had been appointed by God himself; while the Reverend William Sewell, headmaster of St Peter's College, Radley, would frequently inform his pupils that the "divisions of men" were ordained by God and that he had struck a line "between those who are gentlemen and those who are not". In 1854, Dickens, on receiving a volume of Sewell's sermons, demonstrated his disapproval by sending the copy back to him unread. In *Lark Rise to Candleford*, Flora Thompson describes the local rector's favourite subject as being "the supreme right of the social order as it then existed".

Oliver is at the very bottom of the social ladder: not only is he an orphan, born to an unmarried mother, but he is also a child of the workhouse. The lowliness of his position is made clear by the contemptuous Noah Claypole, his fellow apprentice at Sowerberry's. Despite being a charity boy himself, he mockingly refers to Oliver as "work'us".

At this key moment in the narrative, the writer echoes the words from the Gospel, "Who is my neighbour?" Mr Brownlow could have crossed over on the other side. After all, he paid his contribution to the poor rate. Perhaps, if his conscience prompted him, he might even take Oliver to the nearest workhouse infirmary, but that was surely the extent of his Christian duty. Instead, he has him placed in a coach and takes him into his own home. Ignoring the risk to his own health, he nurses Oliver back to health with the help of his housekeeper, Mrs Bedwin. From this point on, the charitable angel brings about a transformation in the boy's life, culminating in his adopting him as his own son.

Most significantly, however, is the fact that Oliver is heir to a fortune. This neglected, forgotten, workhouse orphan has an inheritance; but it is only through the intervention of Mr Brownlow that it comes to light. Dickens's message was clear: if compassionate individuals were willing to step in and fulfil their Christian responsibility, they could change the lives of those around them.

Rose Maylie's introduction in Chapter 28 of *Oliver Twist* represented a key moment in the writer's fictional expression of his faith. Inspired by Mary Hogarth, she is the first of Dickens's female angels. Rose, and those who were to follow, embodied the Christ-like qualities of self-sacrifice, atonement, love, grace, mercy, and forgiveness. In doing so, they affirmed the author's belief that true religion was not defined by doctrine, dogma, or formal observance, but by the practical demonstration of Christian virtues. His use of female angels was an act of genius. While inconsistent with the biblical representation of angels being male, the angelic nature of women was, to an extent, already embedded within the culture of the period. What the author did so perceptively was to take an already established idea and develop it.

Very early in his career, Dickens had explored the cultural idea of women being angels. In only his fourth sketch, "Horatio Sparkins" (*Monthly Magazine* 1834), he refers to the poet, the Reverend Robert Montgomery, who the previous year had published a poem entitled "Woman, the Angel of Life". In Chapter 8 of *The Pickwick Papers*, Rachael Wardle, in response to Tracy Tupman calling her an "angel", replies: "All women are angels, they say." Alfred Jingle also refers to her as being "the dearest of angels" and, later in the book, Tony Weller, Sam's father, questions the value of calling a "young 'ooman a angel". Some years later, in a far more poignant manner, he returned to the theme in Chapter 34 of *Dombey and Son*. With reference to Alice Marwood, who has recently returned from being transported, he writes:

> *Lost and degraded as she was, there was a beauty in her face and form, which, even in its worst expression, could not be recognized as such by anyone regarding her with the least attention. As she subsided into silence, and her face, which had been harshly agitated, quieted down; while her dark eyes, fixed upon the fire, exchanged the reckless light that animated them for one that was softened by something like sorrow; there shone through all her way-worn misery and fatigue, a ray of the departed radiance of the fallen angel.*

One of the dominant paradigms of the period regarding women, which the author was able to tap into, was the idea of the "Angel in the House". In 1840, the marriage of Queen Victoria and her subsequent motherhood in the same year was to play a significant role in the development of what was essentially an idolized image of domestic womanhood. Although some commentators have suggested that the term was adopted from the title of Coventry Patmore's popular narrative poem, Dickens had actually used the phrase ten years earlier, with reference to Meg Veck, in his 1844 Christmas story, *The Chimes*.

In 1852, the influential Birmingham Congregationalist, John Angell James, wrote: "There are few terms in the language around which cluster so many blissful associations as that delight of every English heart, the word HOME... One of the most hallowed and lovely, and beautiful sights in our world is, woman at home." This was a popularly held sentiment among many writers at the time. The "Angel in the House" icon was also highly visible within the narrative and genre paintings of the period. Charles West Cope's *Prayer Time* (1860) is a fine example. Set in a tastefully appointed room, with a fireside and Bible, a seated mother watches over her kneeling, praying daughter. The hearth was often used symbolically to denote domestic warmth, security, and contentment, angelically fostered within the home.

Speaking at the Leeds Mechanics Society dinner, on 1 December 1847, Dickens defined women as "those who are our best and dearest friends in infancy, in childhood, in manhood, and in old age, the most devoted and least selfish natures that we know on earth, who turn to us always constant and unchanged, when others turn away". In doing so, he was to highlight many of the attendant virtues, such as grace, gentleness, simplicity, and selflessness, which were connected both with his female angels and the "Angel in the House" motif.

The author was not the only contemporary literary advocate of women being spiritually superior to men – Tennyson, Ruskin, Thackeray, and many others endorsed this view – but his female angelic characters are unique. Even though Rose Maylie, Madeline Bray, Nell Trent, Florence Dombey, Agnes Wickfield, Esther Summerson, Amy Dorrit, and Lizzie Hexam all prove to be exemplary housekeepers in their respective homes and possess all the necessary "Angel in the House" virtues, their role was more profound. Not just culturally familiar spiritual symbols, they were the fictional messengers of Dickens's gospel.

The sound of Rose's "sweet female voice", first heard at the top of the stairs in Mrs Maylie's Chertsey cottage, was to resonate throughout the pages of *Oliver Twist*, bringing Christian virtue and light as it did so. Appearing on the opening page of Chapter 29, Rose's carefully crafted initial description clearly alludes to the ethereal aspect of her character:

> *The younger lady was in the lovely bloom and spring-time of womanhood, at that age, when, if ever angels be for God's good purposes enthroned in mortal forms, they may be, without impiety, supposed to abide in such as hers. She was not passed seventeen. Cast in so slight and exquisite a mould; mild and gentle; so pure and beautiful; that earth seemed not her element, nor its rough creatures her fit companions. The very intelligence that shone in her deep blue eye, and was stamped upon her noble head, seemed scarcely of her age, or*

of the world and yet the changing expression of sweetness and good humour, the thousand lights that played about the face, and left no shadow there; above all the smile, the cheerful happy smile.

The symbolic relationship between physical beauty and angelic character, used with regard to Rose, was to be repeated with reference to her successors. Madeline Bray, who appears in Dickens's next novel, *Nicholas Nickleby*, is described as having "a countenance of most uncommon beauty"; Florence Dombey, Agnes Wickfield, and Esther Summerson are all "beautiful"; while Lizzie Hexam is said to be "handsome" and Nell Trent "pretty". Whereas the angelic identity of Dickens's three charitable angels is confirmed by obscure references to inns, landmarks, court rooms, and the comments of other people, Rose is introduced to the reader as an "angel" in human form. Later in the novel, following her eventual recovery from her illness, Harry Maylie refers to her as being "a creature as fair and innocent of guile as one of God's own angels".

As was to be the case with the female angels that were to follow, Rose's angel-like virtues of self-sacrifice, atonement, and love were expressed within the context of her relationships with those around her. In Chapter 35, after her recovery, Harry Maylie proposes to her. Despite loving him, she selflessly turns him down. There are two reasons for this. Firstly, Harry, aged twenty-five, has been lined up to pursue a promising career in politics through the influence of his relatives. Rose is aware of her unsuitability, as her deceased mother was involved in a scandalous affair, and recognizes that, by accepting, she would jeopardize his career. Secondly, she acts out of love for her adopted mother, Mrs Maylie, who is eager for her son to become an MP.

Towards the end of the narrative, Harry Maylie proposes again. In repeating her refusal, Rose once more reveals her virtue and selflessness:

"The same reasons which influenced me then, will influence me now, if I ever owed a strict and rigid duty to her [Mrs Maylie] whose

*goodness saved me from a life of indigence and suffering, when should
I ever feel it, as I should to-night? It is a struggle", said Rose, "but
one I am proud to make, it is a pang, but one my heart shall bear."*

Only when she realizes that Harry has turned his back on his
parliamentary prospects in favour of becoming a clergyman does
she feel able to follow her heart's desire and marry him. His change
of direction from politics to the Church is a clear indication of Rose's
spiritual influence upon him.

Her angelic qualities are also revealed in her compassion for the
orphan Oliver, who, following an unsuccessful attempted burglary at
the Maylies' home, has been shot and injured. Taken upstairs, she
takes responsibility for nursing him through the night

It is, however, in relation to Nancy that Rose's angelic influence is
most apparent. On calling to see Rose, to pass on some information
about Oliver, Nancy is harshly treated by the hotel employees. Upset
and hurt, she is overcome by the compassion, kindness, and non-
judgmentalness of the "dear, sweet, angel lady". Several chapters
later, on the occasion of their final and fatal meeting on London
Bridge, Nancy once again contrasts Rose's angelic virtues with those
of the false religionists:

*"haughty, religious people would have held their heads up to see me as
I am to-night, and preached of flames and vengeance," cried the girl.
"Oh, dear lady, why ar'n't those who claim to be God's own folks as
gentle and as kind to us poor wretches as you, who, having youth, and
beauty, and all that they have lost, might be a little proud instead of so
much humbler?"*

Rose, as with the other female angels, is deliberately distanced from
both church and chapel attendance. Formalized religious observance
is replaced with the practical expression of genuine Christianity. This
approach is most obvious with Dickens's third angel, Nell Trent.
Though living in the confines of the church and her responsibilities

for showing people around and opening and closing the building on Sundays, she is not actually depicted attending a service.

Despite Rose's heartfelt pleading, Nancy refuses the assistance offered to her and leaves. Not realizing that she has been watched by Fagin's spy, Noah Claypole, she returns to her room. It is here that she is brutally murdered by Bill Sikes. It is just prior to her death that the efficacy of Rose's actions and words are revealed: "raising herself, with difficulty, on her knees, she drew from her bosom a white handkerchief – Rose Maylie's own – and holding it up, in her folded hands, as high towards Heaven as her feeble strength would allow, breathed one prayer for mercy to her maker." In her dying moment, Dickens shows her receiving salvation. It was this passage that was to so move him and his audience during the course of his public readings.

12

NICHOLAS NICKLEBY: CHARITABLE AND FEMALE ANGELS

On 9 November 1837, just nine days before the celebratory dinner to mark the success and completion of *The Pickwick Papers*, the 25-year-old Dickens again signed a contract with Chapman and Hall. This time it was for his third novel, *Nicholas Nickleby*.

Following the now familiar format, it was to appear in monthly instalments and then in book form. Under the agreement, he was to be paid £150 for each number, with the first being published on 1 April 1838. Added to this, he was able, for the first time, to negotiate a deal whereby the copyright of the novel became his after a period of five years. He was also able to secure a third share in the rights of *The Pickwick Papers*.

Such was the writer's reputation that the very first issue sold around 50,000 copies – a hundred times that of the opening instalment of *The Pickwick Papers*. It was to retain its popularity right through to the final number, which was published on 1 October 1839. The single-volume book, including an engraving of Daniel Maclise's iconic portrait of the author, appeared twenty-two days later. Once again, Chapman and Hall were able to celebrate a highly profitable collaboration with Dickens. On the book's completion, as they had done previously, they presented him with an extra payment. The sum of £1,500 was twice what he received for *The Pickwick Papers*.

The timing of the payment could not have been better. With the addition of two more children – Mary, named after his deceased sister-in-law (6 March 1838) and Kate (29 October 1839) – the need for live-in servants to assist Catherine, and the increasing necessity to accommodate overnight guests, Dickens had spent the autumn looking for a suitable new property. By November, he had settled upon 1 Devonshire Terrace, York Road, near Portman Place. Built in the 1770s, the elegant, sizeable, Georgian house, complete with coach-house, tall bay windows, and large, walled garden, was set in a private location, opposite Regent's Park. He paid £800 for the remaining eleven-year lease, with an annual rent of £180, and it was to be the family home for the next ten years.

In what was to become a regular feature of his future career, during the course of writing *Nicholas Nickleby*, Dickens spent several months away from home. Finding a change of scene relaxing and a boost to his creativity, the family stayed in various locations, including Twickenham, Petersham, and the Isle of Wight. He would commute to London to attend frequent meetings with Chapman and Hall, and the book's illustrator, Phiz. One of Dickens's favourite places at this time was Broadstairs in Kent. In the early autumn of 1837, when the family first visited, it was little more than a fishing village, with three winding streets leading down to the white chalk cliffs, overlooking the semicircular bay. It was here, at 40 Albion Street, on Friday, 20 September 1839, that *Nicholas Nickleby* was completed.

When Dickens was a boy living in Chatham, a peculiar incident took place which remained with him into adulthood. Walking around the area next to Rochester Castle, he came across a child, a little older than himself, sitting on a wall, fiddling with a pen-knife. As he watched, he was shocked to see him cutting his arm until it bled. On asking him why he did such a thing, the crying boy explained that his step-father planned to send him to a Yorkshire school, and rather than being subjected to the terrible cruelty they were notorious for, he preferred to contract blood poisoning and avoid having to go.

Around twenty years later, in *Nicholas Nickleby*, Dickens launched a one-man crusade to expose the neglect and widespread abuse prevalent at these schools, which had effectively become the dumping ground for unwanted children. Towards the end of January 1838, just before he started the novel, he determined to investigate some of the establishments in person. Using the name of the book's illustrator, Hablot K. Browne, with whom he travelled, Dickens posed as the friend of a widowed mother, who was seeking to place her child in a school.

On a cold winter's morning, they caught the "Express Coach", which departed from the Saracen's Head, Snow Hill. They stayed at Grantham overnight and then took the Glasgow Mail to Greta Bridge. On the morning of Thursday, 1 February, they set off from The George and New Inn for the small moor village of Bowes, to visit the school run by William Shaw. Six years previously, the schoolmaster, whose terrible neglect led to ten boys completely losing their sight, had been sued by their parents. Found guilty and ordered to pay £500 in damages, he was, unbelievably, allowed to carry on in his role.

Following the meeting with Shaw, Dickens wandered into the churchyard and discovered the graves of no fewer than thirty-four pupils who had died in the district's schools. One gravestone in particular caught his eye, that of the nineteen-year-old George Ashton Taylor of Trowbridge, Wiltshire, who died suddenly at Shaw's Academy. Reading the epitaph, with the snow lying thickly on the ground, the form of Smike, the novel's most tragic character, came into his mind. The one-eyed Shaw was to appear as Wackford Squeers, the tyrannical headmaster of Dotheboys Hall. After the publication of *Nicholas Nickleby*, such was the ground-swell of public opinion against Yorkshire schools that the government introduced strict regulations and closed down the worst establishments. The response clearly demonstrated that the author was not only a great storyteller, but also a powerful agent for social change.

On the opening page of Chapter 18 of *Nicholas Nickleby*, Dickens describes charity as being "the one great cardinal virtue". Charles Cheeryble, the final charitable angel, is the novel's embodiment of this principle. Although he resembles both Samuel Pickwick and Mr Brownlow in appearance, bachelorhood, and social status, there is one important difference: he is not retired. In making this distinction, the author is able, for the first time, to demonstrate the application of benevolence and kindness within the workplace. In direct contrast to the inhumane exploitation and heartless capitalism associated with the "dark satanic mills", the employees of the Cheerybles (Charles runs the firm with his twin brother Edwin) are treated with dignity and respect. Also, their City premises, just off Threadneedle Street, serve not only as the base of their successful merchant business, but also as the centre for their charitable activity.

In common with that of Wackford Squeers, Dickens's characterization of the Cheeryble brothers was drawn from real life. At the end of October 1838, he had toured the Midlands and the north of England to see the atrocious conditions endured by those working in the cotton mills. After visiting Liverpool and being joined by Forster, they went on to Manchester. Prior to their departure, William Harrison Ainsworth, who had previously lived in that city, provided Dickens with a letter of introduction to some of his friends there. One November evening, at the home of one of them, Gilbert Winter, he met the extraordinary brothers, William and Daniel Grant. Self-made men, they ran their successful merchant and manufacturing business from their offices at Cheeryble House, Canon Street, Manchester.

In the book's Preface, Dickens wrote:

> *Those who take an interest in this tale will be glad to learn that the Brothers Cheeryble live, that their liberal charity, their singleness of heart, their noble nature and their unbounded benevolence, are no creations of the author's brain, but are every day (and oftenest by stealth) promoting some munificent and generous deed in that town of which they are the pride and honour.*

Beyond the author's clever use of his name, a combination of "cheery" and "cherub" (child angel), there are several distinct references to Cheeryble's angelic status, all of which occur during his confrontation with the novel's principal evil character, Ralph Nickleby. In the first, he associates him with the angelic ability "to appear in men's houses, whether they will or no, and pour out speech in unwilling ears". Following on from this, having identified mercy as an attribute of angels, Cheeryble exhibits the virtue in his dealing with Nickleby. Next, in describing him as being "truth itself", Dickens is clearly associating Charles Cheeryble with the divine. The mutual aversion between the agents of good and evil also reveals his angelic character.

Like Samuel Pickwick, in the exuberance and extent of his benevolence, Charles Cheeryble's charitable activities have a workplace focus. Nicholas Nickleby has, as an act of kindness, been employed by Cheeryble, and when he first visits the Threadneedle Street offices, he is introduced to a man named Mr Trimmers. Described by Cheeryble as one of his best friends, he regularly provides him with information about dock-workers, warehousemen, and their families who are in desperate need. On this occasion, Trimmers informs Cheeryble about the family of a man killed that morning in the East Indian docks. His immediate response is to make a donation of £20.

Next, Nicholas notices that "among the shipping-announcements and steam packet lists, which decorated the counting-house [office] walls, were designs for almshouses, statements of charities and plans for new hospitals." He is further struck by the healthy, cheerful appearance of all the warehousemen and porters employed by the firm, and the respect they show Charles Cheeryble. There can be no doubt that this is due to the kindness of their employer. This point is confirmed several pages later, on the occasion of their chief clerk's birthday celebrations, which take place at the Cheerybles' home, contrary to the strict social discrimination of the period. After Tim Linkinwater's birthday toast – the brothers have given him a costly gold snuff-box and a banknote worth ten times its value – one of their employees gives a brief speech commending Charles and his brother, Edwin, for their benevolence.

It is not only the employees and those connected with their business that benefit from Charles Cheeryble's generosity. He also transforms the lives of the urban migrant Nickleby family. Nicholas, in the desperate hope of finding work, has gone to a General Agency Office (the Victorian version of an employment agency), and while there he meets the charitable angel. Drawn by Charles's "kind face" and "radiant countenance", he finds himself confiding in this complete stranger. In response, Cheeryble takes Nicholas back to his offices and employs him as a clerk at a very generous salary. He provides the family with a cottage in Bow. Sensing that Nicholas is a proud young man, he agrees a monthly rent, but it becomes clear that he has come up with a scheme of reimbursing him the money without his knowledge. Cheeryble also arranges "a loan" to furnish the cottage and regularly purchases gifts for Mrs Nickleby, which happen to be the things they most require.

The final person who directly benefits from the charitable angel's kindness is the novel's female angel, Madeline Bray. Cheeryble was in love with her mother, who foolishly rejected him for the dissolute Walter Bray. Nonetheless he generously responded to his former sweetheart's plea for financial help, made just before her death. Now, her daughter, dutifully struggling to care for her father, has been forced to rely upon her "dear friend and benefactor". Aware of Bray's nasty, vindictive character, Cheeryble has provided for them both under the pretence of buying various pieces of Madeline's art through his agent Nicholas. His last benevolent act towards her is to become her legal guardian.

Samuel Pickwick, Mr Brownlow, and Charles Cheeryble are the embodiment of Dickens's idea of true Christianity. To him, faith was practical. It had to be seen at work within society as a whole, not confined within the walls of churches and chapels. With the exception of Mr Pickwick, who attends church for two weddings and a Christmas Day service, while at Dingley Dell, the charitable angels are completely divorced from formal religious observance, as we have seen. They are not overtly spiritual people, but agents of social change, applying Christian values to transform the lives of the poor.

Closely resembling Rose, in age and appearance, Madeline Bray, Dickens's second female angel, once again connects external beauty with inner virtue. Straight away she is described as being "a young lady who could be scarcely eighteen, of very slight and delicate figure, but exquisitely shaped. She raised her veil, for an instant, while she proffered the inquiry, and disclosed a countenance of most uncommon beauty." Whereas Rose's selflessness and self-sacrifice are revealed in relation to Harry Maylie and his mother, Dickens uses Madeline's relationship with her father for the same purpose. This father–daughter motif was to be repeated on no fewer than three occasions: Agnes Wickfield (*David Copperfield*), Amy Dorrit (*Little Dorrit*), and, most significantly, Florence Dombey (*Dombey and Son*).

Madeline's female angelic virtues are accentuated by the undeserving and nasty nature of her father, Walter Bray, who is responsible not only for his daughter's hardship, but also for the premature death of her mother. To fund his previously indulgent lifestyle, he borrowed substantial sums of money from both Arthur Gride and the novel's principal villain, Ralph Nickleby. His failure to repay these debts results in both him and Madeline being confined to the Kings Bench Debtors' Prison. His health having deteriorated, Madeline is forced to work day and night to support them both. In doing so, she is forced to take on a variety of jobs, which not only involve arduous work, but also expose her to numerous indignities. Ungrateful for all her efforts on his behalf, he also treats her badly.

Such is the extent of Madeline's angelic self-sacrificing love that, by staying with her undeserving father, she is denying herself the help that others wish to provide. The Cheeryble brothers pleaded with her to leave and to allow them to take care of her. Also, had she left, she would have received the substantial sum of £12,000, which was the proceeds from her maternal grandfather's will. After two years of hardship, Madeline demonstrates the full extent of her angelic qualities when she consents to sacrifice herself in marriage to redeem her father. Gride, one of Walter Bray's principal creditors, agrees to clear all his debts and to provide a new life for him in exchange for his daughter's hand. The personal cost of this atonement is heightened by the nature of her elderly intended husband. Newman Noggs, Ralph Nickleby's clerk, describes the miser Gride as being "a hoary wretch – a devil born and bred, and grey in devil ways".

Nicholas Nickleby, on learning of the wicked scheme, resolves to confront Walter Bray and dissuade Madeline from sacrificing herself. On entering their home, he is struck by the "change in the lovely girl before him, which told him, in startling terms, how much mental suffering had been compressed into that short time". In response to his passionate plea for her not to marry Gride, she declares that it is "her duty to do so; and with the help of heaven" she will, of her "own free will" pursue the path that will redeem her father's debt. Dickens figuratively uses the idea of personal sacrifice to pay a financial debt as an analogy for Christ's atoning death to redeem individuals spiritually. Right up to the day of the wedding, Madeline retains her resolve to sacrifice herself. Just before the ceremony is due to take her place, her father dies, releasing her from the responsibility. The shock of her father's death and the mental anguish she endured in the time before the wedding take a severe toll on her health and result in her suffering a life-threatening illness. She eventually recovers to marry Nicholas.

13

THE OLD CURIOSITY SHOP AND
THE TICKING OF THE CLOCK

Sitting in the coffee room of the King's Head Inn (Barnard Castle, County Durham) in 1838, Dickens briefly broke off his conversation with Hablot K. Browne to look out of the window. Gazing towards the Market Square, his attention was inexplicably drawn to William Humphrey's Watch and Clock-Maker's shop. His interest aroused, he braved the cold February air, crossed the square, and entered the shop. As he did so, he encountered a beautiful old timepiece, Master Humphrey's Clock, which had been made by the present owner some years before. The distinctive metronomic voice of the clock and its peculiar appearance fascinated him. On leaving the shop, he had a definite sense that, at some point, it would feature in his writing. A few days later, having collected sufficient material on Yorkshire schools for *Nicholas Nickleby*, he returned to London. During his lengthy journey, and in the subsequent weeks and months, he continued to hear the ticking of the clock and wondered when its time would come.

A year later, in the May or early summer of 1839, while still working on *Nicholas Nickleby*, Dickens began to explore with Chapman and Hall the possibility of launching his own weekly publication. Modelled on popular eighteenth-century periodicals, the plan was that it would contain a miscellany of anecdotes, short stories, satire, historical articles, facts, and information, all of which would be written by the author himself. During their discussions, the writer came up with the idea of introducing a central character, an old man, a dreamer and philosopher, who lives in a strange, shadowy old house. His only companion is an "old, quaint, queer-cased grandfather clock", from whose dark, deep weight compartment he occasionally draws various manuscripts. He, together with his unusual friends, who had formed a little club, were to be both the contributors and the narrators of the weekly journal. The name of the periodical was, of course, *Master Humphrey's Clock*.

Dickens had every reason to be delighted with the prospects of his new venture. Not only was he to have complete editorial control of the publication, he had also managed to negotiate extremely favourable terms. In addition to his salary of £50 per week, he was also, for the first time, to receive a 50 per cent share in the profits. Whereas, up to this point, he had always received a fixed payment, regardless of the sales, now he would benefit directly from the success of his work. The publishers were also liable for all the associated costs of producing the periodical, including printing, distribution, advertising, and the salaries of the two illustrators, George Cattermole and Phiz. With copies also being sold in Germany and the United States, the author realistically anticipated an annual income of around £5,000.

By the end of 1839, he had started work on the first instalment. It was not, however, the only project he was undertaking at that time. On 23 November, the marriage of Queen Victoria was announced. Chapman and Hall, seeking to capitalize on the occasion, commissioned Dickens to write *Sketches of Young Couples*. Illustrated by Phiz, the collection of eleven pieces was published on the Queen's wedding day, 10 February 1840.

By mid-January, the contents of the opening number, containing "Gog and Magog, the two Guildhall Giants", was complete. Three months later, on Saturday, 4 April 1840, the first weekly issue of *Master Humphrey's Clock*, priced at threepence, went on sale. Distinctive and larger than the instalments of *Nicholas Nickleby*, it consisted of twelve creamy white pages of text in a white wrapper. Innovatively, rather than having the illustrations at the front, they were placed within the text. Seeking to maximize their profits, Chapman and Hall also published a green wrapped monthly shilling version and three bound six-monthly volumes containing all eighty-eight issues.

As was his normal practice, Dickens made arrangements to be away from London when his new work first appeared. On this occasion, he travelled with Catherine to Birmingham on the day before it came out. Shortly afterwards, they were joined by John Forster, who could barely contain his excitement: The opening number had sold around 70,000 copies. It was an unprecedented success. Or so it seemed. However, sales of the second number fell drastically, and not even the reintroduction of his former stellar double-act, Mr Pickwick and Samuel Weller, could stem the tide. By the third week, its circulation had fallen by 30 per cent.

The public had flocked to buy the opening number in the expectation that it would contain the opening instalment of the author's latest novel. They wanted a story, not a Dickensian version of an eighteenth-century periodical. The situation was not too dissimilar to that faced by Dickens four years earlier, when the fate of *The Pickwick Papers* hung in the balance. Once again, the writer intuitively understood what was required and rose to the challenge. During the course of a hastily convened editorial conference, which took place at Chapman and Hall's office in the Strand, he announced his plan to expand a short piece he had begun into a full-blown narrative. The public wanted a new book: he would give them one. Once again, he was to demonstrate a remarkable flexibility, ingenuity, and connection with his readership. Such was his resilience that he was able to transform a potentially serious threat into an opportunity to further enhance his already impressive reputation.

A few months earlier, Dickens, along with his wife and his friends John Forster and the artist, Daniel Maclise, went to Bath to visit the essayist and poet, Walter Landor. During their three-day stay at York House Hotel, a seed of an idea for a short story had begun to develop in his mind. In between sightseeing and spending time with Landor, he began to loosely sketch various plot and character details. By the end of his stay, he was in a position to discuss with Forster a possible title: "Should it be *The Old Curiosity Dealer and The Child* or *The Old Curiosity Shop?*", he asked. They decided on the latter.

Determining, with any certainty, the inspirational source of this or any other story that Dickens wrote is not feasible, such was the extent of his creative imagination. However, in this case, aspects of the lead character, the thirteen/fourteen-year-old Nell Trent, can be traced to the Evangelical tracts of the period. Two such examples are *The Dairyman's Daughter* and *The Young Cottager*, both of which were translated into six languages and sold around 2 million copies. Based on the Reverend Legh Richmond's experiences as a curate on the Isle of Wight, both have female heroines who die prematurely: Elizabeth Wallbridge (*The Dairyman's Daughter*), who dies of TB at the age of thirty-one, and Jane, who dies at the age of twelve. Also, two years prior to the writer starting *The Old Curiosity Shop*, the Reverend Edward Caswall, author of *Sketches of Young Ladies*, the companion to Dickens's own *Sketches of Young Gentlemen* (1838), wrote a book entitled *Morals of the Graveyard*. Published by Chapman and Hall and illustrated by Phiz, it was another possible inspiration for Nell. Essentially a fable, designed for the moral improvement of children, it featured a young girl, often referred to as "the little maid", who would regularly visit a graveyard with her grandfather.

Following the emergency editorial conference, Dickens decided to replace a piece about a witch "with a little-child story, which is SURE to be effective". Thus, in issue number four (25 April 1840), *The Old Curiosity Shop* made its debut. Up to week eleven, it was just one of several stories that filled the pages of the periodical; after that, until its conclusion in the forty-fourth issue (6 February 1841), *Master Humphrey's Clock* became the vehicle for the instalments of his new novel. Having anticipated a period of being free from the constraints of serialized novel writing, he now found himself, for the first time, working to a weekly deadline. Any pressure he felt was, to a large extent, offset by the fact that not only had his new novel restored the fortunes of the *Clock*, but it had actually increased its readership to around 100,000.

As with *Nicholas Nickleby*, Dickens combined his time at Devonshire Terrace with visits to Broadstairs. Throughout June 1840, four months into *The Old Curiosity Shop*, he once again stayed at 37 Albion Street, with Catherine and their three children. On his return in September, he rented Lawn House, a small villa set between a cornfield and the sea. His frequent night-time walks along the cliffs, during these two months, proved an important source of inspiration. At some point in August, he went with Catherine to visit his parents in Alphington, near Exeter. On the twentieth of the same month, the christening of his second daughter, Kate, took place. The author's fourth child, Walter, was born on 8 February the following year, two days after the final instalment of *The Old Curiosity Shop* appeared.

Throughout this whole period and until the novel was complete, Dickens, along with his readers, found himself becoming more and more involved with the narrative and in particular with the fate of the central character, Nell Trent. Second only to *The Pickwick Papers* in sales during the author's lifetime, *The Old Curiosity Shop* was hugely influential in creating the bond which was to exist between the writer and the public throughout the remainder of his career. It was to set the seal upon his fame.

Essentially *The Old Curiosity Shop* is the story of a thirteen/fourteen-year-old girl who seeks to rescue her grandfather from his deluded aspirations of acquiring wealth through gambling, whilst being mercilessly pursued by the villainous dwarf Quilp, to whom he owes money. Nell, in mirroring the popular religious classic of the period, *Pilgrim's Progress*, flees London in the hope of finding some blissful place in which they can make a new start. They eventually find refuge in a small peaceful village, after having passed through the industrialized Midlands, securing temporary shelter and work at a waxworks attraction, attending a horse-racing meeting and being befriended by an ageing schoolmaster. But such is the degree of suffering endured by little Nell in the course of their journey that, soon after faithfully carrying her grandfather to this safe haven, she dies.

While *The Old Curiosity Shop* contained all the elements that had made his previous three novels so successful – the lively humour, the brilliant life-like characters (including Dick Swiveller, the Marchioness, Kit Nubbles, and Quilp), his photographic descriptive powers, and wonderful storytelling – it was the book's compelling pathos, specifically in relation to Nell Trent, that defined its appeal. To his readers, these individuals were as real as themselves, none more so than the heroine, who virtually became their own adopted child.

It was not only the public who were gripped by the story. Dickens himself, particularly in the stage leading up to Nell's death, felt increasingly burdened. He grew daily more miserable towards the end and delayed its conclusion as long as was practically possible. In a letter to the book's illustrator, George Cattermole, he confided: "I am breaking my heart over the story and cannot bear to finish it." He eventually did, on either 17 or 21 January 1841, at four o'clock in the morning. The fictional demise of the fourteen-year-old girl evoked painful memories of Mary Hogarth and her tragic death. Although it had taken place almost four years previously, the feelings of grief and loss were still agonizingly real.

As the proposed fate of Nell became apparent, the author received scores upon scores of letters imploring him not to kill her off. Such was the suspense and interest in the United States that huge crowds gathered at New York Harbour to await the arrival of the crucial instalment. Soon the speculation ended. Nell was dead, and the public on both sides of the Atlantic mourned.

14

DEATH, THE RESURRECTION, AND CHILD ANGELS

The Old Curiosity Shop, with its emphasis on death and the resurrection, has been rightly identified as one of Dickens's most religious novels. It was these very themes that so touched his readers. When Nell died, the spontaneous widespread mourning that ensued was not for the fictitious fourteen-year-old girl; rather, it represented the heartfelt grief of thousands upon thousands of people who had come to associate her with the children they had lost. The staggering scale of infant and child mortality during the writer's lifetime reveals just why such an empathetic work proved so popular.

In 1839, the year prior to the commencement of *The Old Curiosity Shop*, almost half of the 45,000 funerals that took place in London were for children under ten. At a meeting, where Dickens was also a speaker, Edwin Chadwick estimated that, between 1820 and 1850, nearly 30,000 children/young people died each year in the nation's capital. In the 1840s, across the country as a whole, the infant mortality rate[8] was around 150, whereas the UK figure for 2015 was just 4. Comparisons with some of the poorest countries in Africa today demonstrate just how high the figures were: Angola 96, Central African Republic 92, and Burkino Faso 61.

Dickens frequently refers to infant and child mortality within his work. In Chapter 2 of "Our Parish", he refers to the death of the

---

8   The infant mortality rate is the number of deaths of infants under one year old per 1,000 live births.

washerwoman's child, while in the "Bloomsbury Christening" (also in *Sketches By Boz*), he refers to the cantankerous Nicodemus Dumps speedily regaining his composure as his eyes rest on a paragraph quoting the number of infant deaths from the bills of mortality. Mrs Thingummy, Agnes Fleming's nurse in *Oliver Twist*, has lost eleven of her thirteen children, and in *Sketches of Young Couples*, written just before *The Old Curiosity Shop*, there are three specific references, one of which links sizes of families to infant mortality. At the beginning of *Great Expectations*, the five little gravestones of Pip's brothers are mentioned. The inspiration for this was taken from the thirteen Comport children's graves at St James's churchyard, Colling in Kent. Septimus Crisparkle, the Minor Canon of Cloisterham Cathedral, who appears in Dickens's final incomplete novel, *The Mystery of Edwin Drood* is so named because "six little brother Crisparkles before him went out one by one as they were born, like six little rush-lights as they were lighted."

As a child growing up in Chatham, Dickens had not been protected from the harsh reality of death. On frequent occasions, he accompanied the family's maid, Mary Weller, as she attended numerous pregnant women during their deliveries. Sadly, often as not, the babies died. Many years later, he recalled an instance of four or five dead infants having been laid out "side by side on a chest of drawers". Shortly before completing the first instalment of *The Old Curiosity Shop*, a curious incident took place which was strangely in keeping with the mortality theme of his forthcoming novel. A month after moving into Devonshire Terrace in December 1839, he was summoned to the nearby Marylebone Workhouse to sit in on a coroner's jury. On sitting down in his allotted seat, he was approached by a fellow juror, who, on discovering that Dickens had three young children, offered his services and handed him his business card. Dickens was bemused when he realized that his family was seen as potential customers for the local undertaker.

On 22 February 1851, Dickens, in his *Household Words* piece, "Births Mrs Meek's of a Son", refers directly to the infant/child mortality rates of the period: "I learn from the statistical tables that one child in five dies within the first year of its life and one child in three within the fifth." Within two months of writing these words, his eight-month-old daughter, Dora, died.

Death, and its associative imagery, are closely linked to Nell throughout the narrative. Her name, for instance, is a deliberately chosen homophone of knell: the sound of a bell ringing to announce a death or funeral. In Chapter 9, Nell, looking out of a window of her grandfather's shop, sees a man passing with a coffin on his back and two or three others silently following him to a house where somebody is dead. Seven chapters later, she and her grandfather meet the Punch and Judy man, Tom Codlin, in a graveyard. In the next chapter, rising early in the morning, she revisits it alone; Dickens writes: "She felt a curious kind of pleasure in lingering among those houses of the dead and read the inscriptions on the tombs of the good people, passing on from one to another with increasing interest." In Chapter 45, while struggling through the large industrial town, where "contagious disease and death had been busy with the living crops", Nell observes carts "filled with made coffins".

During the closing stages of her life, her association with death intensifies. On the very first night in her new home, close by a graveyard, Nell's thoughts, prompted by her surroundings, are drawn to think about death: "The glare of the sinking flame, reflected in the oaken panels, the aged walls where strange shadows came and went every flickering of the fire – the solemn presence within, of that decay which falls on senseless things, the most enduring in their nature: and, without, and round about on every side, of Death."

Early in the morning, in Chapter 53, as she sets off for the church, Dickens writes: "The neighbouring stream sparkled, and rolled onward with a tuneful sound; the dew glistened on the green mounds, like tears shed by Good Spirits over the dead." Shortly afterwards, she meets the elderly sexton.[9] Following a lengthy conversation about mortality, they visit an old well under the belfry of the church, which is used by the author as an allegory of death and the grave. Harry, Mr

---

9   A sexton is an individual employed to care for the churchyard, ring the church bell, and dig the graves.

Marton's favourite pupil, dies, as does Willy, the younger brother of a child whom Nell has befriended. Finally, as has been foreshadowed, Nell herself dies.

In the same way that the harsh reality of death pervades the novel, so, too, does the certain hope of the resurrection. In the person of Nell, both are juxtapositioned to great effect. Of all the references to the resurrection in the novel, only one, which occurs in a conversation between Mr Chuckster and Dick Swiveller, does not involve her. Although *The Old Curiosity Shop* can be viewed as Dickens's most concerted fictional expression of his personal belief in this key Christian doctrine, references to it do appear elsewhere in his work, most noticeably in *A Tale of Two Cities* (1859).

The first reference to the resurrection in *The Old Curiosity Shop* occurs in Chapter 6. In conversation with Mrs Quilp, Nell recalls how, when she was a little girl, her grandfather would "try to make her understand that her deceased mother was not lying in her grave, but had flown to a beautiful country beyond the sky, where nothing died, or ever grew old".

Just as he did in his final unfinished novel, *The Mystery of Edwin Drood*, in seeking to represent the idea of the resurrection, Dickens symbolically drew upon aspects of creation. In Chapter 53, Nell, having read the Bible, and considered the interaction of nature and death among the tombs of the baronial chapel, decides to climb the winding stairs to the top of the church tower. As she does so, she experiences:

> *the glory of the sudden burst of light; the freshness of the fields and woods, stretching away on every side and meeting the bright blue sky; the cattle grazing on the pasturage; the smoke that, coming from among the trees, seemed to rise upward from the green earth; the children yet at their gambols down below – all, everything so beautiful and happy! It was like passing from death to life; it was drawing nearer to heaven.*

In conversation with the elderly sexton, the girl earnestly states: "Perhaps the mourners learn to look to the blue sky by day and to the stars by night, and to think that the dead are there and not in graves." The remaining instances focus on Nell's demise, which, in keeping with the resurrection motif, occurs early on Sunday morning.

Of her death, Dickens writes how her "young spirit has winged its early flight". The accompanying illustration, "At Rest", also contains two associated images. At the specific request of Dickens, George Cattermole included slips of evergreen foliage on the girl's pillow. Nell's death takes place in the depth of winter – there had been a heavy fall of snow covering the countryside – and its inclusion, at the specific request of the author, can be interpreted as a symbolic representation of the resurrection: the certain hope of spring, new life, within the death of winter. The second image is the closed Bible resting by the girl's right hand. Throughout the narrative, whenever she was depicted reading the Bible, it was connected with death and resurrection. This was not the only occasion when Dickens was to use this device: he was to repeat it in the last chapter of "Our Parish" (*Sketches By Boz*), *The Pickwick Papers*, and *Dombey and Son*.

With his funeral quote from the *Book of Common Prayer's* "Order for the Burial of the Dead" – "Earth to earth, ashes to ashes, dust to dust" – Dickens was able to evoke further resurrection imagery. His readers, who were very familiar with the text of the service, would have immediately recalled the words that followed them: "in the sure and certain hope of the Resurrection to eternal life, through our Lord Jesus Christ". The final allusion appears in the last chapter, when Kit Nubbles reassures his children that Nell, having died, had gone to heaven.

Despite the religious sentiment of *The Old Curiosity Shop* attracting criticism from the Christian press on both sides of the Atlantic, it, nonetheless, struck a chord in the hearts of thousands upon thousands of bereaved parents. And it was a story through which Dickens sought to introduce one of his own beliefs – that children who died became angels.

In various letters to grieving friends he would repeat this conviction. When corresponding with William Bradbury (March 1839), he reassures him that his young daughter was already half an angel before she died. Two years later, just a few months after the completion of *The Old Curiosity Shop*, he wrote to comfort Basil Hall: "It must be something to you, even in your grief, to know that one of the Angels called you Father upon earth." Writing to the Reverend James White and his wife in May 1848, he consoled them with the thought that their dead child was "among the Angels of God". After his death, a poem was discovered in his desk that contained the following lines:

> *Oh, there is nothing on earth half as holy,*
> *As the innocent heart of a child.*
> *They are angels of God in disguise.*

This belief was found in his novels as well as his letters. The first reference is in Chapter 29 of *The Pickwick Papers*. On Christmas Eve, at Manor Farm, the aged mother of Mr Wardle entertains the assembled guests with a story involving a sexton who has a strange encounter with a band of goblins and their king. During the course of his abduction, the cantankerous Gabriel Grub undergoes a Scrooge-like transformation following his forced observation of a family's tragic bereavement:

> *The scene was altered to a small bed-room, where the fairest and youngest child lay dying; the roses had fled from his cheeks, and the light from his eye and even as the sexton looked upon him with an interest he had never felt or known before, he died. His young brothers and sisters crowded round his little bed, and seized his tiny hand so cold and heavy; but they shrunk back from his touch, and looked with awe on his infant face for calm and tranquil as it has in rest and peace as the beautiful and sleeping child seemed to be, they saw that he was dead, and they knew he was an Angel looking down upon, and blessing them, from a bright and happy Haven.*

In the very first number of *Master Humphrey's Clock*, before *The Old Curiosity Shop* even began, Dickens was already introducing his readers to the idea of a connection between children and angels. In the opening chapter, Master Humphrey describes children as being "little people who are so fresh from God". After this, he recounts a childhood birthday memory in which he and his friends are gathered round his mother, eagerly admiring a picture containing a group of infant angels. Studying the subjects carefully, he recognizes in each a likeness to one of his young companions.

Other than *The Old Curiosity Shop*, the first most noticeable occasion when deceased children become angels is to be found in Dickens's seventh novel, *Dombey and Son* (1848). In describing the death of the child Paul Dombey, Dickens writes: "The old, old fashioned Death! Oh thank GOD, all who see it, for that older fashion yet, of Immortality! And look upon us, angels of young children, with regards not quite estranged, when the swift river bears us to the ocean!" Fifteen chapters further on, his sister, Florence, sees "her dead brother shining like an angel".

The next reference to dead children becoming angels occurs in "A Child's Dream of a Star". In 1850, having just launched *Household Words*, Dickens was returning home on the night train from Brighton. As he gazed thoughtfully up at the starlit sky, he remembered how he and his older sister, Fanny used to sit together as children in his St Mary's Place attic bedroom, looking up at the stars. Finding it difficult to come to terms with her death from TB two years earlier, he often found his thoughts drifting back to their childhood days. For the previous few days he had been somewhat concerned that the second number of his new journal lacked something of a more sentimental nature. By the time he reached his destination, an idea for a short story had formed in his mind.

"A Child's Dream of a Star" begins with the child narrator having to come to terms with the death of his sister and baby brother. On each occasion, he is comforted by the thought that they have been taken up along a sparkling road to heaven by a company of angels. On their arrival, they are met by their deceased relatives and friends who, like themselves, have joined the angelic host. As a young man, the narrator loses his mother, and then his daughter when he is a mature man. He finds solace in the knowledge that they too are now angels and in the presence of their loved ones. Finally, now an old man, on his deathbed, he describes how his "age is falling from him like a garment and he is moving toward heaven as a child".

As was the case with death and the resurrection, the references to children becoming angels in *The Old Curiosity Shop* focus on the female angel, Nell Trent. In Chapter 26, following the death of Mr Marton's favourite pupil, Harry, she dreams of him being "not coffined and covered up, but mingling with angels and smiling happily". Approaching her own death, she visualizes him again. This time, "along with a column of bright faces", she sees him looking down on her while she is asleep. At the same time, she hears music in the air and the sound of angels' wings.

Later in the narrative, the younger brother of Willy, a boy who has just died, finds Nell alone in the church. In a highly agitated state, he runs up and embraces her and states: "She is not one yet! No, No, not yet… you must not be one dear Nell. We can't see them. They never come to play with us, or talk with us. Be what you are. You are better so." Confused, she asks him to explain what he means. The child looking up into her face, replied: "they say that you will be an Angel before the birds sing." Dickens confirmed Nell's angelic transformation, in the close of her deathbed scene; "So shall we know the angels in their majesty after death." In George Cattermole's final illustration of the book, she is depicted being carried heavenwards by four angels, all of whom are of a similar age and appearance to herself.

For Dickens, Nell does not just become an angel after death – there are frequent references to her earlier angelic status. Numerically, these references far exceed those used for his other female angels. The first appears in the form of a night-time blessing spoken by her grandfather in the opening chapter: "Sleep soundly Nell, and angels guard thy bed." The next occurs on the morning of their departure from London. Dickens writes of the air "falling like breath from angels on the sleeping town". On three separate occasions, Nell dreams of angels and, in Chapter 44, the furnace-man, who has kindly offered them shelter, gives Nell a gift of two penny pieces that were "shining brightly in the eyes of Angels". Some twenty chapters later, Nell is described as being an angel by her friend Kit and a "Good Angel" by her great-uncle. On the night of Nell's death, her grandfather tells Kit the deep snow has been "strewn by Angel hands" and Dickens, referring to her lifeless body, declares: "So shall we know the angels in their majesty after death!" The final allusion occurs when the elderly mourners at Nell's funeral whisper among themselves that she had seen and talked with angels.

Even though Nell's suffering and deprivation are most conspicuous during her pilgrimage to redeem her grandfather, Dickens leaves his readers in no doubt as to the extent of her heartbreak and sorrow prior to her flight:

> *It was not the monotonous day unchequered by variety and uncheered by pleasant companionship, it was not the dark dreary evenings or the solitary nights, it was the absence of every slight and easy pleasure for which young hearts beat so high, or the knowing nothing of childhood but its weakness and its easily wounded spirit; that had wrung such tears from the Nell. To see the old man struck down beneath the pressure of some hidden grief, to mark his wavering and unsettled state, to be agitated at times with a dreadful fear that his mind was wandering and to trace in his words and looks the dawning of despondent madness; to watch and wait and listen for confirmation of these things day after day, and to feel and know that, come what might, they were alone in the world with no one to help or advice or care about them – these were the causes of depression and anxiety.*

The mental, emotional, and physical anguish endured on behalf of her grandfather during the journey comes to a head in a large, noisy industrial town. Just before being given refuge by the furnace-man, she is "shivering with the cold and damp, ill in body, and sick to death at heart". Following their overnight stay by the furnace fire,

Nell explains to her grandfather: "We shall be very slow to-day dear, my feet are sore, and I have pains from the wet of yesterday in all my bones." Despite all her suffering, Dickens reveals the selflessness of her angelic character: "So very weak and spent she felt, so very calm and unresisting, that she had no thought of any wants of her own, but prayed that God would raise up some friend for him." With hope, strength, and energy all but gone, Nell resolves to disguise her true desperate state from her grandfather and heroically staggers on. Eventually, however, she collapses senseless in the street. The elderly schoolteacher, Mr Marton, comes to her aid and takes it upon himself to provide a home and support for Nell and her grandfather, but it is too late.

Four chapters from the end of the novel, during the course of a conversation between Nell's great-uncle and Mr Garland, Dickens directly refers to the redemptive power of the fourteen-year-old girl and her actions:

If you have seen the picture gallery of any one old family, you will remember how the same face and figure – often the fairest and slightest of them all – come upon you in different generations; and how you trace the same sweet girl through a long line of portraits – the Good Angel of the race – abiding by them in all reverses – redeeming all their sins.

The Old Curiosity Shop serves as an excellent example of the author's ability to weave spiritual content into his work. The book is not obviously about death, the resurrection, and angels; rather, it is a story of a girl's attempt to rescue her grandfather, and the journey they undertake together. Dickens cannot be described as a religious writer, as we have noted earlier, but instinctively, in an age when the Church and its teachings were beginning to be challenged by the creeping tide of intellectual doubt, he rightly perceived that the most effective means of communicating religious truth rested in appealing directly to the hearts of his readers. Such a direct sentimental approach was clearly vindicated by the book's success.

15

A CHRISTMAS CAROL

No author has been more closely associated with Christmas than Dickens. Although it is true that he did play a major role in changing what was a church/community-based occasion into a family-centred celebration, complete with dancing, songs, games, and stories, this was by no means his chief purpose. As George Orwell correctly observed, he was a change of heart man, and he knew there was no better time to promote this approach than Christmas. It is, of course, one thing to appreciate such an opportunity, quite another to come up with a story to execute it. With *A Christmas Carol* (1843) and *The Chimes* (1844) he successfully did it not once, but twice.

Prior to *A Christmas Carol*, the writer's first Christmas story appeared in *Bell's Life in London* on 27 December 1835. Originally called "Christmas Festivities", its title was changed to "A Christmas Dinner" when it appeared in *Sketches By Boz*. A short piece, focusing on the writer's theme of a convivial family gathering, it involves the reconciliation of a daughter and her mother. Margaret has committed two crimes – marrying without her parents' consent and doing so beneath her social status – and has been ostracized by her family. On Christmas Day, she arrives at her former home. Despite her mother's initial chilliness, the peace and goodwill of the day wins her over and, much to everyone's surprise, her husband turns out to be very pleasant and engaging.

His next reference to Christmas appears in Chapter 28 of *The Pickwick Papers*. Mr Pickwick with his friends and servant Sam Weller enjoy a most entertaining Christmas Eve party at Manor Farm,

Dingley Dell, following the wedding of Mr Wardle's niece, Bella Allen. At the end of the evening, Mr Wardle's aged mother recounts a story told to her many Christmas Eves ago by her husband, now deceased. Entitled the "Goblin and the Sexton", it involves a cantankerous, child-hating individual by the name of Gabriel Grubb. Digging a grave on Christmas Eve, he is abducted by goblins and carried down to their underground kingdom. Admonished by the king, he is shown three images from the "Great Storehouse". As a result of the sad family scenes he witnesses, he is returned to the churchyard a changed man. The seeds of this short narrative were to germinate and grow within Dickens's imagination. Seven years later, they would come to fruition and produce one of the most popular Christmas stories ever written.

Late one mid-October night in 1843, the front garden gate of 1 Devonshire Terrace creaked open, and the owner of the house, wearing a large grey coat and hat, stepped out. While his respectable neighbours and, indeed, his own family were safely tucked up in bed, the 31-year-old father of four set off into the dark, empty streets. For the next six weeks, Dickens would maintain this strange nocturnal ritual. Walking between fifteen and twenty miles a night, he was not to return home until close to dawn. Navigating through the highways and byways of the capital, which he knew intimately, any that observed him, as he laughed and cried out loud, might have thought he was drunk, or in some way deranged. Far from suffering from the effects of alcohol or some mental affliction, he was pacing out the words, sentences, and paragraphs of one of his most celebrated works, *A Christmas Carol*.

Around a fortnight earlier, he had attended the opening of the Athenaeum Club in Manchester. Set up to provide education and stimulation for the city's underprivileged, the enterprise, and those like them, held a special place in his heart. Looking out over the audience before him, many representatives of the very people he so passionately sought to help, Dickens found himself profoundly moved. As he paced the streets, night after night, it was not only "the bright eyes and beaming faces" of those who attended the

Athenaeum Club that spurred him on to write the first of his Christmas books. About the same time as his visit to Manchester, Dickens received a letter from Angela Burdett Coutts (see Chapter 19) regarding a Ragged School situated in one of the worst areas of London. The Ragged School movement, with which Dickens was familiar, sought to provide education for the children of the poor in some of the country's most deprived urban locations. Having been approached by Samuel Starey, a lawyer's clerk responsible for the school, the heiress asked Dickens to visit the school on her behalf to assess what needed to be done.

On arriving at Field Lane School, in the south-eastern corner of Holborn, he found seventy pupils, male and female, crammed into three first-floor rooms of a dilapidated house. Frequently the target of young yobs, much of the school furniture lay smashed and scattered around the rooms. Impressed by Samuel Starey and all the teachers, who effectively funded the school themselves, Dickens enthusiastically informed Miss Coutts of all the necessary improvements to be undertaken.

The school was not, however, the sole cause of his rising sense of social indignation. Several months earlier, he had received from his friend and fellow social reformer, Dr Southwood Smith, a copy of the Child Employment Commission's second report. Detailing the harrowing exploitation of tens of thousands of children, some as young as five or six, forced to work in mines, factories, and foundries, it contained dreadful first-hand accounts of their terrible injuries, barbaric treatment, and fatalities.

Dickens also had before him the evidence of his own eyes. The scenes he regularly witnessed on his walks through the deprived areas of Whitechapel or Seven Dials (in the Rookery, 2,850 people were crammed into just 95 small decrepit houses, around 30 per dwelling) were enough to convince him that something had to be done. Initially, he had resolved to submit an evocative article to the influential *Edinburgh Review*, but this was quickly superseded by the first of his Christmas books. A beautifully crafted parable, which encapsulated the selfish, materialistic attitudes of the period in the person of Ebenezer Scrooge, its central message is one of personal and societal redemption. Unashamedly sentimental, it sought to convert the Christian message of Christmas into practical intervention on behalf of the poor.

At the same time as Dickens was undertaking his nightly composition of *A Christmas Carol*, he was also working on the instalments of his latest novel, *Martin Chuzzlewit* and was around halfway through. Sales had, despite his high expectations, proved disappointing. Whereas *The Pickwick Papers* and *Nicholas Nickleby* had sold 40,000 copies a month, and *The Old Curiosity Shop* 100,000 a week, *Chuzzlewit's* monthly circulation was only 20,000. Indeed, its mediocre performance played a significant role in the ending of the writer's eight-year relationship with Chapman and Hall.

On 7 September 1841, when he signed the original contract for the book, the publishers had included a clause at his request, stipulating that they would pay him £150 a month for the fourteen months prior to publication. The advance, to fund his trip to America, was to be repaid from his 75 per cent share of the profits. In addition to this, it was agreed that, in the highly unlikely event of low sales, the sum would be recovered by reducing his monthly salary by £50. At this point, neither party would have envisaged this caveat having to be enforced.

Predictably, with a new novel by such a celebrated writer, the first instalment, which appeared on New Year's Day 1843, sold well. However, sales of the subsequent numbers fell. As he had done with *The Pickwick Papers* and *Master Humphrey's Clock*, Dickens came up with a creative approach designed to boost circulation. At the end of the fifth number, Martin Chuzzlewit (junior) announces his intention to go to America. Although the subsequent nine American chapters and the introduction of the novel's stand-out comic character, Sairey Gamp, did help, the resulting monthly increase of 3,000 copies was far from dramatic.

Around about this time (June 1843), the author turned up at the offices of Chapman and Hall in the Strand to discuss some amendments to the number in which Mrs Gamp was to first appear.

While there, William Hall, in an unguarded moment, expressed his concerns about *Chuzzlewit's* sales. In doing so, he referred to the £50 salary reduction clause. Dickens was furious, and stormed out of the office. On his return home, he lambasted the publishers in the presence of John Forster. He took great exception to Hall's remarks.

Ironically, when *Martin Chuzzlewit* appeared in book form in July 1844, sales went exceptionally well. Why a complete novel should sell far better than its instalments is a mystery. It is, nonetheless, worth noting that throughout 1843 the book industry was severely affected by an economic downturn. Perhaps, after all, Dickens's belief that *Martin Chuzzlewit* was "in a hundred points immeasurably the best of his novels he had yet written" was, to an extent, justified. What can be said with absolute certainty is that it had the longest title of any of his books: *The Life and Adventures of Martin Chuzzlewit, His Relatives, Friends and Enemies. Comprising all his Wills and his Ways; with an Historical Record of What he Did and What he Didn't; Showing moreover Who inherited the Family Plate, Who came in for the Silver Spoons, and Who for the Wooden Ladles. The Whole forming a Complete Key to the House of Chuzzlewit.*

The writing of *A Christmas Carol* was a liberating experience for Dickens. It was also to provide a welcome boost to his confidence, following the relative disappointment of *Martin Chuzzlewit*, which, from the start, had been a real uphill struggle to write. Freed from the pressures of working to instalment deadlines, he experienced a surge of creative energy during the course of his night-time walks. So much so, that *A Christmas Carol* was finished in six weeks, even though he was working on *Martin Chuzzlewit* at the same time. There was also another key difference: whereas on all previous occasions he had received a lump sum payment during the course of his writing and a share of the profits afterwards, he insisted on covering all the publication costs himself and being paid on a commission basis only. In doing so, it enabled him, for the very first time, to take complete control of the book.

It is evident, from studying the corrections, redrafting, and deletions contained on the original manuscript, that he took meticulous care to ensure that the quality of the content matched his aspirations. This labour of love also extended to the presentation and pricing of the book. Very early on in the process, he employed John Leech (one of the unsuccessful applicants to replace Robert Seymour on *The Pickwick Papers*), who produced a total of eight illustrations, including one on the blue and red title page. Bound in red cloth, with a gilt design on the cover, spine, and on the edges of the pages, *A Christmas Carol in Prose, Being a Ghost Story of Christmas,* was an attractive volume, especially considering the relatively low price of five shillings, set by Dickens himself.

Despite a few teething problems – two days before publication, it was discovered that the yellow paper clashed with the title page – the book came out on 19 December 1843. It was an immediate success, selling 6,000 copies on the first day and 2,000 on each of the next two. The second print run sold out by 31 December. By May of the following year, it had reached its seventh edition and had been the subject of three separate dramatizations.

A Christmas Carol is a contemporary parable and combines an allegory of the excessive materialism and charitable neglect of the age with a compassionate appeal on behalf of the disadvantaged and powerless. It is also a story of how spiritually inspired redemption can transform society. Governments and their agencies, even if inclined to do so, could not hope to address the overwhelming needs of the time, nor force people to do so. Any meaningful social improvement depended upon individuals experiencing a change of heart, and this is exactly what Dickens intended to achieve.

Ebenezer Scrooge embodied the soulless materialism of the age. The prominent churchman, Thomas Arnold (headmaster of Rugby School), much admired by the author, condemned the wicked covetousness of the period, which determined that the sole aim of man was the maximization of profit. He also highlighted the exploitative nature of employers: "it was in the interest of every employer to get as much as he can done for the smallest sum possible." It was this very attitude that led to women and children, as young as four, being forced to work ninety-six hours a week in mines for two shillings.[10] Not until four years after *A Christmas Carol* came out did John Fielder's Ten Hour Act restrict their weekly working hours to fifty-eight.

Scrooge, a selfish miser, who bullies and underpays his clerk, Bob Cratchit, and cares nothing for the poor, is, in common with Zacchaeus from Luke's Gospel, the unlikeliest candidate for spiritual transformation that one could imagine. Nonetheless, not only does he become a changed man, but, more importantly from Dickens's perspective, he changes the lives of those around him.

The book has three key passages on the subject of the poor. The first, which takes place on Christmas Eve, involves two men who have visited Scrooge's office in the misplaced hope of collecting a donation towards helping those in need.

"At this festive season of the year, Mr Scrooge," said the gentleman, taking up a pen, "it is more than usually desirable that we should make some slight provision for the Poor and destitute, who suffer greatly at the present time. Many thousands are in want of common necessaries; hundreds of thousands are in want of common comforts, sir?"

"Are there no prisons?" asked Scrooge.[11] [After the Poor Law Amendment Act of 1834 poverty was criminalized.]

"Plenty of prisons," said the gentleman, laying down his pen again.

"And the Union Workhouses?" demanded Scrooge. "Are they still in operation?"

"They are still," returned the gentleman, "I wish I could say they were not."

"The Treadmill and the Poor Law are in full vigour, then?" said Scrooge.

"Both very busy, sir."

---

10   A shilling was twelve old pence or a twentieth of a pound (equal to 5p in decimal currency).

11   This was written after the Poor Law Amendment Act of 1834 when poverty was criminalized.

"Oh! I was afraid, from what you said at first, that something had occurred to stop them in their useful course," said Scrooge. "I'm very glad to hear it."

"Under the impression that they scarcely furnish Christian cheer of mind or body to the multitude," returned the gentleman, "a few of us are endeavouring to raise a fund to buy the Poor some meat and drink, and means of warmth. We choose this time, because it is a time, of all others, when Want is keenly felt and Abundance rejoices. What should I put you down for?"

"Nothing!" Scrooge replied.

"You wish to be anonymous?"

"I wish to be left alone," said Scrooge. "Since you ask me what I wish, gentlemen, that is my answer. I don't make merry myself at Christmas and I can't afford to make idle people merry. I help to support the establishments I have mentioned – they cost enough and those badly off must go there."

"Many can't go there; many would rather die."

"If they would rather die," said Scrooge, "They had better do it then, and decrease the surplus population."

Scrooge shows clearly that he shares the two prevalent ideological objections to helping the poor, neither of which Dickens agreed. The first is that, by paying his rates, he is absolved of the duty to do more. When, at the end of the Third Stave, he is confronted by two hideously deprived children, he cries out to the Ghost of Christmas Present, "Have they no refuge or resource?"; the Spirit turns on him with his own words: "Are there no prisons... Are there no workhouses?" When exposed to the realities and struggles experienced by the poor, the hard-hearted man of business begins to sympathize with their plight. His heart is changed. Dickens sought to achieve the same effect in his readers.

The second ideological argument related to the Malthusian view of population. Thomas Robert Malthus, an English economist, wrote *An Essay on the Principle of Population* (1798), which surmised that the population of a country is likely to exceed the resources available to sustain it. In this case, in the absence of birth control, poverty or war would diminish the excess population. Naturally, the many who held this view applied it to the poor, and Scrooge had been one of them.

Dickens, with Tiny Tim as his example (based on his sister Fanny's sickly four-year-old son, Henry), exposes the godless nature of Malthusian population theory as applied at that time. Scrooge, once again in the company of the Ghost of Christmas Present, is forced to contemplate the possible death of Bob Cratchit's son:

> *"I see a vacant seat," replied the Ghost, "in the poor chimney corner, and a crutch without an owner, carefully preserved…"*
>
> *"If these shadows remain unaltered by the future, none other of my race," returned the Ghost, "will find him here. What then? If he be like to die, he had better do it, and decrease the surplus population."*
>
> *Scrooge hung his head to hear his own words quoted by the Spirit, and was overcome with penitence and grief.*
>
> *"Man," said the Ghost, "if man you be in your heart, not adamant, forebear that wicked cant until you have discovered What the surplus is, and Where it is. Will you decide what men shall live, what men shall die. It may be, that in the sight of Heaven, you are more worthless and less fit to live than millions like this poor man's child."*

Dickens is showing that every single individual has value in God's eyes, which is not linked to their wealth or social status. He adds to this the inference that the destitute are of special concern to the Lord of all humankind.

The second key passage involves Scrooge's supernatural Christmas Eve visitation from his deceased business partner, Jacob Marley, who had died seven years previously:

> *"Man of the worldly mind!" replied the Ghost, "do you believe in me or not?"*
>
> *"I do," said Scrooge. "I must. But why do spirits walk the earth, and why do they come to me?"*

"It is required of every man," the Ghost returned, "that the spirit within him should walk abroad among his fellowman, and travel far and wide; and of that spirit that goes not forth in life, it is condemned to do so after death. It is doomed to wander through the world – oh, woe is me! – and witness what it cannot share, but might have shared on earth and turned to happiness!"

Again the spectre raised a cry, and shook his chain and wrung his shadowy hands.

"You are fettered," said Scrooge, trembling. "Tell me why?"

"I wear the chain I forged in life," replied the Ghost...

"... the weight and length of the strong chain you bear yourself? It was full as heavy and as long as this, seven Christmas Eves ago. You have laboured on it, since. It is a ponderous chain!"...

"But you were always a good man of business, Jacob," faltered Scrooge...

"Business!" cried the Ghost, wringing its hands again. "Mankind was my business. The common welfare was my business, charity, mercy, forbearance, and benevolence, were all my business..."

"At this time of the rolling year," the spectre said, "I suffer most. Why did I walk through the crowds of fellow-beings with my eyes turned down and never raise them to the blessed Star which led the Wise Men to a poor abode! Were there no poor houses to which its light would have conducted me!"

Here, Dickens is suggesting that he believed individuals not only have a responsibility to care for the poor, but that there will be a price to pay if they fail to do so: it will have eternal consequences. Far from being detached from the affairs of the world, God is watching and recording people's actions. Directly contradicting the self-centred perspective of the period, Jacob Marley redefines the nature of business and, in doing so, reminds the reader that Christ himself was born into a humble home.

The final key passage comes at the end of Stave Three, just prior to the departure of the Ghost of Christmas Present, when Scrooge witnesses a horrifying sight:

"Forgive me if I am not justified in what I ask," said Scrooge, looking intently at the Spirit's robe, "but I see something strange, and not belonging to yourself, protruding from your skirts. Is it a foot or a claw?"

"It might be a claw, for the flesh there is upon it," was the Spirit's sorrowful reply. "Look here."

From the folding of its robe, it brought two children; wretched, abject, frightful, hideous, miserable. They knelt down at its feet, and clung upon the outside of its garment.

"Oh, Man! Look here. Look, look down here!" exclaimed the Ghost.

They were a boy and girl. Yellow, meagre, ragged, scowling, wolfish… Where graceful youth should have filled their features out, and touched them with the freshest tints, a stale and shrivelled hand like that of age, had pinched and twisted them, and pulled them into shreds. Where angels might have sat enthroned, devils lurked; and glared out menacingly. No change, no degradation, no provision of humanity, in any grade, through all the mysteries of wonderful creation has monsters half so horrible and dread.

Scrooge started back, appalled. Having them shown to him in this way, he tried to say they were fine children, but the words choked themselves, rather than be parties to a lie of such enormous magnitude.

"Spirit! Are they yours?" Scrooge could say no more.

"They are Man's," said the Spirit… "This boy is Ignorance. This girl is Want. Beware of them both, and all of their degree, but most of all beware this boy, for on his brow I see that written which is Doom, unless the writing be erased."

Dickens is warning his contemporaries that potential angels, through neglect, can become devils. The two children were representative of the tens of thousands that inhabited the streets of London, and other cities, in need of education and care. He is also warning that ignoring the issues of social inequality might have catastrophic consequences. He is evoking memories of the French Revolution of 1789. The fear of a similar class war in England remained even in the 1840s, and there had been serious civil disturbances surrounding the Reform

Act. If the poor were not helped, they might be forced to fight for what they were denied.

As a result of his supernatural encounter with his deceased partner, Jacob Marley, and the three Ghosts of Christmas, Scrooge is transformed. Although far from resembling an orthodox Christian conversion, the change he undergoes is profound. On finding himself restored to the normality of his own bedroom, he describes himself as being "as happy as an angel" and, on leaving his house, makes his way directly to a church, prior to visiting his nephew Fred.

At the end of the narrative, Dickens includes the phrase "and as for Tiny Tim, he did not die". The prevailing determinism of the time decreed that the sickly boy, a child of a poor clerk, should die. Yet, because of the unlikely charitable intervention of one person, he lives. His health, his future, and that of the whole Cratchit family, are secure. Scrooge no longer believes in abdicating his responsibility for the poor: their welfare has become his business. Dickens hoped his readers would follow Scrooge's example.

16

THE CHIMES

Dickens had little time to sit back and enjoy the success of *A Christmas Carol*. As well as the continuing demands of writing the monthly instalments of *Martin Chuzzlewit*, his fifth child (third son), Francis Jeffrey, was born on 15 January 1844. Around the same time, the author took upon himself the responsibility of finding his brother, seventeen-year-old Augustus, a suitable job – as he had done for his other brothers. His efforts, once again, proved fruitful, and the wealthy City merchant, Thomas Chapman, who was also Chairman of Lloyds Registry of Shipping, offered him an office position.

On 10 February the accounts from the sales of *A Christmas Carol* arrived from Chapman and Hall. Having anticipated around £1,000 from the sale of the first 10,000 copies, Dickens was extremely disappointed and anxious at only receiving £460. This was mainly his own fault: he had insisted on the costly format of the book and had fixed the relatively low price of five shillings. Nevertheless, he blamed the publishers. This, along with the earlier incident regarding *Martin Chuzzlewit* and the £50 reduction in his monthly salary, proved too much. By the time Dickens travelled up to Liverpool on 26 February to speak at the Mechanics Institute, his business relationship with Chapman and Hall was, for the time being, over.

By the beginning of the summer, he had signed an agreement with Bradbury and Evans, the printers of *Nicholas Nickleby*. Negotiations had to be handled carefully, not least as Chapman and Hall were one of their important customers. On 1 June, they advanced the substantial sum of £2,800, secured against a 25 per cent share of the proceeds of whatever he wrote over the next eight years. Shortly after signing the contract, Dickens, much to his relief, had completed the twentieth and final instalment of *Martin Chuzzlewit*.

Two days after it appeared, on 2 July 1844, Dickens left England for Genoa, Italy, together with his family. At this point, this consisted of Dickens, his wife Catherine, and their five children: Charley (seven-and-a-half), Mary (six), Kate (four-and-three-quarters), Walter (almost three-and-a-half), and Francis (six months). Catherine's sister, Georgina, was with them, as was the pet spaniel Mr Snittle Timbery. Servants accompanied them, and the party of twelve was completed by Louise Roche, the French courier.

Arriving a fortnight later, Dickens's first impressions of Genoa were far from favourable. He found the famous streets of palaces – the Strada Nuova and the Strada Balbi – a disorderly jumble of dirty houses, full of filth and sickening smells. The passages leading from them appeared even more squalid than those he had seen in the worst parts of London. Whatever positive images the grandly named Villa di Bella Vista (the House of the Beautiful Views) summoned up, they were quickly dispelled. The "pink jail", as Dickens named it, was a "lonely, rusty, stagnant, old staggerer of a domain". Extremely expensive, despite its somewhat dilapidated state, it nevertheless offered two compensations: the view across the Bay of Genoa and of the Alps in the distance, and the fact that it had only been rented for a month.

In late September, the Dickens family escaped and moved to the nearby Palazzo Peschiere (the Palace of the Fishponds). The contrast between the two residences could not have been more marked. As they arrived, the sun shone on the stately terraces leading up to the Palazzo; the groves of camellias, orange, and lemon trees must have proved a beautiful sight. In front of the property, from which its name was derived, were seven fountains, replete with goldfish. With views equal to that of their previous villa, they were delighted to remain there for the rest of their stay.

On his return, a year later, Dickens wrote an account of his experiences. *Pictures From Italy: Travelling Letters Written on the Road* was published in a single volume by Bradbury and Evans at the end of March 1846. Around half of it had already been serialized in *The Daily News*, a Liberal newspaper for which Dickens acted as editor for a short time.

On finishing *Martin Chuzzlewit*, Dickens, rather than starting another novel, decided to concentrate on his second Christmas book. By early October, unable to think of a title, he still had not started. The truth of the matter was that he was desperately missing the creative stimulus of the London streets. This was the first time he had attempted to write a story away from England. Whereas *A Christmas Carol* was composed within familiar surroundings, in Italy he was painfully aware of being away from home. Added to this, the continual clashing and clanging of bells of Genoa was driving him to distraction.

It was at this disruptive, frustrating time that he experienced what amounted to a vision of Mary Hogarth. It had been six years since he had last dreamt of her, when he had been in Yorkshire preparing for *Nicholas Nickleby*. While in Italy, and unable to sleep because of the return of his childhood back and side pain, possibly due to stress, Mary appeared to him, draped in blue like one of Raphael's Madonnas. Even though he was unable to see her face, he instinctively recognized her. Stretching out his arms, with tears streaming down his face, he asked her for some token to prove that she had really visited him. Then, desperate in case she left him, he asked "What is true religion?" The spirit hesitated, during which time Dickens suggested that the forms of religion did not generally matter, "if we try to do good". He then went on to say, "Perhaps, the Roman Catholic is the best." "For you," it said, "for you, it is the best." At this point, he awoke and went straight to Catherine to relate what had taken place. He was never to forget what occurred. Yet, when he recorded his experiences of his travels in *Pictures From Italy*, such was his criticism of Roman Catholicism that the original illustrator, Clarkson Stanfield, a Catholic himself, resigned.

A week later, Dickens still had no title for his next Christmas book. Then, suddenly, the clanging bells of Genoa struck a chord in his imagination. His second Christmas book was to be called *The Chimes: A Goblin Story of Some Bells That Rang An Old Year Out And a New Year In*. On the morning of 10 October, he was up at 7.00 a.m, and, after breakfast, he began to write. In less than four weeks the story was complete. On 6 November, three days after finishing, he set off for London to deliver the manuscript in person and to read it to his friends. On Saturday, 14 December, six days after Dickens had departed on his return journey to Italy, "the little book", with illustrations by Clarkson Stanfield, Daniel Maclise, and John Leech, went on sale. It proved popular, selling 20,000 copies on the first day alone, twice that of *A Christmas Carol*. Four days later, its stage adaptation had its opening night at the Adelphi Theatre.

The Chimes was Dickens's most sustained and powerful attack on society's failure to adopt the principles of social justice and compassionate intervention. Within its pages, he vigorously opposed those ideologies and beliefs that, in his view, prevented or stifled collective or individual Christian intervention on behalf of the poor. Added to this, his portrayal of Alderman Cute amounted to little less than a full-scale public denunciation of the notorious London magistrate, Sir Peter Laurie, and the inhumane values he represented.

Whereas the ghosts in *A Christmas Carol* reveal scenes from Scrooge's past, present, and future, the visions of the bells in The Chimes relate solely to the tragic future of Toby's daughter Meg, her husband, Richard, their baby, and a young girl, Lillian Fern. Although, in the end, readers are relieved to learn that Toby had dreamt the whole thing, they are left in no doubt that the harrowing scenes contained within the book represented the waking reality for thousands upon thousands of people. Dickens hoped, once again, that the book's disturbing images would generate direct action on behalf of the abandoned poor.

Toby Veck is a licensed ticket porter: someone who is paid to deliver letters and small parcels within the City of London. At the end of the "First Quarter", he sits down at his customary post by the church, next to the steps leading to Alderman Cute's house.[12] It is

---

12   The term Alderman relates to the position of a borough magistrate.

midday on New Year's Eve, and, as usual, Toby's faithful daughter, Meg, is bringing him in his lunch. On this occasion, she has prepared him a "special" meal of tripe and hot potatoes, to pre-empt her announcement that she and Richard, a blacksmith, plan to marry the following day, after a three-year delay.

A few minutes later, Alderman Cute, Filer (an economist), and Deedless (a banker) appear on the steps. Unable to resist the opportunity of patronizing the lower classes in front of his two friends, Cute decides to impart to Toby, Meg, and Richard a sample of his "insightful" wisdom as to the true condition of the poor:

> *"Now, you know," said the Alderman, addressing his two friends, with a self-complacent smile upon his face which was habitual to him, "I am a plain man, a practical man; and I go to work in a plain practical way. There is not the least mystery or difficulty in dealing with this sort of people if you only understand 'em and can to talk to 'em in their own manner. Now, you Porter! Don't you ever tell me, or anybody else, my friend, that you haven't always enough to eat, and of the best; because I know better..."*

> *"You see, my friend," pursued the Alderman, "there's a great deal of nonsense talked about 'Want' – 'hard up', you know; that's the phrase, isn't it? And I intend to Put it Down. That's all!" said the Alderman, turning to his friends again, "you may Put Down anything among this sort of people, if you only know the way to set about it."*

On learning from Richard of his planned marriage to Meg, Filer exclaims:

> *"Put that down indeed, Alderman, and you'll do something. Married! Married! The ignorance of the first principles of political economy on the part of these people; their impudence, their wickedness... A man may live to be as old as Methuselah," said Mr Filer, "and may labour all his life for the benefit of such people as these; and may heap facts on figures; and he can have more hope to persuade 'em that they have no right or business to be married, than he can hope to persuade 'em that*

they have no earthly right or business to be born. And that we know they haven't. We reduced it to a mathematical certainty long ago!"

Cute and Filer are referring to two more prevailing attitudes towards the condition of the poor. First, as in the case of the Alderman, there was denial that the problem of widespread neglect even existed. Five years after *The Chimes* was first published, the Bishop of London, in his report on London's public health, made reference to Dickens's representation of the appalling squalor of Jacob's Island in *Oliver Twist*. Peter Laurie, on whom Cute was based, incorrectly informed the members of the writer's own parish that the island did not exist.

Filer, the economist, in challenging Richard and Meg's right to marry, or even to be born, is referring again to the prevalent Malthusian doctrine of the period. The poor should remain celibate; they should be convinced that sexual relations, even within marriage, is a sin. Society can not support them, therefore, inevitably, they must die.

Following on from his initial pronouncement, Cute then goes on to describe to Meg the inevitable depressing downward cycle of despair and disaster that awaits her should she marry:

"After you are married, you'll quarrel with your husband and come to be a distressed wife. You may think not; but you will, because I tell you so. Now, I give you fair warning, that I have made up my mind to Put distressed wives Down. So, don't be brought before me. You'll have children — boys. These boys will grow up bad, of course, and run wild in the streets, without shoes or stockings. Mind, my young friend! I'll convict 'em summarily, every one, for I am determined to Put boys without shoes and stockings Down. All young mothers, of all sorts and kinds, it's my determination to Put Down. Don't think to plead illness as an excuse with me; or babies as an excuse with me; for all sick persons and young children I am determined to Put Down. And if you attempt, desperately, and ungratefully, and impiously, and fraudulently attempt to drown yourself, or hang yourself, I'll have no pity for you, for I have made up my mind to Put all Suicide Down! If there is one

> *thing," said the Alderman, with his self-satisfied smile, "on which I*
> *can be said to have made up my mind more than on another, it is to*
> *Put Suicide Down."*

Distressed wives, young mothers, sick people, and young children are not to be helped, but "Put Down". The emphasis on suicide is a deliberate reference to Sir Peter Laurie. Around the time *The Chimes* appeared, about 2,300 people a year died by throwing themselves in the Thames alone. If the individual proved to be unsuccessful in their attempts to kill themselves, then Laurie and other magistrates, rather than showing compassion or offering help, would send them to prison, or the house of correction.

In the vision induced by the spirit of the bells, Toby Veck witnesses the fulfilment of Alderman Cute's chilling prediction: Richard has been transformed into a drunk, wasted by vice; Meg is driven to despair and plans to drown herself and her baby in the Thames; and Lillian Fern, barely more than a child is forced, due to poverty, into prostitution. At the time, this was common: 30,000 girls and women in London shared the same fate.

After his speech, Cute hands Toby Veck a letter to be delivered to Sir Joseph Bowley. Staying in his London residence to celebrate his wife's birthday, Bowley is the squire of a country estate. The purpose of the magistrate's letter is to inform him that someone from his parish is due to appear before him. Will Fern, having come to London in the hope of finding work to provide for himself and his young niece, has been arrested for vagrancy. New to the city, he could find nowhere to rest and was discovered sleeping in a shed.

On delivering the letter, Toby is treated to a sample of Sir Joseph Bowley's paternalism:

> *Your only business in life is with me. You needn't trouble yourself*
> *to think about anything. I will think for you; I know what is good*
> *for you; I am your perpetual parent. Such is the dispensation of an*
> *all-wise Providence! I do my duty as the Poor Man's friend and*
> *Father; and I endeavour to educate his mind by inculcating on all*

occasions the one great moral lesson which that class requires: that is, entire Dependence on myself. They have no business whatever with themselves. If wicked and designing persons tell them otherwise, and they become impatient and discontented, and are guilty of insubordinate conduct and black-hearted ingratitude; which is undoubtedly the case; I am their friend and father still. It is ordained. It is the nature of things.

Though many shared Sir Bowley's view that the social order had been ordained by God, Dickens did not. It was not providence that condemned the multitudes to depravation and poverty; rather, it was the failure of individuals and society. The poor needed education, decent housing, and life chances, beyond that of fighting to survive.

When Lady Bowley hears mention of Fern's name, she confesses that she is not surprised to find him accused of a crime. She tells her guests, gathered for her birthday celebration:

Last winter, when I introduced pinking and eyelet-holing[13] among the men and boys in the village, as a nice evening employment, and had the lines

> *O let us love our occupations*
> *Bless the squire and his relatives*
> *Live upon our daily rations*
> *And always know our proper station*

set to music: he refused to attend, pronouncing that he was no girl but a man.

Dickens was to produce three more Christmas books, but he did not return to the subject of social justice in any of them.

---

13   Eyelet-holing was a synonym for sewing.

17

THE SIMPLE FAITH OF DICKENS

As we have seen, Dickens possessed, throughout his life, a simple, sincere, and, above all, practical faith. Uninterested in matters of doctrine and petty sectarian squabbles, he passionately believed that the role of the Church, and those individuals within it, was to live out the example of Christ. This was especially the case with regard to social justice and the plight of the poor. Christianity was not about ritual or formal religious observance, but a matter of individual conscience and attitude of heart, which manifested itself in actions, rather than words.

The author's personal beliefs were rooted in the teaching of the New Testament in general, and in the four Gospels in particular. George Dolby, Dickens's reading tours manager, wrote of his "great reverence" towards the Bible: "It was the book of all others he read most and which he took as his one unfailing guide in his life." In a letter to a clergyman, R. H. Davies (Christmas Eve 1856) the writer states: "There cannot be many men, I believe, who have a more humble veneration for the New Testament, or a more profound awareness of its all-sufficiency, than I have."

Added to this, at the conclusion of his will, Dickens strongly urged his family to adopt his personal position: "My dear children humbly try to guide yourselves by the teaching of the New Testament in its broad spirit, and to put no faith in any man's narrow construction of its letter here and there."

Dickens's positive commitment to the efficacy of the New Testament did not extend to the Old. In corresponding with his friend, Frank Stone (Monday, 13 December 1858), he writes: "Half the misery and hypocrisy of the Christian world (as I take it) comes from a stubborn determination to refuse the New Testament as a sufficient guide in itself, and to force the Old Testament into alliance with it." His reliance upon the New Testament was in keeping with that of the Unitarians, one of only two denominations with whom he identified throughout his adult life.

On the afternoon of Saturday, 22 January 1842, the American Mail steam-packet, *Brittania* sailed safely into Boston Harbour, much to the relief of its eighty-six passengers. The eighteen-day voyage from Liverpool had been one of the stormiest experienced for years. Before even having the opportunity to disembark, Dickens found himself surrounded by a posse of journalists, all eager to secure an interview for their respective publications.

That evening, at the Tremont Hotel, he, along with Catherine and her maid, Anne Brown, barely had time to finish their dinner before invitations to various social events began flooding in. Despite all the celebrity attention he received – he had to employ a secretary to assist him with the enormous volume of correspondence that arrived on a daily basis – the author found time to meet the city's leading influential Unitarian, Dr William Ellen Channing. The time they spent together was to have a profound effect on Dickens.

It was not only his personal acquaintance with Channing that attracted the author to Unitarianism. While in Boston, it became apparent that nearly all the cultivated men he met belonged to the denomination. He also discovered that a number of Harvard University professors were also Unitarians, including the poet, Henry Wadsworth Longfellow, who became a friend of Dickens and stayed with him in London. So was John Forster and his friend, the social reformer, Dr Southwood Smith.

Shortly after returning home in July 1842, Dickens, now thirty, began attending Essex Street Chapel in the Strand. It was here, in 1774, that the original Unitarian congregation first met, led by the former Church of England clergyman, Theophilus Lindsey. Unitarian beliefs, most noticeably their rejection of the doctrine of the Trinity, had started to develop in the seventeenth century. One of the movement's founders, John Biddle, published his "Twelve Arguments Drawn Out of Scripture" in the 1640s. In it, he contested, based on his reading of the Greek text of the New Testament, that the Trinitarian argument was not based on Scripture.

Dickens, however, was to stay at Reverend Thomas Madge's Chapel for only a short time. Just nine months after their meeting in Boston Dr Channing died. Such was his reputation that a memorial service was arranged on the 20 November at Little Portland Street Unitarian Chapel. Eager to pay his respects, Dickens went to the service and was so impressed by the Reverend Edward Tagart's tribute and sermon that he decided, along with Catherine and their five children, to join the church. He was to attend the chapel, situated in the West End of London, near his Devonshire Terrace home, regularly for almost two years. His departure, in July 1844, coincided with the family's extended visit to Italy. Some fifteen years later, and then, until his death in 1870, he would occasionally return to hear the sermons of James Martineau, Tagart's successor.

Despite his decision to leave Little Portland Street, the author was to remain on extremely friendly terms with the Reverend Edward Tagart until the minister's death in 1858. There can be no doubt that his attendance at the chapel was considerably influenced by his high regard for its minister. Dickens found many of the Unitarian beliefs compatible with his own. As already mentioned, both believed in a Christ-centred, New Testament faith, which, although falling short of rejecting the Old Testament altogether, viewed its contents as belonging to a previous dispensation. Unitarians were also committed to the principle of faith in action and the cause of social reform. Dr Channing's tireless campaign against slavery in the United States exemplified this approach.

Dickens described Unitarianism as "the religion that has sympathy for men of every creed and ventures to pass judgement on none". He also appreciated their liberal, non-dogmatic, rational, humanitarian approach, and their rejection of eternal punishment.

Importantly, as will be discussed in Chapter 23, they shared the writer's rejection of the doctrine of original sin. Unitarianism, with its practical sympathetic approach, sat comfortably with Dickens and mirrored much of his own personal religious ideology.

While it would be wrong to characterize Dickens's involvement with Unitarianism as a mere passing fancy, his long-term denominational commitment was to the Church of England, the Established Church. His parents, though somewhat lukewarm in their own faith, were regular churchgoers, so growing up he attended services at the local parish churches where his family lived. The churchgoing habit, cultivated in his childhood, was to remain with him throughout his adult life. At the age of twenty-five, within a year of his marriage, having moved to Doughty Street, Bloomsbury, he rented a pew at the nearby popular Foundling Hospital Chapel. Two years later, in 1839, his move to Devonshire Terrace rendered his regular attendance impractical, but he still went along to the services at the chapel on an occasional basis.

On moving to Gad's Hill Place in the late 1850s, where he stayed until his death in 1870, Dickens first attended St Mary's Higham and then the newly built St John's in Mid-Higham. At the latter, which was closer to his home, he had his own pew in the chancel, which he shared with his sister-in-law, Georgina Hogarth, and his children when they visited. There is also ample evidence of the writer attending services within his writings. In "Our Watering Place" (*Reprinted Pieces*), he refers to going to Broadstairs parish church in the course of his frequent visits to the town; in "City of London Churches" (*The Uncommercial Traveller*), reference is made to his numerous visits to various churches. He arranged for all his children to be baptized in the Church of England, even when he was going to Unitarian services: when Frank, his fifth child was baptized, Dickens was attending Little Portland Street Unitarian Chapel. His circle of friends contained several clergymen: Reverend William Harness, Reverend Brookfield, Reverend James White, Reverend Sidney Smith, and Reverend Chauncey Hare Townsend to whom he dedicated *Great Expectations*.

Then, as now, the Victorian Church of England contained various groups, who held different emphases. For much of the author's lifetime, two of the most influential were the Evangelicals and the Tractarians, also known as the Puseyites, after one of the movement's leaders, Edward Pusey. Such was the interest they generated that the philosopher, John Stuart Mill, observed: "What is it that occupies the minds of three-fourths of those in England who care about any public interest or any controversial question? The quarrel between Puseyite and Evangelical." Dickens disliked both groups. He took exception to the Evangelical emphasis on the doctrine of original sin and the depravity of man, and was troubled by their insistence on addressing just the perceived spiritual needs of the poor, rather than seeking to first alleviate the physical conditions they were forced to endure. Also, as will be seen in Chapter 23, Dickens vehemently objected to the disproportionate amount of money the Evangelical missionary societies spent overseas, while neglecting the poor at home.

In common with the Tractarians, the Evangelicals sought to separate religion from social concern. Originating in Oxford in 1833, the Tractarians, so called because of their use of tracts to disseminate their views, wanted to restore the Catholic doctrines and practices that had characterized the Church prior to the Reformation. Dickens felt this focus on worship and the sacraments to be an unnecessary distraction from the practical application of Christian faith within society. Dickens, with his pronounced liberal Christian views and commitment to practical faith, belonged to the broad church stream of the Church of England, which was similar to Unitarianism in its tolerance, lack of doctrinal emphasis, and reliance upon the New Testament, rather than the Old. The clearest indications of his sympathies towards the broad church are to be found in a letter to John Forster, regarding A. P. Stanley's biography of the influential early Victorian broad churchman, Thomas Arnold (Headmaster of Rugby School). In it, Dickens writes: "I respect and reverence his memory beyond all expression. I must have that book. Every sentence that you quote from it is the text-book of my faith."

Despite the religious indifference of his parents, Dickens's family home life as a child was not without Christian influence, as we have seen. It was also during his formative years that he began his lifetime commitment to personal prayer. Visiting his friend, Lady Lovelace, just before she died, he confided to her that throughout his adult life he prayed twice daily.

At the time of his childhood in Chatham, Dickens's religious experience was not limited to the home environment and church services. In keeping with the educational system of the period, both schools he attended encouraged Christian observance. At his first school in Rome Lane, the six-year-old, as reflected in Paul Dombey's education at Mrs Pipchin's (*Dombey and Son*), prayed and read, or listened to the Bible being read, on a daily basis. The same pattern would have continued at William Giles's school. In the autobiographical account of Paul Dombey, a pupil at Dr Blimber's is asked to recite the first chapter of Ephesians in front of the class. This is the very same text that Arthur Clennam in Little Dorrit read in a "horrible tract" while a child. From this, it would appear likely that the writer took part in scriptural recitation at school and remembered this passage.

Another positive Christian influence on young Charles from his Chatham days was his schoolmaster, William Giles, and his family. Giles took a personal interest in his bright, intelligent pupil. Such was the impression that he made upon him that, some twenty-seven years later, Dickens formed part of the committee set up to celebrate the schoolmaster's fiftieth birthday. He also had previously, in August 1838, sent Giles a copy of every book he had written up to that point (*Sketches By Boz, Sunday Under Three Heads, Sketches of Young Couples*, and *The Pickwick Papers*).

Of all the members of his family, it was his eldest sister, Fanny, who possessed the most fervent faith. Having met her husband, Henry Burnett, at the Royal Academy of Music (he had taken the lead role in Dickens's operetta, *The Village Coquettes*), she moved to Manchester where they took up responsibility for the music at Rusholme Road Congregational Chapel. At no time was her sincere spirituality more evident than in her long illness, when she was suffering from tuberculosis. Dickens was with her shortly before she died in August 1848, and he told John Forster how calm and happy she seemed as a result of her complete reliance upon "the mediation of Christ". She told Charles how she "felt sure that they would meet again in a better world".

The sincerity of Dickens's faith was clearly demonstrated with regard to his children. In October 1861, when his son Henry (Harry) left home to go to Cambridge University, he wrote to him:

> As your brothers have gone away one by one, I have written to each of them what I am now going to write to you. I most strongly and affectionately impress upon you the priceless value of the New Testament and the study of that book as the one unfailing guide in life. Deeply respecting, and bowing down before the character of Our Saviour, you cannot go very wrong, and will always preserve at heart a true spirit of veneration and humility.

Two months later, he wrote a similar letter to his youngest son, Edward, who was emigrating to Australia:

> I put a New Testament among your books because it is the best book that ever was or will be known in the world, and because it teaches you the best lessons by which any human creature, who tries to be truthful and faithful to duty can possibly be guided. As your brothers have gone away, I have entreated them all to guide themselves by this book, putting aside the interpretations and inventions of men. I now most solemnly impress upon you the truth and beauty of the Christian religion, as it came from Christ Himself, and the impossibility of your going far wrong if you humbly respect it.

On the day before he died, in what was quite possibly his last ever letter, Dickens wrote: "I have always striven to express veneration for the life and lessons of Our Saviour, because I feel it; and because I rewrote that history for my children – everyone of whom knew it from having it repeated to them – long before they could read, and almost as soon as they could speak." This history was entitled *The Life of Our Lord*. He started it in June 1846, while at the Villa Rosemont, Lausanne, in Switzerland and finished it at some point three years later. It is a child-like account of the life of Jesus, based on the Gospel of Luke and the Sermon on the Mount in Matthew. The author insisted that the narrative, designed to recapture the essence of Christianity for his children, remain private. In fact, it was not published until it was serialized in the *Daily Mail* newspaper in March 1934.

Dickens's purpose in writing the account for his children is described in the book's opening passage:

> *MY DEAR CHILDREN, I am very anxious that you should know something about the History of Jesus Christ. For everybody ought to know about Him. No one ever lived, who was so good, so kind, so gentle, and so sorry for all people who did wrong, or were in anyway ill or miserable, as he was. And as he is now in Heaven, where we hope to go, and all to meet each other after we are dead, and there be happy always together, you never can think what a good place Heaven is, without knowing who he was and what he did.*

In addition to effectively retelling the story of Jesus' life, he was also able to introduce to his children two central aspects of his own beliefs: the necessity for faith to be shown through works and the Christian responsibility of individuals and society to care for the poor. With reference to the former, he informed them that "people who have done good all their lives long, will go to heaven after they are dead", and at the close of the book he wrote in bold letters: "REMEMBER! – It is Christianity TO DO GOOD always."

Within the opening section of "Chapter the Third", he explains his views about how God sees the poor and how he hoped his children would treat them:

> *That there might be some good men to go about with Him, teaching the people, Jesus Christ chose Twelve poor men to be his companions.*

These twelve are called "The Apostles" or "Disciples", and he chose them from among Poor Men, in order that the Poor might know – always after that; in all years to come – that heaven was made for them as well as for the rich and that God makes no difference between those who wear good clothes and those who go barefoot and in rags. The most miserable, the most ugly, deformed, wretched creatures that live, will be bright Angels in Heaven if they are good here on earth. Never forget this, when you are grown up, never be proud or unkind my dears to any poor man, woman, or child. If they are bad, think that they would have been better, if they had had kind friends and good homes, and had been better taught.

As well as encouraging his children to read the New Testament, and having written for them their own personal Gospel narrative, Dickens also actively encouraged them to emulate his daily habit of prayer. His daughter Mamie remembers his "writing special prayers for us as soon as we could speak". In his previously mentioned letter to his son Henry, he wrote: "I impress upon you the habit of saying a Christian prayer every night and morning. This has stood by me all through my life." To Edward he offered similar advice: "Never abandon the wholesome practice of saying your own prayers, night and morning. I have never abandoned it myself, and I know the comfort of it."

18

THE PRIVATE AND PUBLIC
CHARITY OF DICKENS

A n appreciation of the genuineness of Dickens's faith can be readily drawn from the remarkable extent of his own charity. In examining the degree by which he exercised this "one great cardinal virtue" (*Nicholas Nickleby*), it becomes apparent that no disparity existed between his fictional and his personal conviction of its importance. To Dickens, charitable activity epitomized the principle of Christianity in action: faith expressed through works. Both within his own family and in the public sphere, the constancy, commitment, breadth, and sheer volume of his benevolence was truly amazing. Even more so when measured against the enormous pressures of maintaining his literary output. The author's children grew up not only hearing about the Christian faith, but seeing, at first-hand, their father's practical application of its teaching.

Dickens began helping to support his parents and siblings at the age of seventeen. For the rest of his adult life, he would, in some shape or form, assist them financially and practically. Following his father's arrest for debt in November 1834, for non-payment of rent and an outstanding wine merchant's bill, the writer took it upon himself to raise the necessary funds to prevent his parents returning to debtors' prison. Five years later, he once again intervened on his father's behalf. On this occasion, this involved their move to Mile End Cottage, Alphington, near Exeter in Devon. He was to continue to subsidize his father at regular intervals until the latter's death in

March 1851, and he continued to care for his mother for the rest of her life as well.

The dutiful son was also the kindly elder brother. Charles used his influence to find suitable employment for his three younger siblings: Frederick, Alfred, and Augustus. Also, to help the family, he took Frederick in as soon as he could afford his own property (13 Furnival Inn, Holborn). His brother was to live with him for several years, even after his marriage to Catherine. Dickens's charitable kindness also extended to his brothers' families. When, in July 1860, Alfred died of tuberculosis in Manchester, Dickens arranged and paid for the funeral, provided temporary lodging for Alfred's widow, Helen, and their five children, near his home in Gad's Hill, and then found them somewhere permanent to live in Hampstead Heath. Thirteen years earlier, when his youngest brother, Augustus, abandoned his blind wife and child, Dickens once again stepped in to provide for them.

It was not only members of his family who benefited from his abounding charity. Many of his friends, such as Daniel Tobin, an old school friend from Wellington House Academy, whom he employed as a literary assistant, had very good reason to thank God for his generosity and kindness. In 1843, the actor Edward Elton, who belonged to the same theatrical company as the author's good friend William Macready, drowned when the ship he was sailing in from Hull, sank in the Irish Sea. He left seven orphans, as his wife had predeceased him. On hearing the tragic news, Dickens agreed to chair a fundraising committee and act as a trustee to provide for Elton's children. As part of this, he arranged a benefit performance of *Hamlet* at the Haymarket theatre. Together with other events, the sum of £1,000 was raised.

Towards the end of his editorship of the *Bentley's Miscellany* (1839), the writer received a submission of some songs from a self-educated carpenter, John Overs, who came from a poor background and was struggling to provide for his family. Dickens took it upon himself to support him. After helping Overs revise his book, entitled *Evening of a Working Man*, he wrote letters of recommendation to various publishers, as well as writing an introduction. His intervention resulted in its publication. In 1844, following Overs's premature death due to illness, the author's support for the bereaved family included providing an excellent education for two of the sons.

The well-being of his fellow writers was close to his heart. An example was the consideration shown to two of his friends, John Poole and James Leigh Hunt. Even though they had been reasonably successful in their literary careers, both fell upon hard times. In July 1847, Dickens organized a charity performance of Ben Johnson's *Every Man in His Humour*, to raise money for them and their families. Appearing in the play as Captain Bobadil and taking on the role of director, he worked tirelessly to ensure that the two performances in Liverpool and Manchester were a great success. He was also instrumental in persuading Queen Victoria to grant a pension of £100 a year to John Poole.

On 5 June 1857, the author returned home (with Douglas Jerrold), after enjoying a day in Greenwich and on the Thames. A journalist, regular contributor to *Punch*, and a playwright whose reputation had been established with his play *Black-Eyed Susan* (1829), Jerrold was one of Dickens's closest friends. When Jerrold died, he set up a relief fund for his widow and family, and set about organizing various events. Within a month of his friend's death, he had arranged a benefit performance of *The Frozen Deep* to be staged at London's Gallery of Illustration in Regent Street. Attended by Queen Victoria, Prince Albert, and the King of Belgium, the evening went exceptionally well. It was repeated on 18 and 25 July. The following month, Dickens, who directed and acted in the play, booked the Manchester Free Trade Hall. This was an ambitious step; with 4,000 seats it was a huge venue for a largely amateur cast. Nonetheless, the production on consecutive nights (21 and 22 August) met with a favourable response.

In addition to his exhaustive involvement with *The Frozen Deep*, the author somehow found time to give two public readings of his work. The first at St Martin's Hall, London attracted an audience of 2,000 people. As a result of his readings and *The Frozen Deep* performances, the substantial sum of £2,000 was raised for the Jerrold family.

Within a month of moving into 1 Devonshire Terrace in December 1839, Dickens was summoned to his local workhouse in Marylebone to serve as a juryman at a coroner's inquest. Shortly after arriving, he and the other jurors were escorted downstairs to the workhouse mortuary. Awaiting him was the disturbing sight of a dead baby, laid upon a clean white cloth within a box. When they returned upstairs, they learnt that the child's mother, Eliza Burgess, was accused of murdering her newborn son. On first seeing her, the writer was immediately struck by her pale, frightened appearance. His sympathetic nature was further aroused on learning that the woman, who was working as a maid, had been orphaned as a child.

The facts of the case, as represented to the jury, were that on Sunday, 5 January 1840, the heavily pregnant accused had been working in the kitchen of her employer's house at No. 65 Edgware Road. On hearing the front door bell, she hurried upstairs and, in doing so, the baby was born. When she got back to the kitchen, she cut the umbilical cord and cleaned up the newborn, who, at this point, was dead. Placing the child in a box, she hid him under the dresser. On being questioned by her mistress, she confessed to the birth and showed her where she had hidden the baby. Both she and the child were duly taken to the workhouse infirmary in Marylebone, where she spent the next nine days before the coroner's inquiry.

The case hinged on whether her newly born son had died at birth, or whether Eliza Burgess had killed him. After an unofficial conversation with Mr Wakeley, the coroner, Dickens took the former view and argued vigorously against those jurors who claimed that the maid had murdered the baby. Such was the passion of his conviction and his desire to help Eliza that he managed to persuade his fellow jurors. A verdict of "Found Dead" was decided upon, which effectively removed the threat of the death penalty. On hearing the result, the maid fell to her knees to thank the jury and then passed out.

On returning home later the same day, Dickens immediately arranged for food and other provisions to be sent to Eliza in prison. He also employed the well-respected barrister, Richard Donne, to defend her at the Old Bailey. The case came to trial on 9 March.

With the support of a previous employer, who was willing to take her back into service and the defence mounted by his barrister, she was convicted of the lesser crime of "unlawfully concealing the birth of a male child". The sentence was a lenient one. It would not be an exaggeration to suggest that the author's compassionate intervention saved and restored Eliza Burgess's life.

One further incident serves to demonstrate the writer's spontaneous Christian charity to strangers. In the autumn of 1854, he received a letter from a Frederick Maynard, requesting his advice and help. The correspondence revealed that his sister, Caroline, had been the mistress of a gentleman. When this man's business failed, he abandoned her and their small child, and she was forced into prostitution. Desperately wanting to help his sister and her child, Maynard had written to Dickens.

On receiving the letter, he had no hesitation in inviting them into his home. Initially the author suggested that they should emigrate, with his help, to South Africa. Changing his mind, he instead helped her to move to another part of London, in the hope that she could make a living running a guesthouse under the guise of being a widow. When the venture proved unsuccessful, it was decided that, with Maynard, she should take her little girl and emigrate to Canada, which they did in 1856. Such was the sincerity of his faith that Dickens felt compelled, regardless of his onerous workload, to help the Eliza Burgesses and the Maynards, and all those like them.

As well as his compassionate benevolence towards individuals, Dickens tirelessly supported numerous charitable institutions and initiatives. Of his 115 public speaking engagements, over half were for organizations that sought to provide education for the poor and labouring classes. Examples of these include his speeches at the Liverpool Mechanics Institute, the Literary Mechanics Institute in Reading, the Polytechnic Institution in Birmingham, and the opening of the country's first free lending library in Manchester (September 1852).

Apart from education, he also supported thirteen hospitals. Among these were the Hospital for Sick Children, on behalf of which he gave a charitable reading in April 1858. He also spoke at a special fundraising dinner, which raised around £3,000, and published a leading article, "Drooping Buds", in his journal, *Household Words* (April 1852). Also, in June 1844, he addressed a fundraising dinner at the London Tavern for Doctor Southwood Smith's sanatorium in Devonshire Place House – the first nursing home in London.

In addition, he frequently delivered speeches on behalf of those initiatives that sought to help those connected with the literary world and the theatre, the two professions closest to his heart. The very first speech he gave at the age of twenty-five (3 May 1837) was for the Literary Fund, and he was to speak on no fewer than ten separate occasions at events organized to raise money for the General Theatrical Fund.

One particular charitable enterprise within the Arts to which the writer was especially committed was the setting up of The Guild of Literature and Art. Having decided on the details, he and his partner in the enterprise, the novelist Edward Bulwer Lytton, turned their attention to raising the £10,000 needed to launch the scheme. It was determined that the best way to achieve the target was through staging a series of fundraising plays. So Dickens and his friend, Mark Lemon jointly came up with a farce entitled *Mr Nightingale's Diary*. Lytton wrote *Not So Bad as We Seem*, a historical costume comedy set in the reign of George II.

As was customary, the writer threw himself wholeheartedly into the project. He assumed the role of director, organized the rehearsals, painstakingly edited Lytton's play, and took a combined total of six parts. Somehow, he also found time to persuade the Duke of Devonshire to allow the first two performances (on 16 and 27 May 1851) to take place at his Piccadilly residence, Devonshire House. On the opening night, Queen Victoria and Prince Albert were once again in attendance, as was the Duke of Wellington. Following their initial London success, the thirty-strong company embarked on a national tour, which included Bath, Bristol, Reading, Liverpool, Manchester, and Birmingham. By the end of the tour, they had achieved their £10,000 target. For most of it, Dickens was also writing instalments of *Bleak House*. In 1854, Lytton, who had recently been elected Tory MP for Hertford, introduced a Parliamentary Bill incorporating the Guild. Dickens, in his capacity as chairman, remained committed to the project for the rest of his life.

The writer's involvement with various charities was not restricted to occasional guest appearances at fundraising events. He also held positions of responsibility at no fewer than eleven organizations. These included Vice-President of the Royal Hospital of Incurables, Honorary Governor of the Hospital for Sick Children, Trustee of the Royal General Theatrical Fund, and Chairman of the General Theatrical Fund. He also worked closely with Doctor West to establish Great Ormond Street Hospital in 1851. His personal banking records show that on at least forty-three separate occasions, he made donations to various charities and was a lifelong subscriber to the Hospital for Incurables.

On the Monday following *The Pickwick Papers* celebratory dinner, the author left his Doughty Street home. In his pocket was a cheque for £500 from Chapman and Hall. His decision on that November morning to open an account at Coutts and Company Bank, rather than at any of its numerous competitors, proved an important one.

During the course of the following year, as his reputation continued to grow, he attracted the interest of one of the bank's partners, Edward Marjoribanks, and it was he who first introduced Dickens to Angela Burdett Coutts; probably the richest woman in London. She was the heiress to two enormous fortunes, one of which was through her grandfather's connection with Coutts Bank. The youngest daughter of the radical reformer, Sir Francis Burdett, she was determined to use her wealth to benefit those neglected by society.

From the first, a strong bond of friendship and sense of shared purpose developed. In 1839, a year after they met, the author's obvious esteem for his new friend was confirmed by her becoming godmother to his first child, Charley. Conscientiously discharging her duties, she funded her godson's education at King's College School and then, as a twelve-year-old, at Eton. She also found him a job at Baring Brothers when he was eighteen.

Two years younger than the writer, the reserved Miss Coutts discovered in him someone who passionately shared her Christian commitment to helping those in need. She placed complete trust in Dickens's judgment and advice, and their relationship, over the next twenty-five years or so, was to bring hope and relief to a vast number of people. At their frequent meetings at her Piccadilly mansion, the pair would discuss all manner of projects aimed at providing education, improved housing, and restoration for those who had fallen victim to depravation.

Of all the charitable enterprises they undertook together, one in particular stands out as a testimony to Dickens's enduring practical faith. On 26 May 1846, five days before setting off for Lausanne, where he was to begin *Dombey and Son*, the author contacted Miss Coutts with an outline plan to set up a rescue home for young women. It was his intention to help those already known to be prostitutes and those likely to drift into it. At the time, there was estimated to be around 30,000 prostitutes in London, some of whom Angela Burdett Coutts could see every night from the window of her Piccadilly home.

Dickens's idea was that the women – who would be recommended by the police, prison governors, magistrates, and privately – would receive an education, which included homemaking skills, singing, and other subjects, and then be given the opportunity to start a new life overseas in Australia (as do Emily and Martha in *David Copperfield*), Canada, or South Africa. The plan was well received.

In May of the following year, he found a suitable house near Shepherd's Bush. Six months later, Urania Cottage was opened to receive its first residents. Fittingly, the name, when translated from the Greek, meant heavenly and spiritual. For the next decade, the author poured his heart and soul into the project. He even composed a letter, which was read to every young woman considering taking up a place:

If you ever wished (I know you must have done so, sometimes) for a chance of rising out of your sad life, and having friends, a quiet home, means of being useful to yourself and others, peace of mind, self-respect, everything you have lost, pray read attentively; I am going to offer you, not the chance but the certainty of all these blessings, if you will exert yourself to deserve them. And do not think that I write to you as if I felt myself very much above you, or wished to hurt your feelings by reminding you of the situation in which you are placed. God forbid! I mean nothing but kindness to you, and I smile as if you were my sister.

The writer interviewed every potential resident and appointed all the staff. He instilled a regime in which the inmates were "tempted to virtue", not "frightened, dragged or driven". Dickens oversaw every detail of the home's daily routine, from the sleeping arrangements, clothing, and reading material, to the soup they made for the poor. The first three residents left for Australia in January 1849, and twenty-seven more emigrated over the next five years. Urania Cottage was a great success, thanks, in the main, to the writer's extraordinary ten-year commitment to the project.

A further charitable enterprise in which the author advised Miss Coutts was her idea of creating good quality housing in a deprived slum area of London. Whereas she had originally envisaged building small separate houses, he persuaded her that well-constructed blocks of flats, with gas, water, drainage, and access to spacious public gardens would prove more desirable and cost-effective. Miss Coutts agreed. Ten years later, in 1862, the first model Columbia apartments in Nova Scotia Gardens, Bethnal Green were occupied.

Throughout his life, Dickens practised and retained a genuine Christian faith. Although, as will be seen in Chapter 24, the author had, in common with us all, feet of clay, his fundamental belief in God and the Christian faith were undeniable. The evidence for this can be clearly seen in the private and public expression of his beliefs, and, most importantly, in his actions.

19

THE BATTLE OF LIFE

In 1846, following his extremely brief excursion into the world of newspaper editorship (he was editor of *The Daily News* for around one month), Dickens decided to relocate himself and his family to Lausanne, Switzerland for six months. As far as the author was concerned, it was far from being a holiday. In April, a month before their departure, he had signed a contract with Bradbury and Evans to write a new novel, *Dombey and Son: Whole sale, Retail and Exportation*, which was to be serialized in twenty monthly parts. It was also his intention to write his fourth Christmas book, *The Battle of Life*, while he was away.

So it was that, on the last day of May, the Dickens entourage – Charles, Catherine, Georgina, his sister-in-law, six children, along with Anne (Mrs Dickens's maid), two other female servants, and Louise Roche, the courier who had travelled with them to Genoa, and, of course, the pet spaniel, Timber – clambered aboard two carriages. In their absence, Devonshire Terrace was let out to Sir James Duke.

The journey from London to Lausanne, via Ramsgate, Ostend, Strasburg, and Basle, took eleven days. On their arrival, the party booked into the Hotel Gibbon. Within two days, the writer had found a suitable property within a ten-minute walk of the hotel. The rose-covered Villa Rosemont, situated on a hill above the town, overlooking Lake Geneva, with views of the mountain gorges, rising to the Simplon Pass, was, indeed, an enchanting property. For his study, Dickens chose a first-floor room, which opened on to a long broad balcony. However, in the absence of his box of books, blue ink, and bronze desk ornaments, he made no effort to begin his new novel.

Towards the end of June, his writing materials arrived. Unpacking them, he turned to his companions and, on choosing a book at random, announced: "Now, whatever passage my thumb rests on, I shall take as having reference to Dombey and Son." Amazingly, the novel he chose was Laurence Sterne's, *Tristram Shandy*, and the passage he selected contained the following words: "What a work it is likely to turn out! Let us begin it!" He immediately did so.

Initially, due to the two-year gap since he worked on his last novel, *Martin Chuzzlewit*, Dickens found it an uphill struggle; but, on being encouraged by the favourable response to the first instalment, he quickly found his feet. His enthusiasm was further kindled by the positive response of his newly found Lausanne friends – Richard and Lavinia Watson, William Haldimand, and William de Cerjat and his wife – to a reading of the book's second instalment. Finally, he had every reason to be pleased, as the sales of the early instalments were averaging 30,000 copies, which provided him with around £100 a month income.

Faced with the added pressure of writing *The Battle of Life* at the same time as the novel, he took himself off to Geneva for a week in late September. He made a good start, and his Christmas book was completed within a month.

On 16 November, five days after the completion of the third instalment of *Dombey and Son*, the family, occupying three separate carriages, left Geneva. Five days later they arrived in Paris and quickly found a place to live close to the Champs Élysées, 48 Rue de Courcelles. In addition to completing the fourth and fifth instalment of *Dombey and Son* by Christmas, he also found time to visit London in mid-December to discuss Chapman and Hall's new Cheap Edition collection of his works and to assist the Keeleys' dramatization of The Battle of Life, which was due to open on 21 December at the Lyceum Theatre. The book itself, which was published two days earlier, sold 24,000 copies on the first day, and by the end of January it had sold more than his three previous Christmas works: *A Christmas Carol*, *The Chimes*, and *The Cricket on the Hearth*. In total, he was to receive £1,300 from its sales.

Back in Paris for Christmas, he continued to work on *Dombey and Son*. In January, his oldest son, Charley, now ten, returned to London with Forster to start his first term at King's College School. Shortly after starting, he contracted scarlet fever, a potentially fatal disease.[14] Immediately on hearing the news, Dickens, along with his family, returned to London to be with his son, staying at the Victoria Hotel in Euston Square. On satisfying himself that Charley was on the road to recovery, the author, with his by now customary effectiveness, found a place to rent, 3 Chester Place, Regent's Park, near Devonshire Terrace, which was occupied by Sir James Duke until May.

Charles's grandly named seventh child and fifth son, Sydney Smith Haldimand, was born at Chester Place on 18 April 1847. Between May and August, Dickens spent hardly any time at Devonshire Terrace. In early May, after being attacked by a horse in the street, which prevented him from writing for several days, he went to stay in Brighton with Catherine, Georgina, and Charley for the rest of the month. Following this, he spent the summer with his family at the Albion Hotel, Broadstairs. It was not until September that he settled down again at Devonshire Terrace. *Dombey and Son* was completed the following March. The final instalment, along with the book, appeared in April 1848.

The heroine of the novel was Dickens's fourth female angel, Florence Dombey. As with Madeline Bray, the writer uses the father–daughter context in which to reveal her angelic qualities. Losing her mother at the age of six, following the birth of her brother, Paul, she is overlooked by her proud selfish father. Fixing all his fraternal ambition upon his son and heir, he makes little effort to foster any kind of relationship with his unwanted daughter.

When six-year-old Paul dies in Florence's arms, Mr Dombey, rather than reaching out to his daughter in the hope of finding

---

14 The naturalist Charles Darwin lost two of his children to it.

mutual consolation, withdraws even more from her. Struggling to come to terms with his loss, he travels to Leamington Spa, where he meets the beautiful young widow, Edith Granger.

Despite her conceit, in which she is a match for Mr Dombey, Edith is deeply affected by Florence's sincere, loving nature. Describing her step-daughter as being a "good angel", she pleads with her: "Be near me, Florence, I have no hope but in you!" Feeling trapped and engaged in a battle of wills with Florence's father, Edith enters into a relationship with Mr Dombey's right-hand man, James Carker. Throughout this difficult time, and in spite of being constantly ignored by her father, Florence continues to reach out to him.

In Chapter 47, Edith elopes with James Carker. On learning what has happened, Florence, despite her own personal heartbreak at losing her second mother, rushes to her father to comfort him:

Compassion for her father was the first distinct emotion that made her head against the flood of sorrow which overwhelmed her: Her constant nature turned to him in his distress, as fervently and faithfully, as if in his prosperity, he had been the embodiment of that idea which had gradually became so faint and dim...

Yielding at once to the impulse of her affection, timid at all other times, but bold in its truth to him in his adversity, and undainted by past repulse, Florence hurried downstairs. As she set her light foot in the hall, he came out of his room. She hastened towards him unchecked, with her arms stretched out, and crying "Oh dear, dear Papa!" as if she would have clasped him round the neck.

And so she would have done. But in his frenzy, he lifted up his cruel arm, and struck her crosswise, with such heaviness that she tottered on the marble floor...

She did not sink down at his feet... she did not utter one word of reproach, but she looked at him, and a cry of desolation issued from her heart.

Wrongly thinking she was in league with Edith, he throws the seventeen-year-old Florence out into the street, and she is forced to find shelter at the shop of Solomon Gill. He is the uncle of Walter Gay, whom Florence meets and married. Mr Dombey is a broken man. His business ruined, rejected and deserted, he remains in his room, completely alone. Brooding and wasting away, he determines to commit suicide. At the very moment he is about to end his own life, razor in hand, Florence, by now a wife and mother, bursts into the room and saves him.

Taking him into her own home, she faithfully nurses him for weeks, bringing him back from death. Eventually recovering his health, he remains with Walter, Florence, and their two children, Paul and Florence. Spiritually and emotionally restored by the love of his angelic daughter, he becomes a loving grandfather to both children, but it is young Florence who holds a special place in his heart.

The normal excitement and exuberance that accompanied the completion of a successful novel were tempered by the author's grave concern for his older sister's health. As we have seen, she died of tuberculosis, on 2 September 1848, aged thirty-eight. In organizing the funeral, which took place six days later, he arranged for Fanny, as per her wishes and those of her husband, to be buried in unconsecrated ground within Highgate Cemetery. Within the space of three years, three generations of Dickens's family would be laid to rest.

The Personal History of David Copperfield, the most autobiographical of his novels (its title is a reversal of his initials) was the last to be written at Devonshire Terrace. In the third week of February 1849, Dickens, along with Catherine and their eight children, went to stay at the Bedford Hotel in Brighton. Their latest addition, Henry Fielding, was around one month old at this point. They were joined by John Leech, who had illustrated *A Christmas Carol*, and his wife Annie. During the course of his stay, Dickens began to plan his new book. Originally, he had thought of the title, *Mag's Diversions*, it then moved on to *David Mag of Copperfield House*, and then, eventually, *David Copperfield*. The first instalment was completed by late March and appeared on 1 May. It was an instant success. As with *Dombey and*

Son, the novel was illustrated by Phiz and published by Bradbury and Evans. The last instalment appeared in November 1850, as did the single-volume novel.

Agnes Wickfield, the book's female angel, like Nell Trent, is closely associated with the theme of the resurrection, and she is Dickens's most overtly religious angelic character. Names play an important role in the author's work, as is the case with his choice of Christian name here: Agnes is both an anagram of the French for angel (Anges) and is linked with "Agnus Dei" (Lamb of God), the refrain still sung before Communion in the Anglican Church to this day.

The theme of the resurrection is first introduced in Chapter 2, when David Copperfield's mother is reading the account of Lazarus being raised from the dead. Nine chapters later, at her funeral, Dickens quotes the phrase "I am the Resurrection and the Life saith the Lord", from the Burial Service of the *Book of Common Prayer*. In the illustration "I am Married", which depicts David's marriage to Dora Spenlow, a stone statue of a winged female angel on a plinth is positioned prominently above the wedding party, which includes Agnes. Of particular note is the fact that the angel is pointing heavenwards.

On the evening of her death, Dora asks to see Agnes alone. Following a brief conversation, in which she implores her to marry David when she is gone, Dora, lying upon Agnes's bosom, dies. Eventually Agnes comes downstairs to inform David, her "face, so full of pity, and of grief". Unable to speak, she raises her hands and points her finger upwards to heaven. In the closing words of the novel, David refers to this resurrectionary symbolic moment: "Oh Agnes, Oh my soul; so may thy face be by me when I close my life indeed; so may I, when realities are melting from me like the shadow's which I now dismiss, still find thee near me, pointing upward."

Throughout the book, Agnes – David's "Good Angel" – acts selflessly as his loving sister, confidant, adviser, and friend. Even though she is in love with him, she supports him during the course of his youthful infatuations with Miss Shepherd and Miss Larkins from

Nettingall's Establishment for Young Ladies. Though heartbroken at the news of his engagement to Dora Spenlow, she not only continues her friendship with him, but extends her unconditional love to his bride. While others are fooled by James Steerforth, she discerns the true nature of the man. Warning David of the bad influence he is upon him, she describes Steerforth as being his "Bad Angel". Like Dickens's other female angels, Agnes, "so true, so beautiful, so good", enriches and blesses the man she loves.

The significance of Dickens's time at Devonshire Terrace extended beyond that of his five completed novels. Shortly after Charley started at Eton (January 1850) – his place had been funded by Angela Burdett Coutts, as we have seen – the author energetically set about completing the practical arrangements for his new twopenny weekly journal. Having discussed numerous proposed titles with Forster, he settled on *Household Words*, a phrase taken from Shakespeare's Henry V. Office premises were secured at 16 Wellington Street, a three-storey house, just north of the Gaiety Theatre in the Strand.

On Forster's advice, Dickens appointed his friend, William Wills, as assistant editor. An experienced journalist, who had held a similar position at the Edinburgh-based periodical, *Chambers*, Wills had worked with Dickens at *The Daily News*, and his methodical approach meant he was well suited to the role. Henry Morley and Richard Horne were also employed as reporters and writers. It was also very much a family affair, with both Dickens's father and father-in-law, George Hogarth, on the payroll, along with Forster in an advisory role.

Dickens contributed all thirty-nine instalments of his *Child History of England* and something like a hundred sketches and articles to the journal in the first three years. As well as exercising absolute editorial control, his personal influence far exceeded his 50 per cent share in the journal. As stated beneath the title on the front page, *Household Words*, though published by Bradbury and Evans, was most definitely "Conducted by Charles Dickens".

As explained to Elizabeth Gaskell, one of many anonymous contributors, the purpose of the journal was "to raise up those that are down". It was to lead to "the general improvement of our social condition". To this end, Dickens wrote on many issues that directly affected the disadvantaged: housing, education, accidents in factories, workhouses, and sanitation. Though seeking to expose social injustice, he never lost sight of the need to entertain his readers and he provided a broad spectrum of material in each number. Among the six to nine items, there were never more than two or three devoted to social reform.

The formula worked. The opening 24-page number, which appeared on Wednesday, 30 March, sold a staggering 100,000 copies. This was probably due to the expectation that it would contain the first instalment of Dickens's next novel. His readers would have to wait a further four years for the serialization of *Hard Times* to appear in the journal. Despite the absence of any new book, the weekly circulation remained at around 39,000 for the next nine years.

In the spring of 1851, with the lease on Devonshire Terrace drawing to an end, Dickens began the process of finding a new home. Impressed by a residence by the name of Balmoral House in North London, he was disappointed that his offer was turned down. A few years later, a barge, carrying gunpowder along the Regent's Park Canal, exploded opposite the house, all but destroying it.

On 20 April, the writer went to look at Tavistock House, Tavistock Square, Bloomsbury, just north of the British Museum. Leased by his good friend the artist Frank Stone, the plain brick house, situated in a desirable location, was in a dilapidated condition, probably due to the current owner's lack of finance. Nonetheless, Dickens quickly saw the potential of the eighteen-room property. By July, he had agreed to pay £1,500 for a 45-year lease. While the cost of actually leasing the house was reasonable, the extensive renovations and refurbishments were not. The success of the work undertaken was, to a large extent, due to the daily oversight of his brother-in-law, Henry Austin. Also, Frank Stone agreed to move out whilst the work was being carried out. The Dickens family stayed at Fort House, Broadstairs, while they were waiting for the house to be completed.

Closing the door of 1 Devonshire Terrace for the last time in May 1851 proved an especially moving experience for Dickens. No doubt, as he observed the blossoming hawthorn trees, he was reminded of the May Day, thirty years earlier, when, as a nine-year-old, he left his beloved Ordnance Terrace home in Chatham. During the course of the family's eighty-mile or so journey to Broadstairs, the memories of the last twelve years spent in the house crowded in upon him. Foremost among these were the images related to the tragic death of his daughter, Dora, a month earlier.

He had returned to London from Malvern, where he had been staying with Catherine, who was recovering from the effects of a nervous breakdown. Dickens had been delighted to be able to spend some time playing with his children in the garden. It was 14 April 1851, and that afternoon he had to chair a meeting of the General Theatrical Fund. Before leaving for the London Tavern, he picked up his eight-month-old daughter, Dora, and gave her a fatherly cuddle. It was to be the last time he would do so. Half an hour before he was due to speak, John Forster, who was also present, received the terrible news from one of Dickens's servants that Dora had suddenly died. Having taken the decision not to tell his friend until after he had delivered his speech, Forster felt tears welling up within him when Dickens referred to the need to leave even the scene of death in order to carry on the battle of life.

At the close of the meeting, with the help of their mutual friend, Mark Lemon, Forster broke the news. Throughout the night, the author kept watch over his daughter. Desperately trying to put on a brave face for the benefit of his other children, his grief overcame him a few days later, when, taking some flowers upstairs to lay on Dora's bed, he broke down in tears. The death of his beloved daughter was not the only bereavement which cast a shadow upon his thoughts as he travelled along. The previous spring, his 66-year-old father also died, following a long illness.

By mid-November, when the family carriage passed through the large iron gates, Tavistock House had been virtually transformed. In showing Catherine, Georgina, and his eight children round, he took particular pleasure in witnessing the delight on Kate and Mary's faces as they saw their carefully designed bedroom for the first time and in revealing his pride and joy, his conversion of the former schoolroom into a theatre.

20

Telescopic Philanthropy and Original Sin

Shortly after moving into Tavistock House, the 39-year-old author settled at his desk, quill pen in hand and blank blue paper in front of him. He had in mind to use his ninth novel to expose the Church's and society's neglect of the domestic poor and to challenge the concept of original sin. Having done so, *Bleak House* proved to be not only one of his most popular books, but also one of his most controversial. For years, as we have seen, Dickens had railed against the imbalance that existed between the Church's overseas missionary activities throughout the Empire and their neglect of the poor on their doorstep. It would seem that he was justified in his concern. In 1847, five years before the first instalment of *Bleak House* appeared, the annual income of the three leading Evangelical overseas missionary societies – the Church Missionary Society, the British and Foreign Bible Society, and the Society for the Propagation of the Gospel to Foreign Parts – was in excess of £100,000. In comparison, the London City Mission, which worked among the city's deprived, received only £14,000.

In Chapter 7 of *The Pickwick Papers*, Dickens had cleverly contrasted the fervent opposition of the inhabitants of the borough of Muggleton to slavery abroad with their failure to help liberate the poor domestic slaves of England's prevailing inhumane industrial regime.

Muggleton is an ancient and loyal borough, mingling a zealous advocacy of Christian principles, with a devoted attachment to commercial rights; in demonstration whereof, the mayor, corporation, and other inhabitants, have presented at diverse times, no fewer than one thousand four hundred and twenty petitions against the continuance of negro slavery abroad and an equal number against any interference with the factory system at home.

In Chapter 3 of the *Mudfog Papers*, "The Full Report of the Second Meeting of the Mudfog Association for the Advancement of Everything" (1838), the writer refers to Mr Tickle's "newly-invented spectacles, which enabled the wearer to discern, in very bright colours at a great distance, and rendered him wholly blind to those immediately before him". In rejecting Tickle's invention, the President points out that "a large number of most excellent persons and great statesmen could see with the naked eye, most marvellous horrors on the West India plantations, while they could discern nothing whatever in the interior of Manchester Cotton Mills."

In the pages of *Bleak House*, Dickens launched his most concerted assault on "Telescopic Philanthropy" (the heading for Chapter 4). The motif is expertly introduced in the form of Mrs Jellyby. Obsessed with the well-being of the African natives in "Borrioboola-Gha, on the left bank of the Niger", she completely neglects her own children.

On the way to Bleak House, the home of their guardian, John Jarndyce, Esther Summerson, Richard Carstone, and Ada Clare stay at the Jellybys. On their arrival, they observe a small crowd gathered round the house. They discover that one of the young boys has managed to get his head stuck between the railings. Throughout the whole comic process of the beadle and the milkman attempting to extricate him, his mother, aware of the situation, makes no attempt to intervene or comfort him.

On entering the house, they accidentally tread on several more children gathered on the dimly lit stairs. As they enter Mrs Jellyby's room, one of the children, Peppy, falls down the whole flight of stairs, making a tremendous noise as he does so. His mother shows no concern whatsoever. In describing her, Dickens writes: "She was a pretty, very diminutive, plump woman, of forty to fifty, with handsome eyes, though they had a curious habit of seeing to look a long way off. As they could see nothing nearer than Africa. She had very good hair, but was too occupied with her African duties to brush it."

As Mrs Jellyby discusses her plans for Borrioboola-Gha, Peppy enters. He is a pitiful sight, with a strip of plaster on his forehead, cuts to his knees, and covered in dirt and bruises. Rather than receiving comfort from his mother, he is dismissed with the words: "Go along, you naughty Peppy!" As he leaves the room, she once again fixes "her fine eyes on Africa". His readers clearly understood the Jellyby metaphor.

Although those in the Church, preoccupied with overseas missionary work, disliked his portrayal of Mrs Jellyby, it was the image of Jo, the destitute, illiterate orphan, sitting on the doorstep of the Society for the Propagation of the Gospel in Foreign Parts, eating his dirty bit of bread for his breakfast, that provoked the strongest criticism. This powerful denunciation of "Telescopic Philanthropy" caused a great deal of indignation. A letter received on 8 July 1852, from the Reverend Henry Christophson, was typical of the responses Dickens received:

> *I venture to trespass on your attention with one serious query, touching a sentence in the last number of Bleak House. Do the supporters of Christian missions to the heathen really deserve the attack that is conveyed in the sentence about Jo seated in his anguish on the doorstep of the Society for the Propagation of the Gospel in Foreign Parts? The allusion is severe, but is it just? Are such boys as Jo neglected?*

If the correspondent anticipated a conciliatory reply, he was sorely disappointed. The passion of the writer's conviction on the subject is evident from the tone of his response the following day:

> *There was a long time during which benevolent societies were spending immense sums on missions abroad, when there was no such thing as a ragged school in England, or any kind of associated endeavour to*

*penetrate to those horrible domestic depths in which schools are now
to be found, and where they were, to my certain knowledge, neither
placed nor discovered by the Society for the Propagation of the Gospel
in Foreign Parts. If you think the balance between the home mission
and the foreign mission justly held in the present time, I do not. Indeed,
I have very grave doubts whether a great commercial country holding
communication with all parts of the world, can better Christianise
the knighted portions of it than by the bestowal of its wealth and
energy on the making of good Christians at home, and on the utter
removal of neglected and untaught childhood from its streets, before it
wonders elsewhere. These are my opinions, founded, I believe, on some
knowledge of facts and some observation. If I could be scared out of
them let me add in all good humour, by such easily impressed words as
"anti-Christian" or "irreligious": I should think that I deserved them
in their real signification.*

The author also used *Bleak House* and, three years later, *Little Dorrit*,
to challenge the prevailing Evangelical doctrine of original sin and
the idea that people, especially the poor, were essentially wicked.
Dickens's opposition to these ideas was not based on any strongly
held theological ideas. It was the product of his conviction that
people retained an element of the divine characteristics of their
Creator, and, more importantly, that adopting such a standpoint
hampered the effectiveness of the Church's response to those in
need. His views on the subject were very much in keeping with those
of the Unitarians. His friend and minister at Little Portland Street
Chapel, Reverend Edward Tagart, wrote on the subject:

*Whilst by other professing Christians the nature of men is viewed
as wholly sinful and inclined to evil, and therefore deserving God's
wrath and damnation, to us it appears that the nature of man though
imperfect is, on the whole good, and designed for good – that sin can
only consist in actual transgression – and we reject, as unscriptural
and irrational, the imputation of Adam's guilt to his posterity.*

Dickens found the concept of original sin to be most disturbing in relation to children. Three years prior to attending Little Portland Street Chapel, he stated his opinion on the subject in a letter to the children's author, Mrs Godfrey:

I think it is monstrous to hold the source of inconceivable mercy and goodness perpetually up to them [children] as an avenging and wrathful God who – making them in His wisdom children before they are men and women – is to punish them awfully for every venial offence which is almost a necessary part of that stage of life. I object decidedly to endeavouring to impress them with a fear of death, before they can be rationally supposed to become accountable creatures, and so great a horror do I feel at the thought of imbuing with strict doctrines those who have just reflection enough to know that if God be as right and just as they are told He is, their fathers and mothers and three fourths of their relations and friends must be doomed to Eternal Perdition.

In *Nicholas Nickleby*, he makes the point that people, far from being born into original sin, have the faint image of Eden stamped upon them in childhood.

The Church's response to the social depravation of the period was, from Dickens's perspective, compromised by a belief in people's inherent sinfulness. They held that the suffering of the poor and labouring classes was symptomatic of their sin. The Evangelical Bishop of Chester, John Bird Sumner, who was later appointed Archbishop of Canterbury, wrote, in an address to his diocesan clergy, that "the real cause of nine parts in ten of the misery which abounds in the world is sin". Another prominent Evangelical of the period, the Reverend Thomas Gisbourne, in his ironically entitled work, *Friendly Observations Addressed to the Manufacturing Population of Great Britain*, observed: "The late and present distress of the Manufacturing Population of Great Britain must be deemed, in the case of the multitudes, in a very considerable degree, attributable to themselves." William Wilberforce, the champion of the abolition of slavery movement, held a similar view. The solution, they argued, rested not in programmes for social improvement or charitable intervention, but rather in spiritual regeneration and moral teaching.

Dickens held the opposite view. Before any meaningful Christian dialogue could take place, the housing, education, and welfare of those living in poverty needed to be improved: the imperative was physical rather than spiritual. On 10 May 1858, as the guest of honour at a dinner of the Metropolitan Sanitary Association, he proposed the following toast:

> *Give him [the poor man] and his a glimpse of heaven. Give them water, help them to be clean. Take the body of the dead relative from the room where the living live with it, and where such loathsome familiarity deprives death itself of awe. Then, but not before, will they be brought willingly to hear of Him whose thoughts were so much with the wretched and who had compassion for all human sorrow.*

He then went on to read the following powerful excerpt from his *Household Words* article, "Nobody's Story":

> *What avails it to send a missionary to me, a miserable man or woman living in a foetid court where every sense bestowed upon me for my delight becomes a torment, and every minute of my life is a new mire added to the heap under which I lie degraded? To what natural feeling within one can we hope to touch? Is it my remembrance of my children? It is a remembrance of distortion and decay, scrofula and fever. Would he address himself to my hopes of immortality? I am so surrounded by material filth that my Soul can not rise to the contemplation of an immortal existence! Or, if I be a miserable child, born and nurtured in the same wretched place, and tempted, in these better times, to the ragged School, what can the few hours teaching that I get there do for me against the noxious, constant, ever renewed lesson of my whole existence. But give me my first glimpse of Heaven through a little of its light and air – give me water – help me to be clean – lighten this heavy atmosphere in which my spirit droops...*

> *gently and kindly take the body of my dead relation out of the small*
> *room where I grew to be so familiar with the awful change that even*
> *its sanctity is lost to me – and, Teacher, then I'll hear, you know how*
> *willingly, of Him whose thoughts were so much with the Poor, and*
> *who had compassion for all human sorrow!*

Dickens's rejection of the concept of original sin and the innate sinfulness of individuals, especially the poor, is expressed in *Bleak House* through Esther Summerson and Jo. Esther, despite her angelic qualities, is forced to suffer a condemnatory upbringing at the hands of her harsh puritanical godmother, Miss Barbary:

> *She was a good, good woman! She went to church three times every*
> *Sunday, and to morning prayers on Wednesdays and Fridays, and to*
> *lectures; and never missed. She was handsome, and if she had ever*
> *smiled, would have been (I used to think) like an angel – but she never*
> *smiled. She was always grave, and strict. She was very good herself, I*
> *thought that the badness of other people made her frown all her life.*

The illegitimate child of Miss Barbary's sister, Lady Dedlock, Esther is harshly treated, in accordance with her aunt's Evangelical belief in original sin. Reflecting on her childhood, she remembers the occasion of her twelfth birthday:

> *Dinner was over, and my godmother and I were sitting at the table*
> *before the fire. The clock ticked, the fire clicked; not another sound. I*
> *had happened to look timidly up from my stitching, across the table at*
> *my godmother, and saw in her face, looking gloomily at me, "It would*
> *have been far better, little Esther, that you had had no birthday, that*
> *you had never been born!"*

She goes on to say:

> *For yourself, unfortunate girl, orphaned and degraded from the first of*
> *these evil anniversaries, pray daily that the sins of others be not visited*

upon your head, according to what is written… Submission, self-denial, diligent work, are the preparations for a life begun with such a shadow in it. You are different from other children, Esther, because you were not born like them, in common sinfulness and wrath. You are set apart.

Shortly afterwards, Dickens issues a scriptural admonishment to those self-righteous individuals characterized by Miss Barbary:

It must have been two years afterwards and I was almost fourteen, when one dreadful night my godmother and I sat at the fireside, I was reading aloud, and she was listening. I had come down at nine o'clock, as I always did, to read the Bible to her; and was reading from St John,[15] how our Saviour stooped down, writing with his finger in the dust, when they brought the sinful woman to him. So when they continued asking him, he lifted up himself and said unto them, he that is without sin among you, let him cast a stone at her!

Almost immediately, on hearing these words, Miss Barbary collapses and dies a week later.

In Chapter 25, the illiterate orphan Jo has the misfortune of finding himself at the home of Mr and Mrs Snagsby, where he is brought into the presence of Reverend Chadband, an Evangelical preacher. Despite his protestations to be "left alone", Jo is forced to sit through a sermon, delivered to a small, select congregation, seated in the Snagsbys' sitting room. Seated for all to see, he is the sole subject of Chadband's discourse:

We have here among us, my friends, a Gentile and a Heathen, a dweller in the tents of Tom-All-Alone's and a mover-on upon the surface of the earth. A brother and a boy; devoid of parents, devoid of relations, devoid of flocks and herds, devoid of gold and silver and of precious stones because he is devoid of the light that shines in upon some of us.

---

15 John 8:2–11.

It is not long until the heathen Jo falls asleep, only to be awoken again by a further lambasting from Chadband.

Eventually, bewildered and confused, the boy decides to leave. Making his way downstairs, he meets the Snagsbys' maid, Guster. Handing him her own supper of bread and cheese, she kindly asks Jo about his parents. He stops in the middle of a bite and looks petrified, "for this Christian saint has patted him on the shoulder, and it is the first time in his life that any decent hand has been so laid upon him".

Whereas Chadband denounces Jo as being a heathen and suggests that he is parentless and poor due to spiritual darkness, Dickens's representative, Guster, actually feeds him and shows him compassion. In so doing, she has a profound effect upon the boy. In *Bleak House*, Dickens not only managed to create a highly successful novel, but also communicated elements of his own beliefs to his huge audience. This was his genius: storytelling which entertained, but, at the same time, championed Christian social responsibility.

21

LAW, GRACE, AND FEET OF CLAY

Sitting in his Tavistock House study on a late spring morning, staring at the blank page before him, Dickens prophetically wrote the title of his eleventh serialized novel: *Nobody's Fault*. Within a year of its completion, in June 1857, he would be separated from his wife and desperately seeking to convince himself and everyone else that the breakup of his 22-year marriage was Catherine's fault rather than his own.

In exploring the twin themes of law and grace, *Little Dorrit*, as it became known, remains the author's most overtly religious novel. It also proved immensely popular. The second monthly number, which came out on New Year's Day, 1858, sold 35,000 copies. By May, its circulation had exceeded that of all the previous novels.

Within his working notes for the novel, Dickens describes the need to "set the darkness and vengeance of the Old Testament against the New". This he achieved through his characterization of Mrs Clennam and the contrasting angelic heroine, Amy Dorrit. It can surely be no coincidence that her Christian name is a homophone of the Latin word for love. While Arthur Clennam's self-righteous mother vehemently condemns those around her, and has subjected him to a harsh, loveless, puritanical upbringing, Amy has sacrificed her own childhood and youth to care for her thankless, imprisoned father and resentful sister and brother.

Returning home from China, following the death of his father, Arthur reflects on his childhood experiences of Sundays:

... when his mother, stern of face and unrelenting of heart, would sit all day behind a Bible – bound, like her own construction of it, in the hardest, barest, straitest board, with one dinted ornament on the cover like the drag of a chain, and a wrathful sprinkling of red upon the edges of the leaves – as if it, of all books were a fortification against sweetness of temper, natural affection and gentle intercourse.

Entering his mother's home, he once again observes the framed pictures of the Ten Plagues of Egypt placed upon the wall. It being a Sunday,

[Mrs Clennam] put on her spectacles and read certain passages aloud from a book – sternly, fiercely, wrathfully –praying that her enemies (she made by her tone and manner expressly hers) might be... utterly exterminated. As she read on, years seemed to fall away from her son like the imaginings of a dream, and all the old dark horrors of his usual preparation for the sleep of an innocent child to overshadow him.

Mrs Clennam's vengeful belief in a wrathful God has resulted in her replacing the New Testament divine virtues of grace and mercy with a system of self-justification. According to the author this was by no means peculiar to her: "Thus was she always balancing her bargain with the Majesty of heaven, posting up the entries to her credit, strictly keeping her set-off, and claiming her due. She was only remarkable in this, for the force of emphasis with which she did it. Thousands upon thousands do it, according to their varying manner every day."

Amy, the antithesis of Mrs Clennam, first appears in Chapter 3. Twenty-two at the time, she has been employed by Arthur's mother for two years. Working twelve hours a day to support her father and two siblings, as she has done for the last nine years, she gives little thought to her own welfare and selflessly cares for those around her. Referred to as the "child of the Marshalsea", on account of her having been born in the debtors' prison, she lost her mother when she was eight. By her own choice, she remains in the prison to support her father, William Dorrit, and her older brother and sister, Edward and Fanny.

In the narrative, Dickens uses the metaphor of the prison both to undermine the legalistic spirit typified by Mrs Clennam and those she represents, and to vindicate the genuine Christian virtue of grace. Arthur's mother, who has not left her room for around twelve years, is spiritually bound by her own guilty secret and harsh, erroneous interpretation of the Old Testament.

Although unsure of the details, Arthur has a vague sense that his parents have wronged someone. His suspicion is at first aroused by the words engraved within his deceased father's gold watch: "Do not Forget". It transpires that Mrs Clennam's husband became involved with a singer, connected with Amy's uncle Frederick. They had a son, Arthur. Forcibly taking him away from his mother and adopting him as her own child, Mrs Clennam imprisoned the natural mother, who eventually went mad and died. Arthur's father was banished to China, where his son joined him when he reached his twentieth birthday.

As the story unfolds, it is revealed that Amy's father is in fact an heir to fortune. Leaving the debtors' prison, her family, including Frederick, embark on a grand tour of Europe. Unlike Fanny, Edward, and her father, Amy remains completely unspoilt by the family's dramatic change in circumstances. On learning that Arthur has suffered financial misfortune, she once again returns to the Marshalsea to save the man she loves.

In Chapters 30 and 31 of Book the Second, the dramatic religious climax of the novel occurs. Blackmailed by the evil Blandois, who has come to know of her secret through meeting Arthur's mother's jailer, Mrs Clennam, gripped by a sort of wild possession, flies from the house to speak to Amy. Blandois has sent her a package detailing all that has taken place. Conspicuously dressed in black, Mrs Clennam's spectral appearance and frantic flight attract the attention of numerous passers-by. Arriving at the prison, and having been shown to Arthur's room, law and grace confront each other.

On confirming that Amy has received the package from Blandois, Mrs Clennam asks her to read the enclosed papers. After she has done so, she kneels at her feet and cries, "Forgive me. Can you forgive me?" Amy replies, "I can, and heaven knows I do! I forgive you freely." After Amy has raised her up, Mrs Clennam continues, "I have done what it was given to me to do. I have set myself against evil; not against good. I have been an instrument of severity against sin. Have not mere sinners, like myself, been commissioned to lay it low in all time!"

In her impassioned response, Amy declares the essence of the author's own Christ-centred beliefs:

> O Mrs Clennam, Mrs Clennam… angry feeling and unforgiving are no comfort and no guide to you and me. My life has passed in prison, and my teaching has been very defective; but let me implore you to be guided only by the healer of the sick, the riser of the dead, the friend of all who were afflicted and forlorn, the patient Master who shed tears of compassion for our infirmities. We cannot but be right if we put all the rest away, and do everything in remembrance of Him.

Immediately after this conversation, Amy agrees to accompany Mrs Clennam back to her home to confront the blackmailer, Blandois. On the way, Dickens signals the profound spiritual metaphor that is about to take place:

> As they crossed the bridge the beauties of the sunset had not faded from the long light films of cloud that lay at peace on the horizon. From a radiant centre over the whole length and breadth of the tranquil firmament, great shoots of light streamed among the early stars like signs of the blessed covenant of peace and hope that changed the crown of thorns into glory.

Approaching Mrs Clennam's, they hear a sudden noise like thunder, and a few seconds later, following another thundering sound, her house collapses into a heap of rubble. At the exact same moment, Mrs Clennam falls to the ground and from that time until her death, three years later, is unable to speak or move.

The destruction of the building and the fate of its owner is used by Dickens to symbolize the relationship between law and grace. The former, representative of the old covenant, had been superseded by the new. Retribution, self-righteousness, and condemnation needed to be replaced by grace, love, and compassion. Individual faith, and the transformation of society, depended upon the adoption of these Christ-like qualities and the rejection of manmade legalism, which sought to justify itself by referring to the retributive depiction of God in the Old Testament. What the Victorian Church needed were Amy Dorrits, not Mrs Clennams.

Within days of completing *Little Dorrit* in June 1857, Dickens attended a production of Talfourd's *Atalanta* at the Royal Theatre in Haymarket. Playing the part of Hippomenes was a pretty, fair-headed actress by the name of Ellen Ternan. The same age as his daughter Kate, she at once caught his eye. She came to his attention again, soon afterwards, when she was recommended to play a part in Wilkie Collins's melodrama *The Frozen Deep* in Manchester, in aid of the Jerrold family. Alfred Wigan suggested both Ellen and her sister, Maria, to perform in the production, and, on 18 August, Maria and Ellen met with Dickens at the Gallery of Illustration to rehearse their respective parts. The performances were a great success.

The following month, on learning that Mrs Ternan and her three daughters (Fanny being the eldest) were performing in *Pet of The Petticoats* at Doncaster theatre, during the popular horse-racing week, Dickens went up to visit them in the company of Wilkie Collins. Within weeks of his return, two significant events took place which foreshadowed the end of his marriage. On 11 October he instructed his wife's maid, Anne Cornelius, to arrange for the marital bedroom to be partitioned. From this point on, they would no longer sleep together. Two days later, he wrote to his friend, John Buckstone, at the Haymarket Theatre, thanking him for employing Ellen and enclosing £50 for her. She was to remain there for two years.

In the spring of 1858, Dickens wrote to Angela Burdett Coutts on the subject of the deterioration of his relationship with Catherine: "I believe that no two people were ever created, with such an impossibility of interest and sympathy, confidence, sentiment, tender union of any kind between them, as there is between my wife and me – but Nature has put an insurmountable barrier between us, which never in this world can be thrown down." The truth of the matter was that he no longer loved his wife. His affections were engaged elsewhere.

By May, he had put forward three possible options for an informal separation: Catherine could have her own apartment at Tavistock House, and appear alongside him at formal and social events; they could take turns alternating between Gad's Hill Place, which he had purchased two years earlier, and Tavistock House; or she could go abroad without her children. She, not surprisingly, rejected all three proposals. Following this, a separation settlement was negotiated between John Forster (Charles's representative) and Mark Lemon (Catherine's representative). Under the terms agreed, his wife would receive an annual allowance of £600, the use of the carriage, and a house, paid for by Dickens, at 70 Gloucester Crescent, on the edge of Camden Town.

On the day that Catherine left Tavistock House, effectively marking the end of their marriage, her sister, Georgina, took their youngest son, Edward, and the girls, Mary (Mamie) and Kate, with her to Gad's Hill Place. With Walter having gone to India, and Frank, Alfred, Henry, and Sydney all at school in Boulogne, the only consolation Catherine Dickens had was the company of her oldest son, Charley, who, while not falling out with his father, decided that his loyalty rested with his mother.

Catherine, understandably, was devastated by the separation. Twenty-two years of marriage, ten children, at least three miscarriages, and now she was cast aside. In writing to her aunt, she revealed her heartbreak:

... you will understand and feel for me when I tell you that I still love and think of their father too much for my peace of mind. I trust by God's assistance to be able to resign myself to His will, and to lead a contented if not happy life, but my position is a sad one, and time only may blunt the keen pain that will throb at my heart, but I will indeed try to struggle hard against it.

Following the separation, until his death, twelve years later, Dickens's attitude towards his wife was one of general indifference.

Though there was some speculation linking the author to Ellen Ternan at the time of the separation, the anger of Catherine's family, most noticeably her mother and youngest daughter, Helen, was directed towards Georgina Hogarth. Now thirty-one, she was only fifteen when she joined the Dickens household. Invaluable in looking after the children when Dickens and her sister were in America (1842), Aunt Georgy quickly became their much-loved surrogate mother. Just as with her older sister, Mary, a special relationship developed between the writer and his sister-in-law. Six years prior to the separation, she had received a proposal from one of the author's friends, the artist, Augustus Egg. Despite her brother-in-law's prompting, she declined the offer, preferring to remain single.

For the rest of his life, Dickens would depend on the woman who "knows everything", to run his household and care for his children. Describing her as "the best, the most unselfish, and most devoted of human creations", she, along with his two daughters and Ellen Ternan (Nell), became the only four women in his life. There can be little doubt that Georgina loved her brother-in-law, and he returned her affection. Along with John Forster, she was appointed as his executor and was bequeathed £8,000, most of his personal jewellery, and his private papers. (Ellen received £1,000, as did Mary [Mamie].)

Although Georgina Hogarth's attachment to the writer was decidedly unusual, following his separation from her sister, it probably was not inappropriate. Dickens's involvement with Ellen

Ternan and the children's love for her, even after their father's death, support this view. The same cannot be said of the intelligent, wilful, and playful Nell. Unable to divorce or marry, Charles, now forty-six, conducted a clandestine relationship with her for the last twelve years of his life.

The period of their relationship between 1862 and 1865 was of particular importance. The information available would suggest that at some point during this time, Ellen Ternan bore Dickens a son while living in France.

Around five miles south of Boulogne, not far from the Norman castle of Hardelot, lies the village of Cordette. There, in an unassuming chalet owned by Monsieur Beaucourt-Mutuel, the couple spent a considerable amount of time. Following the construction of the Boulogne and Amiens railway in 1847, travel between England and France became a lot quicker. Leaving London, Dickens would travel on the train to Folkestone and then catch one of the two daily ferries. It was a journey with which he became very familiar, making it on at least sixty-eight occasions between 1862 and 1865. The timing and frequency of these unaccompanied visits would indicate that Nell was resident there for most or all of the time.

After the death of Ellen in 1914, Dickens's daughter, Kate, confided to her friend, Gladys Storey, that they had had a child, a son. This was later confirmed by the author's son, Henry. This, and other information, appeared in Storey's biography of Kate, *Dickens and Daughter* (1939). The confinement and subsequent birth of the child would have taken place during the Cordette period. There has been some speculation that the baby was actually born in Paris and that the records of the birth were destroyed, due to the fire that took place in 1871. The baby's life must have been short. In June 1863, both Ellen and her mother failed to attend Maria's wedding, which would suggest that the child had either been born close to this date, or died shortly after being born.

Though the exact dates are not known, what is certain is that on their return to England on Friday, 9 June 1865, the first-class carriage in which they travelled contained only Dickens, Ellen, and

Mrs Ternan. As they boarded the 2.38 p.m. tidal train at Folkestone station, on what was a bright, sunny afternoon, any thought that it marked the beginning of a period of recuperation and recovery was abruptly shattered within less than an hour.

Having passed the town of Headcorn, they approached the Staplehurst viaduct over the river Beult – around forty-miles south-east of London. As they approached the bridge, travelling at 50 mph, panic ensued: two rails had been removed, leaving a gap of forty-two feet. The foreman in charge of the work had looked at the wrong timetable and had not expected the train for another two hours. Despite the driver's best efforts, seven of the eight first-class carriages plummeted down the bank into the river. The remaining one, which contained Dickens and the two ladies, was left precariously hanging over the bridge.

Even though he was suffering from anxiety and emotional upheaval, the writer reacted with remarkable energy and kindness. On safely removing Ellen and her mother from the carriage, he set about helping his fellow passengers. Filling his top hat with water and utilizing his brandy flask, he clambered down the bank, helping those he could. In all, ten people died and forty were seriously injured.

Six months after the Stapleton rail disaster, one young man, aged seventeen, Edward Dickenson, had very good reason to thank his Christmas host. As he enjoyed a convivial, seasonal evening as a guest at Gad's Hill Place, he could not help but remember how Dickens had pulled him out of the wreckage, then, personally, took him to Charing Cross Hospital. Afterwards, even though he was a complete stranger, Dickens visited him regularly during his convalescence. The author never fully recovered from the shock of the crash. For the rest of his life, train travel was to prove a trial.

In 1876, six years after Dickens's death, Ellen married George W. Robinson. The son of clergyman, he was a teacher, who went on to become a headmaster at a boys' school in Margate. They had two children: Geoffrey and Gladys. On leaving Margate, they moved to Southsea, Portsmouth, to be near her sisters. Her sister, Maria died of cancer in 1904, and, when Ellen was widowed, six years later, she moved in with Fanny. The sisters lived happily together for three years until Fanny's death.

Ellen died in 1914 and was buried within a few miles of the house where Dickens had been born 102 years earlier. Georgina Hogarth remained close friends with her, and her children, until her death. It was not until her son, Geoffrey, returned to England in 1920, after a period of six years in the army, that he learnt the truth about his mother's relationship with the great writer.

22

THE TRIUMPH OF HIS
LATTER YEARS

The month after Catherine agreed to the separation, Dickens made a serious error of judgment. In an attempt to justify his actions towards Catherine, he decided, against the advice of John Forster, to make a public statement about his marital affairs. Whereas the breakup of the marriage had, in the main, passed relatively unnoticed, even among his wider social circle, it would not do so once it became public knowledge. On Wednesday, 12 June 1858, the numerous readers of *Household Words* were surprised to find a personal announcement from the editor referring to aspects of his private life on the front page. It was to appear in other newspapers around the same time, including *The Times*. When Dickens asked the editor of *Punch*, his close friend, Mark Lemon, who had acted on Catherine's behalf during the separation negotiations, to publish his statement on 17 June, Lemon refused. Extremely annoyed, Dickens approached his publishers, Bradbury and Evans, who were also the proprietors of *Punch*. They supported Lemon's decision. The quarrel that ensued signalled the end of the two men's friendship. There can be no doubt that the fault lay with Dickens.

If the decision to publish his statement was ill-advised, what was to follow was ten times worse. Charles decided to entrust to his manager, Arthur Smith, a much more explicit explanation of his differences with his wife. He passed it on with the vague instruction that Smith was to use his own discretion in deciding who to give the letter to. It somehow ended up in the hands of the London correspondent of the *New York Tribune*, who duly published it. Later in the summer, it appeared in several British newspapers.

The author's anger at Bradbury and Evans's decision not to publish his statement in *Punch* was expressed on both a personal and business level. He strongly disapproved of his son Charley's decision to marry Frederick Evans's daughter, Bessie, and refused to attend the wedding in November 1861. On returning from his reading tour in November 1858, Dickens instructed Forster to approach the publishers with a demand that they sell their interest in *Household Words* to him. When they declined, he threatened not only to resign, but also to set up a rival weekly publication. Two months afterwards, he was busy trying to come up with a suitable title for his new venture. As always, Forster's advice proved invaluable. When Dickens suggested it should be called "Household Harmony", his friend pointed out that in view of recent events such a name would be wholly inappropriate.

A few days later, on 28 January, having considered various names, Dickens once again turned to Shakespeare for inspiration. On reading the quote: "The story of our lives, from year to year" in *Othello*, he settled on *All the Year Round*. By the following month, he had secured premises at 11 Wellington Street, the Strand – only five doors away from the *Household Words* building. With five rooms above the office, it was, after the sale of Tavistock House in 1860, to become his main London residence.

On cutting all ties with Bradbury and Evans, the author returned to Chapman and Hall for both his new journal and all his remaining books. Not for the first time, adverse circumstances and change brought out the very best in Dickens as a writer. From the moment the first weekly edition appeared on 30 April 1859, it was an outstanding success. The print run for the second number was 100,000. By the fifth, it had trebled the circulation of Household Words, the last edition of which came out on 28 May. Arthur Smith purchased the stock, plates, and use of the title on behalf of the author for £3,550. Thereafter, the phrase "with which is incorporated Household Words" was to be found on the title page of *All the Year Round*. By August/September 1861 its sales would exceed that of *The Times* and had reached a staggering 300,000. While its meteoric success was, in part, due to the recruitment of a team of aspiring young writers, including Edmund Yates, George Sala, Percy Fitzgerald, and John Hollingshead, the overriding factor was Dickens himself.

The first issue made an immediate impression, as it contained the opening instalment of his new novel, *A Tale of Two Cities*, which ran until November. In January 1860, the following year, the first of his seventeen *Uncommercial Traveller* pieces appeared, and, in December, *Great Expectations* began. Added to this, each year, he would produce show-stopping Christmas stories. For example, *Doctor Marigold* (1866) sold 256,000. Two of Wilkie Collins's best-known novels, *The Woman in White* and *Moonstone*, were also first serialized in the journal.

When, in March 1859, Dickens settled at his desk to begin *A Tale of Two Cities*, he must have been apprehensive, not having written a novel for nearly two years. Set against the background of the French Revolution, the narrative explores the themes of the resurrection and self-sacrifice.

Inevitably, due to the turmoil and anguish he had been experiencing, aspects and images from Dickens's own life surface within the book. This is especially the case with regard to his sense of imprisonment within his marriage and Sidney Carton's relationship with Lucie Manette, who, in appearance, is very similar to Ellen Ternan. One particular scene, involving Sidney Carton taking a long look at himself in the mirror, stands out. There is a definite sense of Charles examining his own soul and, as with his fictional self, finding causes for regret.

The motif of the resurrection is introduced right at the start of the book, when Jarvis Lorry sends the cryptic message "Recalled to Life" to his employers at Tellson's Bank. Dozing in the carriage, he dreams of digging out of his grave a man who has been buried for nearly eighteen years. The individual involved is Alexandre

Manette. Formerly the doctor of Beauvais (a town thirty miles from Paris), he was falsely imprisoned in the Bastille by the Marquis of St Evrémonde. His English wife, exhausting herself in an attempt to find out about her husband's fate, died when their daughter, Lucie, was two. Believing her father to be dead, they are reunited at the Paris wine-shop run by her father's former servant, Defarge.

The next reference to the resurrection occurs in instalment thirteen. Jeremiah Cruncher, the porter/messenger and general odd-job man of Tellson's Bank has a dark secret. In an attempt to take revenge on the French aristocracy, the Revolutionary Council employ a spy, John Barsad, who assumes the name of Roger Cly, to track down Charles Darnay, the nephew of the evil Marquis of St Evrémonde. On being identified in London as a French agent, Barsad fakes his own death. Sitting outside the bank in Fleet Street, Cruncher spots the funeral procession. That night, along with two other men, he enters the churchyard on the pretence of going fishing with a view to stealing the body and selling it to members of the medical profession. Individuals who committed such crimes were referred to as "Resurrection Men".

Dickens's third and most poignant reference, relates to Sidney Carton's Christ-like sacrifice. Irresponsible, despite having the potential to be a great lawyer, Carton settles for a supportive role, working for the barrister, Stryver. Involved in acquitting Charles Darnay, who has been falsely accused of being a spy, Carton meets and falls in love with Lucie Manette. Becoming painfully aware of his own shortcomings, he realizes that he can never marry her, so he pledges his friendship and protection to her and her loved ones.

Darnay, now married to Lucie, goes to Paris in the hope of rescuing his deceased uncle's employee, Gabelle. When he arrives, he is arrested and tried on the basis of being related to the Marquis of St Evrémonde. Lucie, along with her young daughter and father, travel to France to save him. Though initially successful, due to Dr Manette's status as a former prisoner of the aristocracy, Darnay is rearrested and sentenced to death.

In the meantime, Carton, transformed by his love for Lucie, arrives in Paris to fulfil his promise and comes up with a plan to rescue Darnay. Tracking down John Barsad (Roger Cly), he threatens to expose him as an English spy. Fearful for his life, Barsad agrees to take him into the Bastille to see Charles Darnay. While there, as they look very similar, Carton changes places with him. He has also provided the necessary passports to ensure that Darnay and his family can leave the city safely.

Before entering the prison, Carton walks the streets of Paris, reciting the Gospel of John 11:25: "I am the Resurrection and the life. He who believes in me will live even though he dies." These words, also part of the *Book of Common Prayer* Burial Service, were extremely familiar to his readers. Carton's willingness to die at the guillotine is Dickens's ultimate fictional expression of Christ-like sacrifice. In linking his death to love, the fulfilment of a promise, the powerless state of Darnay, and the similarities in appearance of the two men (Christ became like us, so he could die for us), the author develops the analogy of Carton's death and his resurrection hope.

Appearing in thirty-one instalments, between 30 April and 26 November 1859, and published in book form by Chapman and Hall a month later, it was the last novel to be illustrated by Phiz. He, like Mark Lemon before him, was dropped by the author for failing to support him over his separation from Catherine.

Dickens described the novel in glowing terms, saying it was "The best story I have written." The reason for this endorsement is, in part, to be found in its positive affirmation of his belief in the resurrection and the Christ-like values it promotes. There is also a very real sense in which his characterization of Sydney Carton provided the writer with the opportunity to search his own soul and make sense of his own life.

At the conclusion of the publication of Wilkie Collins's novel *The Woman in White*, Dickens, unable to secure the services of either Elizabeth Gaskell or George Eliot, whose books had been serialized by him in the past, decided to publish Charles Lever's, *A Day Ride*. Starting in July 1860, it proved unsuccessful. As a result, for the first, and only time, the circulation of *All the Year Round* began to fall. Following an emergency office meeting, the author, once again, took it upon himself to remedy the situation.

Working on a little sketch for his *Uncommercial Traveller* series, he decided to extend it into a novel of similar length to *A Tale of Two Cities*. So it was that the *All the Year Round* edition of 1 December opened with the first of the thirty-six instalments of *Great Expectations*. Appearing weekly thereafter, it was published in three volumes by Chapman and Hall in July 1861. By the end of August, the fourth edition was going to press.

Set in the period and location of his childhood in Kent, the novel seemed to spring spontaneously from the depths of Dickens's imagination. Dispensing with his normal practice of using working notes, within a couple of weeks of starting at the end of September, he had already written four chapters.

Investing much of his own self into the main character, Philip Pirrip (Pip), the novel is unique in that Dickens was persuaded to change the end. This is of particular importance as Pip's consuming love for Estella mirrors his own for Ellen. Believing he had completed the novel on 11 June, Dickens sent a copy to his friend and fellow-writer, Edward Bulwer Lytton. On reading through it, Lytton suggested that the ending, in which Estella and Pip go their separate ways, should be changed.

After discussing the matter with Ellen, Charles agreed. Pip and Estella meet in the ruined garden of Miss Havisham's former home, Satis House, where they first met. Reunited in love and compassion, they leave holding hands, with Pip "seeing no shadow of parting from her".

Although, as with *Martin Chuzzlewit*, there is little religious content within *Great Expectations*, what is there is extremely revealing of Dickens's own situation and beliefs. Though, throughout much of the narrative, Pip believes his change in fortune is due to the patronage of Miss Havisham, he discovers that his benefactor is, in fact, the convict Abel Magwitch, whom he helped as a boy. Also the father of Estella, Magwitch secretly returns to London. On attempting to return to Australia, he is betrayed by his old adversary, Compeyson, a criminal informant and the man that jilted Miss Havisham on her wedding day. Intercepted on the Thames, Magwitch temporarily evades the police long enough to kill him. Injured in the process, Magwitch is taken to the prison infirmary.

Each day, Pip visits and reads to him from the Bible. The only occasion that Dickens identifies the text being read is the day Magwitch dies. The passage, "The Parable of the Pharisee and the Tax Collector" (Luke 18:9–14), both expresses what Dickens felt constituted genuine heartfelt religion and reveals something of his own spiritual state at the time. It begins with a statement that encapsulates the writer's view of those who adopted a self-righteous, puritanical religious approach: "To some who were confident of their own righteousness and looked down on everybody else Jesus told this parable." The first of the two characters, a Pharisee, exalts his own righteousness before God, emphasizes his own religious observance, and condemns the second man, a tax collector. Under the rule of the Roman Empire, tax collectors were usually social outcasts. But in this case, the tax collector, who does not even feel worthy of looking up to heaven, cries out to God, "Have mercy on me, a sinner." The parable ends with Jesus' words: "I tell you that this man, rather than the other went home justified before God."

On Thursday, 29 April 1858, Dickens stepped onto the stage at St Martin's Hall, Covent Garden, to give his first ever reading for his own financial gain. Prior to this, he had given six readings for the benefit of various charitable institutions and organizations that sought to help the poor and labouring classes. That first evening, just a month before his separation from Catherine, he effectively embarked on a second career, which was to prove far more lucrative than his writing. The audience of 2,000 (hundreds were turned away) was captivated as he read a selection of his work, including Paul Dombey's death. Originally only six readings were planned, but this was quickly increased to sixteen.

A month later, on 2 August, he set off on his first nationwide tour. Starting in Clifton (Bristol), he gave eighty-seven readings in forty-four separate venues, including three in Ireland and five in Scotland. The tour ended in Brighton on 13 November 1858.

There were to be four more. Added to this, there were three separate London events at St James's Hall (St Martin's Hall had burnt down). His final appearance was on 15 March 1870, three months before his death.

His public readings were an unprecedented success, both in terms of popularity and profitability. On the first of his nationwide tours, arranged by Chappell's, the theatrical management company based in New Bond Street, 3,000 people were turned away from the Liverpool venue. For this series, he was paid the sum of £1,500 for thirty readings, £50 a reading. Today, this would equate to something like £2,500 a reading. It has been estimated for the four Chappell tours alone that he earned in the region of £13,000 (around £650,000 in today's money).

Of equal importance to him was the adulation he received from his audience and the contact he had with them. Coming at such a difficult time in his life, it gave him a very real sense that he was loved by his public and that his work had a significance beyond that of mere entertainment. Despite all that had happened, he had remained the people's favourite. Perhaps, most importantly, it enriched his sense of purpose and confidence in his calling.

The theatrical side of Dickens's nature demanded that he produce not mere readings, but a series of dramatic performances. This, to all intents and purposes, is exactly what he did. The material that he used was not lifted from his books, but was rewritten and crafted into carefully designed scripts. Standing behind his specially built reading-desk, he would wait for absolute silence. Dressing identically for each performance, he would rest the elbow of the hand in which he held the book on the desk. Everything was meticulously managed: the stage lighting, focusing upon his face and figure, was affected by the use of dark curtains and gas illumination. He even employed his own gas man.

Using gestures, facial expressions, and intonations in his voice, he would fill the stage with a host of people without moving from his original position. He would jump between characters: one minute he was the elderly, comic Mrs Gamp (*Martin Chuzzlewit*), the next, the tragic child Paul Dombey. One of the most powerful readings was Sikes's murder of Nancy in *Oliver Twist*. Practising outdoors at Gad's Hill Place, his performance frightened those who overheard it. On 14 November 1868, he performed it to a select audience of 100 people at St James's Hall. Many were shocked. Added to his third Chappell's tour the following year, it became a tour de force. It was, however, to prove so emotionally and physically draining that he was advised by his doctor, Frank Beard, to drop it from his repertoire.

Such was Dickens's international acclaim that it was only a question of time before he was invited to undertake an overseas tour. In 1862, he was asked to consider the possibility of going to Australia. Having been offered £10,000 for the duration of eight months, he eventually decided against it. He could not, however, resist the opportunity to return to America. Refusing an initial offer made to him in 1860, he was approached seven years later by the Boston editor and publisher James Fields. The proposition was for him to give eighty readings (later reduced to seventy-six), for the huge sum of £20,000 (around £1,000,000 today).

In early August, three months later, Dickens's friend and reading manager, George Dolby, sailed across the Atlantic to assess the feasibility of the tour. On his return, despite the opposition of his close friends, John Forster and William Wills, Dickens telegraphed his acceptance to Fields on 30 September 1867.

Two months later, he attended a farewell banquet at London's Freeman's Hall organized by Charles Kent, the editor of the *Daily Telegraph*, Arthur Chappell, and Edmund Yates. Among the 550 guests were the Lord Mayor of London, the Lord Chief Justice, and the President of the Royal Academy. The music for the evening was provided by the band of the Grenadier Guards. The hall had been lavishly decorated with laurel leaves and the titles of Dickens's books in gilded lettering.

Though he enjoyed the grandeur of the evening, it was when he eventually left that he was most overcome: on stepping out into Great Queen Street, he was greeted by a cheering crowd, who, despite the lateness of the hour, had wanted to express their support and good wishes. These were the friends with whom he had shared his heart.

A week later, on 9 November, Dickens boarded the Cunard liner, Cuba, at Liverpool docks. Turning to wave goodbye to Georgina, Mary (Mamie), Kate, Charlie, and his friends, he walked along the deck and entered the second officer's cabin, which had been assigned to him. Dolby had gone on ahead the previous month, and his only travelling companion was his valet, Henry Scott.

Despite the negative publicity he had received from the press on his last visit on account of his views on copyright, Dickens's popularity in America had soared. Just before leaving England, he had received £2,000 for two short stories previously published in *All the Year Round*: "George Silverman's Explanation" (*Atlantic Monthly*) and "Holiday Romance" (*Our Young Folk* – a children's magazine). These stories were around half the length of a monthly instalment of one of his novels, and so the sum was enormous. Arriving in Boston on 19 November, he was welcomed into the home of James Fields.

The tour was a great success. Three days after his arrival, the tickets for his opening readings in Boston on 2 December went on sale at the offices of Ticknor and Fields. The first four performances were sold out in eleven hours. From Boston he travelled to New York, where, despite the heavy snow, the crowds still filled the venues. In January and February, he was in Philadelphia, Baltimore, and Washington, where, for the second time, he had a private audience with a president of the United States. His meeting with Andrew Johnson was all the more memorable because it took place on his fifty-sixth birthday.

On delivering his farewell reading in New York, Dickens boarded the Cunard liner, Russia, on 22 April. Invigorated by a refreshing return voyage, for which he had exclusive use of the Chief Steward's cabin, he arrived in Liverpool on 1 May 1868 and at Euston Station, London, the next day. Disappearing to spend a week with Ellen, he returned to a hero's welcome at Gad's Hill on 9 May.

Much of the material the writer chose for his performances – *A Christmas Carol*, *The Chimes*, *David Copperfield*, Paul Dombey's death, and Nancy's murder – allowed him to focus on those spiritual themes which were to feature so prominently in his work: the plight of the poor, social justice, death and the resurrection, and, in Nancy and Scrooge's case, redemption.

Returning from France in August 1863, Dickens discussed with Forster his plans for his next book, *Our Mutual Friend*. It was to be his last completed novel. Preferring to return to his writing roots, and instead of running it weekly in *All the Year Round*, he chose to publish it in twenty monthly instalments (1 May 1864 – November 1865). A two-volume book, illustrated by Marcus Stone, also came out in the November. The green wrappers of Chapman and Hall were to appear once again.

By the time he started to write it, in November 1863, it had been seven years since he completed *Little Dorrit*, his last lengthy novel. Having negotiating a fee of £6,000 (£2,500 on the publication of the initial and sixth numbers and £1,000 at the end), this was the first time that he acknowledged the possibility of dying before a book was completed. The opening number sold 30,000 copies in just three days, and it was to generate more advertising revenue than any of his previous serializations: £2,750.

The novel contains the author's final female angel, Lizzie Hexam. As with those that preceded her, she demonstrates remarkable self-sacrifice and selflessness on behalf of those she loves: her father, Jesse, her younger brother Charley, and Eugene Wrayburn. Saving the life of the latter, she also, through her love, gives him purpose.

Jesse Hexam, a morose, rough, ignorant man, makes a living pulling corpses out of the Thames. Suspected of having a hand in the deaths of some of those he recovers, he exists at the very margins of society, shunned by many. Lizzie, who assists him by rowing his boat, the Bird of Prey, is blighted by her association with him. Urged by Abby Potterson, the proprietor of the Six Jolly Fellowship Porters, to leave her father and "not fling her life away", Lizzie replies: "Thank you! I can't. I won't. I must not think of it. The harder father is borne upon, the more he needs me to lean on."

Having sacrificed her own future, Lizzie harbours great hopes for her brother. Having lost her mother when Charley was born,

Lizzie took upon herself the responsibility of bringing him up, a fact that he acknowledges: "Don't go saying I never knew a mother, for I knew a little sister that was sister and mother both." Understanding the importance of an education, though she forfeited hers to care for her brother and father, Lizzie has, through undertaking a variety of jobs, provided Charley with a place at school. It is her hope that, one day, he will become a teacher. Realizing the negative effect her father is having on Charley, she encourages him to move away from home and accept a full-time place at a school that offers accommodation. Despite the ungratefulness and hostility of both parent and sibling, Lizzie faithfully continues to care for both.

Following the drowning of her father, she moves in with a friend, Fanny Cleaver (Jenny Wren). Working as a needle-woman and managing the stock-room of a seamens' outfitters, she supports herself and her brother. By this point, she has attracted the interest of an idle, dissolute gentleman, by the name of Eugene Wrayburn. On first meeting Lizzie, he is immediately struck by her beauty and demeanour. Having fallen in love, he seeks to win her to himself. Painfully aware of the social gulf that exists between them, Lizzie, not wanting to discredit or disgrace him, rejects his advances even though she loves him. With the help of her Jewish friend, Riah, she leaves London secretly and starts a new life. Prior to leaving, she attracts the unwelcome attention of Charley's dangerously obsessive teacher, Bradley Headstone.

On discovering her whereabouts, Waryburn meets with her to declare his love. In doing so, Lizzie reveals her integrity: "'Think of me, as belonging to another station, and quite cut from you in honour... I am removed from you and your family by being a working girl." "The purity with which in these words she expressed something of her own love and her own suffering made a deep impression on him." A few moments after parting, Eugene is savagely attacked by the insanely jealous Headstone. Beaten about the head with an oar, he falls into the water. Lizzie, hearing a strange sound, hurries to the spot. Seeing someone in the water, she clambers into a nearby boat, praying as she does so. Using all her strength and expertise gained from her time with her father, she manages to pull the body into the boat. On recognizing it to be Eugene, she kisses his disfigured head, does her best to staunch the flow of blood, with strips from her dress, and rows upstream to the nearest inn, praying again as she does so.

Not knowing whether he will live or die, Lizzie consents to marry Eugene in his sickroom at the inn. In the conversation that follows and, subsequently, it becomes clear that as a result of Lizzie's love, he is resolved to repent of his wastefulness and is resolved to devote his energies and purpose towards a worthwhile end. Lizzie has not only saved his life, she has also transformed it.

Our Mutual Friend stands out because of its positive representation of Jews, which was unusual for the time, but which he felt he had to include. In August 1860, having made the offices of *All the Year Round* his London home, Dickens had sold the remaining thirty-six years of the Tavistock House lease on to a business man by the name of Davis. Some three years later, he had received a letter from Davis's wife, a Jewess, Eliza, in which she claimed he had wronged the Jewish people through his depiction of Fagin in *Oliver Twist*. As with many readers, past and present, she failed to notice his positive portrayal of a young Jewish woman who was imprisoned with Lord George Gordon in *Barnaby Rudge*.

Nonetheless, incredibly sensitive to the views of his readers, Dickens set about rectifying the perceived wrong in the pages of *Our Mutual Friend*. This he did superbly by reversing the prevailing Jewish/Christian stereotype. "Fascination" Fledgby, a hard-hearted, ruthless individual, in addition to being a slum landlord, owns a moneylending business, Pubsey and Co. He employs a Jew, Aaron Riah, to run his business and uses him as a smokescreen to conceal his own mercenary devices. Whenever he takes advantage of a customer or feigns reluctance to ease their predicament, Fledgby blames Riah. He would like to help, but his manager will not allow it; he would like to charge less interest, but he is powerless to resist the dictates of Riah. Yet it is the Christian, not the Jew, who is responsible.

Dickens is also at pains to depict the kindly, noble nature of his Jewish hero. Considered by Jenny Wren, a crippled child, with whom he eventually lives, as a kind of fairy godmother, it is Riah who helps Lizzie to escape London, by finding her work at a papermill owned by his Jewish friends. The author is also careful to detail the considerate nature of her employers. On having read *Our Mutual Friend*, Eliza Davis wrote once more, thanking Dickens for redressing the balance and atoning for his portrayal of Fagin. As a token of her gratitude, she also enclosed a copy of a Hebrew and English Bible.

Betty Higden, though only a minor character, is used to powerful effect in the novel. A laundress and a childminder to Johnny – the boy whom Mr and Mrs Boffin had hoped to adopt – she is representative of the godly poor. Elderly and determined, as were many thousands like her, not to enter the workhouse, she leaves her humble dwelling and travels around villages and towns around the Thames area, selling her various small crafts. So as not to be a burden to anyone should she die and to avoid a pauper's grave, she has, around her neck, a purse which contains a shilling to pay for her funeral.

On becoming unwell in a small market town, near where Lizzie Hexam now lives, she panics, thinking she will be taken, on account of being homeless, into the workhouse. She struggles to make her way into the surrounding countryside. Nearing death, she sees a tree by the wayside and, believing it to be the cross, she clings to it. As she settles on the ground, there is a definite link with the contemporary hymn, "Rock of Ages"[16]; the opening line of verse three reads: "Nothing in my hand I bring, simply to thy cross I cling."

In this gesture of simple faith, Dickens directs his readers to consider the atoning love of Christ, and the efficacy of his sacrifice, in which he himself believed. Seeing this old lady, Lizzie hurries to her aid. Looking up at her angelic face, Betty believes herself to be in heaven and dies in her arms.

---

16   Reverend Augustus Montague Toplady.

THE END

On the afternoon of Wednesday, 8 June 1870, Dickens completed the final page of his sixth monthly instalment of his latest novel, *The Mystery of Edwin Drood*. Poignantly, it was to be the last thing he was ever to write. The experience of walking back through the tunnel that linked his writing chalet with the garden of Gad's Hill Place reminded him of the passage he had just written:

> *A brilliant morning shines on the old city. Its antiquities and ruins are surprisingly beautiful, with a lusty ivy gleaming in the sun, and the rich trees waving in the balmy air. Changes of glorious light from moving boughs, songs of birds, scents from gardens, woods and fields – or rather from the one great garden of the whole cultivated island in its yielding time – penetrate into the Cathedral, subdue its dusty odour, and preach the Resurrection and the Life. The cold stone tombs of centuries ago grow warm and flecks of brightness dart into the sternest marble corners of the building, fluttering there like wings.*

The passing from the shade of the tunnel into the brilliant light was also to serve as a spiritual metaphor of his approaching death.

The book, his fifteenth, was not finished and has attracted a great deal of interest and speculation: how would he have finished it? He was exactly halfway through, having just completed the twenty-third chapter before he died. Many have attempted to solve the conundrum as to the identity of Edwin Drood's murderer, with John Jasper, the individual responsible for directing choral services at Cloisterham Cathedral, proving the prime suspect.

What is known, however, is that on 13 December 1869, Dickens signed a contract with Chapman and Hall worth £7,500. This represented the highest amount he had ever received and was, quite possibly, the most ever paid for a single book up to that point in time. The American rights went to Harpers for £1,000. For the last time, on 1 April 1870, the public flocked to buy the first instalment of a new Dickens novel. By the time the final sixth instalment appeared, sales had reached 50,000, 20,000 more than *Our Mutual Friend*. This was in addition to the 300,000 copies of *All the Year Round* that were selling each week.

The unprecedented popularity of Dickens's work in the last few years of his life was, to a large extent, attributable to his public readings. At 8.00 p.m. on Monday, 15 March, Dickens walked out onto the stage of St James's Hall to give his four hundred and fiftieth and final reading. As he did so, the audience of 2,000 people rose to their feet and cheered. Delayed for several minutes, Dickens began, as he had done seventeen years earlier at his first public reading in Birmingham Town Hall, with *A Christmas Carol*. This was followed by the trial from *The Pickwick Papers*.

As on the previous eleven occasions, Frank Beard and Charley were positioned on the front row in the event of his collapsing. There was no cause for alarm, Dickens performed magnificently. Leaving the stage to thunderous applause and cheering, he was coaxed back. Never one to miss an opportunity, on his return he gave a brief farewell speech, which concluded with his advertising *The Mystery of Edwin Drood*. Having done so, he kissed his hand and then was gone.

Just six days before his last reading, Dickens was invited to Buckingham Palace for a private audience with Queen Victoria. She had been a fan since reading *Oliver Twist* at the age of eighteen. Although in Windsor, she made a special trip to Buckingham Palace in London to accommodate the writer, who was unable to travel far because of his health. This was not the only concession that she was to make. Royal protocol demanded that he should stand throughout the meeting. Mindful of the pain he was feeling, rather than remaining seated, the Queen stood with him for the duration of their conversation.

The Queen expressed regret that she had not heard the author read. Refusing to put on a special reading for her benefit, he neglected to tell her of his farewell performance. It was not the first time he had failed to acquiesce to Her Majesty's request. Thirteen years before, after seeing Dickens's production of *The Frozen Deep* at the Gallery of Illustration in Regent's Street, she asked him to put on a private showing for her and her guests. He respectfully informed her that it would not be possible. It was rumoured that Dickens had declined a knighthood, as he always considered himself to be a man of the people. Their meeting ended with the Queen presenting Charles with a copy of the book she had written, *Leaves from the Journal of Our Life in the Highlands*, and he agreed to pass on a special red and gold bound set of his own work. He was most likely amused by her gift, for two years earlier, while he was in the United States, he had chastised William Willis for reviewing Her Majesty's book in the pages of *All the Year Round*: "I would not have had that reference made to the Queen's preposterous book (I have read it) for any set of money. I blush to join the shameful lick-spittle chorus. It is amazing to me, knowing my opinions on such matters that you could have passed it."

On hearing of Dickens's death, the Queen wrote in her diary: "He is a very great loss. He had a large loving mind and the strongest sympathy with the poor classes."

She was not the only reigning monarch to have an audience with the writer. In May, Dickens was invited to dine at Lord Houghton's where he was joined by Victoria's cousin, Leopold II, King of the Belgians, and the Prince of Wales. It was not only royalty who courted the author. In the same month, he dined with the American Ambassador, John Lothrop Motley, and two British prime ministers, Disraeli and Gladstone. Dickens's literary genius served as a passport to the higher echelons of society. Yet he never allowed social ambition to distract him from his crusading ideals and Christian values. Far from aspiring to be part of the establishment, he set himself against it in his fight for social justice.

In April 1870, Constance Cross, a young aspiring writer, came to visit Dickens at his Gad's Hill home. The purpose of the meeting, arranged through their mutual friend, Edward Bulwer Lytton, was for him to pass on some advice. During the course of the conversation, he confided to his guest that it was his heartfelt hope to die at Gad's Hill Place. When asked if he had considered the possibility of failing to complete book he had started, he loosely quoted from John 9: "As long as it is light we must work, for when darkness comes no one can work." This verse is followed by Jesus' declaration that he is the light of the world.

On the night of Sunday, 5 June, after Georgia and Mary had gone to bed, Dickens and his youngest daughter, Kate, stayed up to the early hours. Initially asking her father's advice about whether she should become an actress, they went on to have an unusually candid and heartfelt conversation in which he confessed that he wished he had been "a better father and a better man". Having discussed issues they had never touched on before, including, no doubt, his separation and his relationship with Ellen, he went on to confide in her that he felt he would not live to finish *The Mystery of Edwin Drood*.

The following morning, the two sisters were due to catch a train at Higham Station. Since he disliked partings, their father had breakfasted at 7.30 a.m. and had gone to the chalet to work. Waiting by the porch for the carriage, Kate had an overpowering desire to say goodbye to her father. Running through the garden, along the tunnel, and up the chalet stairs, she found him writing away at his desk. Ordinarily, he would have raised his head for a kiss and said a few affectionate words, but on this occasion he pushed back his chair from his desk, rushed towards her, and took her in his arms. Kissing her, he said, "God bless you Katie." They were to be the last words she would hear her father say.

Two days later, having worked on the book and written several letters, he entered the dining room at 6.00 p.m. Because he looked decidedly unwell, Georgina, the only one present, asked if he felt ill. He replied, "Yes, very ill. I have been very ill for the last hour." Shortly afterwards, he began to speak incoherently. When she suggested that he lie down, he replied, "Yes, on the ground." Those were to be his final words. Isaac, the young houseboy, was immediately dispatched to fetch Dr Steele, who arrived half an hour later. He held out little hope. With the help of the servants, a narrow green sofa was brought in from the drawing room and Dickens was placed upon it.

Around midnight, Mary, Kate, and Frank Beard arrived. Watching him through the night, his daughters took turns placing hot bricks under his cold feet. Initially, Beard believed that Dr Steele's prognosis was incorrect, but the London specialist who was sent for advised them that the writer had suffered a brain haemorrhage. It was now only a matter of time.

In the morning, Charley arrived, and later Ellen. With whispered voices and heavy hearts they all waited. At around 6.10 p.m. on Thursday, 9 June, Dickens gave a deep sigh, and a tear from his right eye ran down his cheek. The great man was dead. Sadly, neither his son, Henry, who heard the news from a railway porter, or his sister, Letitia, arrived in time to witness this final scene.

That evening and throughout the following day, Dickens's favourite flowers, scarlet geraniums and blue lobelias, were laid on and beside his body. As Kate arranged them, tears came into her eyes, as she remembered what she had said to him sometime before: "Well, really, Papa, I think when you're an angel your wings will be made of looking-glass, and your crown of scarlet geraniums."

The dining room windows, which looked out on his beloved glass conservatory and into the garden beyond, were deliberately left uncurtained. So it was that as he lay upon the sofa, his body, surrounded by flowers, was bathed in light. He, who worked so diligently, while it was day, had gone to his eternal rest.

In direct contrast to the subdued, mournful atmosphere of Gad's Hill Place, news of Dickens's death spread quickly throughout England, Europe, and the world. The outpouring of public grief that ensued and the desire to honour his passing quickly presented the family and the grief-stricken Forster, who had arrived on the Saturday from Cornwall, with an unforeseen complication.

Shortly after he died, Charley, aware of his father's wish to be buried quietly in the Kent countryside he loved, approached the clergyman of the parish church of St Peter and St Paul in the nearby village of Shorne. No sooner had they chosen a spot on the east side of the churchyard, the family received a request from the Dean and Chapter of Rochester Cathedral that he be buried there because of the author's long-term affection for the city. The family agreed, and a grave was duly dug in the Chapel of St Mary. How fitting it was that he should be buried within the cathedral in which he set his last, unfinished book.

On Monday, 13 June, following *The Times* editorial calling for Dickens to be buried in Westminster Abbey, the family plans were, once again, superseded. By eleven o'clock that morning, Charley and Forster met with Dean Arthur Stanley to discuss the funeral arrangements. As executor, Forster was charged with the responsibility of insisting that the author's wishes be observed: there were to be just three plain mourning coaches, no funeral pomp of any kind, and no public announcement of the time or place of the burial.

Early the next day, the plain oak coffin was taken from Gad's Hill Place to Higham Station. It was transported by rail to Charing Cross. Family and friends, travelling on the same train, were met by a plain hearse and three coaches. As they entered the Abbey precincts, the great bell tolled. The Dean and Canons met the fourteen mourners and escorted them, and the coffin, through the western cloister door, along the nave, and into the south transept, where Poet's Corner was situated.

The Burial Service was read, the service concluded. The only music that was played was the "Death March" as the mourners departed. It was just as Dickens demanded, simple and no fuss. Neither he, nor anyone else, could have foreseen the spontaneous demonstration of grief, love, and gratitude that was to follow.

Despite the supposedly secret nature of the venue and time of the funeral, a great crowd had already gathered at the Abbey, even before the afternoon papers revealed the details of the burial. Thousands of people came to pay their respects that day. Filing past the open five-foot grave, close to the bust of Thackeray, many dropped in flowers. Very soon it was full to overflowing. By the time the Abbey closed at 6.00 p.m., there were still around 1,000 people outside.

For the next two days, an endless procession passed through. Among the innumerable floral tributes were a considerable number of roughly picked wild flowers, held together with strips of rags. It was these, symbols of affection from the poor and vulnerable, that he would have treasured most.

Just as his life had been subject to a series of providential moments, so, too, was his death. On the Thursday night, there was to be one last visitor: Lord Houghton, who had played some part in calling for Dickens to be buried in the Abbey. On learning from Dean Stanley that the grave was not to be closed until near midnight, he entered the dimly lit building, lantern in hand. It was a scene straight from the pages of one of the author's novels. On returning home, he recalled all that he had seen and felt to his wife, Annabel, the grand-daughter of Lord John Crewe, for whom Charles's grandparents had worked. As she listened, she remembered how her mother, Henrietta, used to tell her of the Crewe Hall housekeeper who kept her and her sister entertained with numerous stories. Storytelling was in Dickens's blood.

On Sunday, 19 June, Dean Arthur Stanley, a broad churchman, after Dickens's own heart, stood in the Abbey pulpit to deliver his memorial sermon for the deceased writer. Using as his text the Rich Man and Lazarus (Luke 16), he went on to explain how the author had removed the veil which separated the rich from the poor and that he had possessed the "dramatic" power "of making things which were not seen be as even though they were seen. It was this remarkable gift that made Dickens, the parabler, the advocate of the absent poor." Those who read his work, thanks to their most influential friend, could no longer feign ignorance of the appalling plight of the poor.

The Times, although it had not always been a fervent supporter of the writer, wrote in his obituary (Friday, 10 June):

We cannot conclude these remarks without paying tribute to the moral influence of the writings of which we have spoken. Mr. Dickens was a man of an eminently kindly nature, and full of sympathy for all around him. We have no doubt whatever that much of the active benevolence of the present day, the interest in humble persons and humble things, and the desire to seek and relieve every form of misery is due to the influence of his works.

On the afternoon that he collapsed, a letter was found on his desk. Addressed to a clergyman who had written regarding *The Mystery of Edwin Drood*, it contained this personal reflection on his work: "I have always striven in my writings to express veneration for the life and lessons of our Saviour."

Anthony Trollope observed that Dickens "was the largest-hearted man he ever knew". His was a religion of the heart, a practical faith that was demonstrated through works and character. Living during a period of unprecedented industrial, social, scientific, and intellectual change, in which long-cherished religious precepts were being challenged, he intuitively understood the importance of appealing directly to the hearts of his readers. His was an unashamedly sentimental approach to communicating Christianity; but it was no less effective for being so. His abiding greatness rested in his unparalleled ability to weave material relating to social reform and faith seamlessly into the fabric of his writing.

SELECT BIBLIOGRAPHY

In the writing of this book, and over the years, I have found the following volumes extremely helpful.

Ackroyd, Peter, *Dickens*, London: Vintage, 2002.

Allen, Michael, *Charles Dickens's Childhood*, London: St Martin's Press, 1988.

Dent, H. C., *The Life and Characters of Charles Dickens*, London: Odhams Press, 1930.

DeVries, Duane, *Dickens' Apprentice Years*, London: Harvester Press, 1976.

Fielding, K. J. (ed.), *The Speeches of Charles Dickens*, Brighton: Harvester Wheatsheaf, 1988.

Forster, John, *The Life of Charles Dickens*, London: Chapman & Hall, 1904.

Johnson, Edgar, *Charles Dickens: His Tragedy and Triumph*, London: Penguin, 1977.

Kaplan, Fred, *Dickens: A Biography*, London: Hodder and Stoughton, 1988.

Langton, Robert, *The Childhood and Youth of Charles Dickens*, London: Hutchinson & Co., 1891.

Pope-Hennessey, Una, *Charles Dickens*, Edinburgh: T & T Clark, 1947.

Tomalin, Claire, *Charles Dickens*, London: Penguin, 2011.

Walder, Dennis, *Dickens and Religion*, London: George Allen & Unwin, 1981.